7/244515/

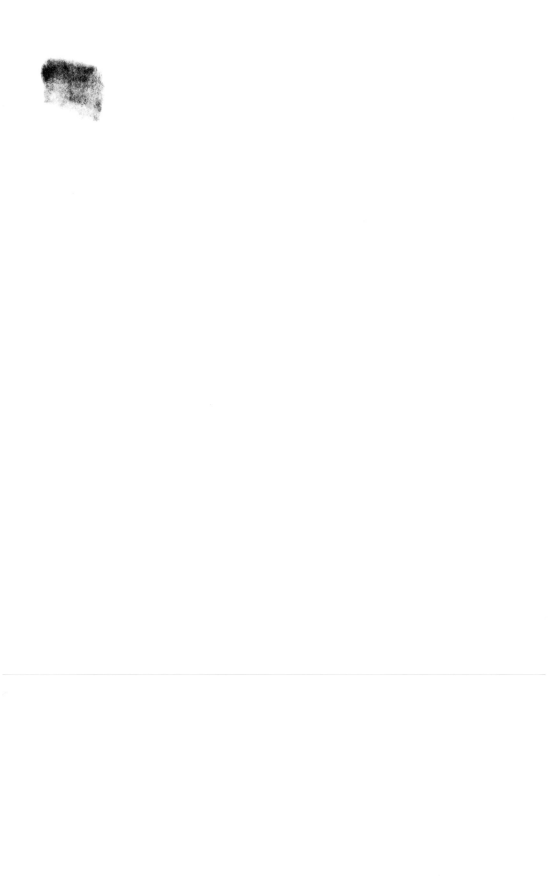

Stone Free

Stone Free

Jimi Hendrix in London, September 1966–June 1967

JAS OBRECHT

THE UNIVERSITY OF
NORTH CAROLINA PRESS
CHAPEL HILL

This book was published with the assistance of the
Anniversary Fund of the University of North Carolina Press.

© 2018 Jas Obrecht

Designed by Richard Hendel
Set in Linoletter and Klavika types
by Tseng Information Systems, Inc.
Manufactured in the United States of America

The University of North Carolina Press has been a
member of the Green Press Initiative since 2003.

Jacket photographs of Jimi Hendrix by Gered Mankowitz
© Bowstir Ltd., 2018/mankowitz.com.

All *New Musical Express* and *Melody Maker* interview
quotations © Time Inc. (UK) Ltd.

Library of Congress Cataloging-in-Publication Data
Names: Obrecht, Jas, author.
Title: Stone free : Jimi Hendrix in London, September 1966–June 1967 /
Jas Obrecht.
Other titles: Jimi Hendrix in London, September 1966–June 1967
Description: Chapel Hill : The University of North Carolina Press, [2018] |
Includes bibliographical references and index.
Identifiers: LCCN 2018020258 | ISBN 9781469647067 (cloth : alk. paper) |
ISBN 9781469647074 (ebook)
Subjects: LCSH: Hendrix, Jimi.—Travel—England—London. | Concert tours—
England. | Rock musicians—United States—Biography. | Guitarists—United
States—Biography.
Classification: LCC ML410.H476 O27 2018 | DDC 787.87/166092 [B] —dc23
LC record available at https://lccn.loc.gov/2018020258

FOR STEVE HILLA—

Here's to a lifetime of friendship

Contents

A gallery of photographs begins on page 101.

Preface

In many respects, Jimi changed the sound of rock
far more than the Beatles. You know, they brought
songwriting to rock and roll, but Jimi changed the
sound of the guitar. —Pete Townshend[1]

This book celebrates what were likely the happiest and most productive nine months of Jimi Hendrix's life. As they begin, he's an under-sung, under-accomplished sideman struggling to get by in New York City. At their conclusion, he's the toast of London and the brightest star of the Monterey International Pop Festival. Even if Hendrix had never played another note or composed another song, his place among rock's most iconic guitarists would have endured.

Through the forces of his personality, imagination, discipline, and unparalleled playing skill, Jimi Hendrix changed the way we hear the guitar. He pushed far beyond his era's musical norms to sculpt new sounds, innovate never-before-heard techniques, and create a new musical vocabulary. As the mood struck, he could be tender, elegant, savage, or sexual—sometimes all within the same song.

By skill and kismet, Jimi landed in the right place at exactly the right moment—London, England, in September 1966. Making every moment count, he organized one of rock's first power trios, the Jimi Hendrix Experience. Within a few months he'd composed an enduring body of songs—"Stone Free," "Purple Haze," "Foxey Lady," "Fire," "The Wind Cries Mary," "Highway Chile," "Manic Depression," "May This Be Love," "I Don't Live Today," and "Are You Experienced?" among them. He became a fashion trendsetter, inveterate jammer, and major concert draw, stunning audiences with his unprecedented volume, flamboyant outfits, and over-the-top stage moves.

While many in Great Britain were instantly drawn to Jimi's music and image—the Beatles, Rolling Stones, and Eric Clapton among them—others were frightened, even angered, by his race, fashion choices, overt sexuality, and his fronting an integrated band. Some reporters used vile and racist stereotypes to describe him. Bobbies hassled him on the street. Stage hands and theater managers sabotaged his gigs. He had to endure comments such as "pansy," "nigger boy," and "blackie." Through it all, Jimi took the high road, remaining intensely focused on his music.

And then there are the recordings. Before returning home to America in June 1967, Jimi recorded three seven-inch singles, the *Are You Experienced* album, and portions of *Axis: Bold as Love*. Each of these releases took listeners to places they'd never gone before. While portions of his music descended from Muddy Waters, B. B. King, Bob Dylan, and others, most of what he played was pure Hendrix—fresh, canny, and perpetually forward-leaning. Many of those who heard it—including a who's who of the era's rock elite— were stunned. "Jimi was intimidating," remembers Carlos Santana. "When you heard him for the first time, you felt like finding another profession until you read in an interview that he felt the same thing, that he learned from Muddy Waters and B. B. King and used to tape-record Buddy Guy's shows. So then you could say, 'It's somewhat attainable.' Jimi was like the Champs-Élysées, that circle in Paris where all the streets connect. When we heard him, some people quit, some got weird, and some found a new way."[2]

While very much a product of their time and the available technology, nearly all of Jimi's recordings broke new ground, lyrically and musically. As Eric Johnson, a brilliant guitarist and mainstay of the twenty-first-century Experience Hendrix tours, points out:

> The voyage of the guitar in modern culture has changed so much from Jimi's time. The electric guitar was a new, fresh instrument in the 1950s and 1960s. And by not having a lot of other options, people had to use this new instrument to orchestrate songs. They didn't have synthesizers or computer gear. The guitar was really the new, upcoming thing. It sounded different and could be plugged into pop music and be cutting

edge. The whole mindset was still, "Let's write great songs. Let's write melodies. Let's just write music, and oh, by the way, we're gonna use the guitar to orchestrate all this music." When Jimi Hendrix came along, that really was his agenda. It's true he was a great guitar player—great in maybe a different definition than now. He wrote great songs and great lyrics and melodies. It was about the music. It was about the song. And it just happened that within that song, you had this terrific, emotional, passionate guitar that became timeless.[3]

"Nowadays the guitar is everywhere," Johnson says. "You see it on the front of magazines—you know, the Strat. The Hard Rock logo is a Les Paul. We've been completely saturated by it. But in Hendrix's time, it was like it came from another planet. There was a certain fire close to the original inception of rock and roll, where you have people like Eric Clapton and Jimi Hendrix. It was all new. You'd hear it and just go, 'My God!' It was an inspiration to last a lifetime."[4]

The enduring influence of Jimi's playing style and recordings helped accelerate the development of stadium rock, heavy metal, fusion, funk, hip-hop, and other styles. Little wonder that, on the cover of its February 6, 1992, issue, *Rolling Stone* magazine declared Jimi Hendrix "The Greatest Guitarist of All Time."

A personal note: Jimi Hendrix was my boyhood hero. While an editor for *Guitar Player* magazine from the 1970s through the 1990s, I wrote of Jimi often and spoke with many of those closest to him. When his father, James "Al" Hendrix, asked me to coauthor his memoir, *My Son Jimi*, I quickly agreed. Our interviews took place in the mid-1990s in Al's modest Seattle home. We pored over family photos, Jimi's youthful artwork and poems, and the postcards and letters he wrote after leaving home. We spoke of Jimi's hard-scrabble upbringing, insecurities, hopes, and dreams. Al showed me his son's instruments and the records he'd spun while teaching himself guitar. Some days we'd sit on the same couch Jimi had used as he taught himself to play. Written entirely in his voice, *My Son Jimi* is very much Al's book. *Stone Free*, by contrast, draws on the recollections of dozens of people—fellow musicians, friends, journalists, managers, studio hands, roadies, and others who knew him. And, most important, there are the words of Jimi himself.

When I first began imagining *Stone Free*, my concept was clear: create a you-are-there narrative detailing the most extraordinary nine-month journey in rock-and-roll history. It's a story that, when laid out in a logical, linear fashion, builds momentum and, like a memorable solo, ends on a climactic high note.

In recent decades, one of the biggest obstacles standing in the way of Hendrix researchers was the difficulty in obtaining copies of accounts published in Great Britain during 1966 and 1967. Many of the publications had long been out of business, and precious few of the original interviews and reviews had been reprinted in books and magazines. Yellowing original copies were few and far between. Then, beginning a few years ago, scans of long-unavailable material began appearing online, along with dozens of bootleg recordings and videotaped performances made during Jimi's initial stay in London. When I began examining these, I knew the time was right for *Stone Free*.

One major issue to consider was interviews—new versus old. Having interviewed hundreds of musicians and music industry figures over the past forty years, I am acutely aware of how stories change over time: events are misremembered, outside forces and after-the-fact additions put spin on the narrative; views are shaped and reshaped. Those who are interviewed often—famous blues and rock musicians among them—tend to repeat the anecdotes that best entertain their listeners, regardless of whether the events occurred exactly as described or not. Over time, these revisions can become "truth" to the teller. With Hendrix, I found, the descriptions and statements spoken by peers during the 1960s often vary from the versions they'd tell decades later. Because of this, I decided to rely on the earliest published accounts as much as possible.

Although I'd gained a wealth of insight into Jimi's ancestors, upbringing, and legacy through my conversations with his father and others, I began *Stone Free* with a sense of trepidation. Reading biographies of actors and musicians whose work I admire, I'd sometimes come away disappointed after learning who these people were away from the spotlight. I am delighted to report that this was not the case with Jimi Hendrix. My boyhood hero proved to be more charming, funny, thoughtful, imaginative, and disciplined than I'd imagined.

1: Setting the Stage

"It's Lonely Out Here by Myself"

It sounds a little silly, but it's the honest-to-God's truth: I used to dream in Technicolor that 1966 was the year that something would happen to me. So eventually it's come true. 1966 is my year—in Technicolor. —Jimi Hendrix[1]

When James Marshall Hendrix boarded a flight from New York City to London on September 23, 1966, his luggage—pretty much everything he owned—showed how hard life had been for him. His small carry-on contained just two satin shirts, a pair of pants, a toothbrush, acne medicine, and plastic hair curlers. His pocket held $40 borrowed on his way to the airport. As the plane ascended and he watched the darkening ocean below, Jimmy James, as he'd been calling himself, could scarcely have imagined what the next few months would bring.

Until then, Hendrix had spent most of his life living hand-to-mouth. On the day of his birth, November 27, 1942, his father was incarcerated in a U.S. Army stockade. His mother, Lucille Jeter Hendrix, a sensitive woman who loved to party, gave her infant firstborn to another family, who took him to San Francisco. Upon his discharge from the military, Al Hendrix journeyed to San Francisco to retrieve the bashful three-year-old. The youngster experienced his father's violent side during the train trip back to Seattle, when he was spanked for misbehaving. Al and Lucille's attempt to reunite proved short-lived, and Jimmy, as his name was spelled before his arrival in London, spent the majority of his childhood living with Al and other relatives. He took up guitar shortly after Lucille's death in 1958. He dropped out of high school, played around Seattle with the Rocking Kings and James Thomas & His Tomcats, and in May 1961 was arrested for being in a stolen car. As an alternative to jail time, Jimmy enlisted in the U.S. Army's elite 101st Airborne Division, where he trained to be a paratrooper. Military life didn't agree with him. After his 1962 discharge he sought work as a professional musician, gigging in small clubs around Nashville with the King Kasuals, featuring his Army buddy Billy Cox on bass.

Jimmy made his first inroads as a session guitarist in 1963, backing Lonnie Youngblood in a New York studio. "I learned a lot about playing guitar from the way Lonnie played tenor sax and the tones he produced," Jimmy would tell author Sharon Lawrence. "He was also a very good friend to me."[2] Lonnie and his wife became like guardian angels to Jimmy, helping him with his hotel bills and buying him an amplifier. Several of the tracks the musicians recorded together hinted at Jimmy's future musical directions—the familiar rhythm style heard on "Go Go Shoes," the Albert King–inspired string bends of "Go Go Place," and especially the gentle, Curtis Mayfield–style filigrees on the Icemen's "(My Girl) She's a Fox," which would reappear on such sublime Hendrix originals as "Little Wing" and "Angel."

Jimmy spent most of the next two years touring in R&B show bands. After joining the Isley Brothers' backup band, he played on their raving, gospel-influenced June 1964 single, "Testify (Part I)" / "Testify (Part II)," soloing with drive and briefly employing the dominant 7–sharp 9 chord he'd later use to power songs such as "Foxey Lady." At another important session that year he backed Don Covay on "Mercy, Mercy," once again drawing inspiration from Curtis Mayfield's style. That summer Jimmy journeyed to Memphis on his own to record for Stax Records, with little to show for his efforts. In September he embarked on an R&B package tour headlined by Sam Cooke and Jackie Wilson. He next became a member of Little Richard's touring band, the Upsetters. The gig required Jimmy to play carefully arranged parts and conform to the manicured image of touring black R&B musicians—slick hair, matching suits, and coordinated, well-rehearsed stage moves. This regimen, like Army life, did not suit him. "You must remember that Jimmy Hendrix U.S. didn't really have a chance to do anything because he was playing behind people," Hendrix later explained.

2

"I had enough respect for a performer to know that I would have to simmer down with what I wanted to do before I went onstage to back him. Like what would have happened if Little Richard started doing his thing and I got all fired up and started doing mine in front of him—playing the guitar with my teeth or start burning up the amp? I was bored to death as a backup man, but I had respect for the people I was playing for."[3]

On the plus side, playing behind Little Richard, one of rock and roll's most flamboyant performers, provided Jimmy with a nightly master class in how to hold an audience's undivided attention. Jimmy made his first known television appearance with Little Richard's band, on the Nashville-based *Night Train* show. In this footage, a smiling Jimmy is seen in the backline, bopping and dipping in time to vocalists Buddy and Stacey's loose cover of Jr. Walker and The All Stars' recent hit "Shotgun." Soon afterward, Little Richard fired Jimmy for failing to show up in time for the tour bus.

Deciding to try his luck in New York City, Jimmy briefly rejoined the Isley Brothers lineup in July 1965. Teenaged Ernie Isley, who'd later take up the guitar and play the brilliant, Hendrix-influenced solos on the Isley Brothers' 1973 hit "That Lady (Parts 1 & 2)," was struck by the ways Jimmy would display his individuality on the bandstand. "Back then the band members wore uniforms," he recalled. "If they had gold ones with black shirts, he might have a gold uniform with a red ruffled shirt and a sash tied around his waist. He always did something that was a little different and individual. It could be a chain or a scarf or a different-colored pair of shoes. He'd play with the guys, but he sort of kept his distance from them. He was, you know, quiet. But there was always an admiration between Jimmy and my brothers."[4] Impressed by Hendrix's performance at an Isleys show in Harlem, R&B producer Henry "Juggy" Murray of Sue Records signed him to a recording and management contract. "Reading a contract meant nothing to Jimmy," Juggy remembered. "He just came in and signed it. And then I didn't hear from him for months."[5] While they did some rehearsals together, Hendrix never completed any releasable recordings for Sue Records.

That July, while staying at the Hotel America on West Forty-Seventh Street in New York City, Jimmy sent his father a handwritten letter. He mentioned that he'd made a few records of his own but was currently out of work again. "I still have my guitar and amp," Jimmy wrote, "and as long as I have that, no fool can keep me from living. There's a few record companies that I visited that I probably can record for. I think I'll start working toward that line because actually when you're playing behind other people you're still not making a big name for yourself as you would if you were working for yourself. But I went on the road with other people to get exposed to the public and see how business is taken care of. And mainly just to see what's what, and after I put a record out, there'll be a few people who know me already and who can help with the sale of the record."

Jimmy, always insecure about his singing voice, added that he was going to start singing:

> Nowadays people don't want you to sing good. They want you to sing sloppy and have a good beat to your songs. That's what angle I'm going to shoot for. That's where the money is. So just in case about three or four months from now you might hear a record by me which sounds terrible, don't feel ashamed, just wait until the money rolls in because every day people are singing worse and worse on purpose and the public buys more and more records. I just want to let you know I'm still here, trying to make it. Although I don't eat every day, everything's going to be alright for me. It could be worse than this, but I'm going to keep hustling and scuffling until I get things to happening like they're supposed to be.... Please write soon. It's pretty lonely out here by myself.[6]

As Jimmy wrote these words, the British Invasion was still going strong, with the Rolling Stones, Yardbirds, Dave Clark Five, and Herman's Hermits riding high in the pop charts and getting heavy play on American AM radio. On the FM side of the dial, derivative rock and pop were giving way to something new and more reflective of the cultural changes afoot in England and America. With the release of landmark albums such as John Coltrane's *A Love Supreme*, Bob Dylan's *Bringing It All Back Home*, the Beatles' *Revolver*, and the Byrds' *Mr. Tambourine Man*, the floodgates for musical self-expression opened wide. Hendrix, who kept up with the latest releases via radio, was especially drawn to Bob Dylan. "Blowin' in the Wind," from 1963's *The Freewheelin' Bob Dylan*, was among his favorite compositions. In early September 1965, he spent his last few dollars on the just-released *Highway 61 Revisited* album, which reaffirmed Dylan's transition to harder-edged rock and roll. "Like a Rolling Stone," with its image of someone having "no direction home, like a complete unknown," hit Jimmy especially hard. He couldn't read music, but he bought a Bob Dylan songbook to study the lyrics. Although Jimmy was likely unaware of this, he and Dylan already had a connection of sorts: alongside of his photo in his 1959 high school yearbook, which identified him as Robert Zimmerman, Dylan had written a single goal: "to join Little Richard."

That fall, with his guitar in pawn and rent overdue, Hendrix met Curtis Knight, a personable but less-than-stellar singer and guitarist, in the lobby of the Hotel America. After speaking together for a while, Knight fetched one his guitars, a right-handed Fender Duo-Sonic, and asked Jimmy to play for him. Taken aback by Jimmy's skill, Knight invited him to meet the members of his R&B band, the Squires. Ace Hall, the group's bassist, recalls, "When Curtis brought Jimmy over to meet me and the band and to go over some of the songs that we was doin' over at the club, Jimmy didn't have a guitar.... He said that he was with the Isley Brothers, Little Richard, and quite a few other little acts, so he was making his mark before he got to us. But when he came with us, he was more free to do the things that *he* liked, that he wanted to do. He was a master at it. He was very sincere about his music. He was loud, but he was sincere. He played a good guitar, he made his point. It was a pleasure to work with him. [But] Jimmy always wanted to be a leader."[7]

After a series of gigs performing soul and R&B covers together at clubs around New York, Knight introduced Jimmy to his producer, Ed Chalpin, with whom he had an exclusive contract. Chalpin's company, PPX Enterprises, specialized in recreating the instrumental backing tracks of current chart hits, which would then be overdubbed by vocalists singing translated lyrics for foreign markets. On October 15, 1965, Chalpin asked Hendrix to sign a one-page agreement. In exchange for "the sum of one (1.00) dollar and other good and valuable consideration," the guitarist agreed to sing and play exclusively for PPX for a three-year period, make available his services "at the request of PPX with a minimum of ten (10) days notice to produce no more than four (4) titles per session," and to participate in a minimum of three sessions per year. The contract also stipulated that "Jimmy Hendrix's services will include singing and/or arrangements, which at the option of PPX shall be written out by [an]other copyist or arranger." After recouping its recording costs, PPX would pay Hendrix one-percent of the "retail selling price of all records sold for his production efforts," as well as "minimum scale for arrangements he produces." The final clauses stipulated that "Jimmy Hendrix shall play instruments for PPX at no cost to PPX Enterprises, Inc.," and that "PPX shall have exclusive rights to assign all masters produced in conjunction with Jimmy Hendrix."[8]

Without consulting a lawyer, Jimmy signed. Fayne Pridgeon, Jimmy's on-again, off-again girlfriend in Harlem, remembered, "He would sign a contract with anybody that came along that had a dollar and a pencil, which got him into a lot of trouble later."[9] After Hendrix became an international sensation, his signature on the PPX contract would lead to years of bitter and expensive litigation, a spate of subpar releases bearing his name, and, as a final step of the settlement, the recording and release of the live *Band of Gypsys* album.

Lawrence Townsend, a renowned intellectual property attorney based in San Francisco, explains some of the difficulties inherent in the agreement:

> To say Hendrix could have benefited from legal advice before signing the PPX contract would be gross understatement. Instead, it's as if he was guided by forces he would later describe as "butterflies and zebra … moonbeams and fairy tales." For $1 and 1 percent of sales of all records produced, Hendrix agreed to "produce and play and/or sing exclusively for PPX" for three years beginning in 1965 in what would prove to be one of the most remarkable five-year runs of creative and performing output in music history. A Rorschach Test for the courts, was it a shackling three-year contract for a studio session musician and arranger where he's on call by PPX at any time on "ten (10) days notice," or could it be worse? Might it cover all of his own creative recording efforts for the next three years? Questions such as these would keep lawyers busy for years, starting with PPX suing Hendrix, his management, and his new label, Reprise.[10]

Hendrix played on a variety of tracks for Chalpin during the ensuing seven months. The most mind-boggling was his appearance
as bassist on actress Jayne Mansfield's syrupy "As the Clouds Drift
By." The Curtis Knight sessions gave him freer rein to showcase
his instrumental abilities. The most intriguing of these recordings, Knight's "How Would You Feel," recast "Like a Rolling Stone"
with new lyrics protesting the discriminatory treatment of African Americans. Knight's melody was virtually the same as Dylan's,
and Jimmy's guitar figures drew heavily from Mike Bloomfield's
playing on the original. The RSVP release's label identified Curtis
Knight as the sole songwriter, and Jimmy Hendrix as the arranger.
Jimmy received his first songwriting credits on Knight's "Hornet's
Nest," an instrumental featuring him playing through a distortion
device, and "Welcome Home." In all, Hendrix would play on thirty-
three tracks for Chalpin.

In between his PPX sessions, Jimmy went back on the road as
a sideman. In November 1965 he sent a postcard from Boston to
let his dad know that he was doing shows with Joey Dee and the
Starliters. Best known for "Peppermint Twist—Part 1," a number-
one hit in 1962, Dee fronted an integrated band, which introduced
Jimmy to playing in front of large, predominantly white audiences.
Recognizing the guitarist's knack for showmanship, Dee allotted
Hendrix a solo each night that climaxed with him playing with the
instrument held behind his head. Though racial segregation had
officially ended with President Lyndon Johnson's signing of the
Civil Rights Act of 1964, when the tour swung through the American South, Jimmy and the other African American Starliters were
required to use black-owned hotels and restaurants.

On January 13, 1966, Jimmy sent word to his family that he was
back in New York City. "It seemed like he was still a little down on
his luck," Al remembered. The postcard read, "Dear Dad—Well, I'm
just dropping in a few words to let you know everything's so-so
here in this big raggedy city of New York. Everything's happening
bad here. I hope everyone at home is alright. Tell Leon I said hello.
... Tell Ben & Ernie I play the blues like they NEVER heard. Love
always, Jimmy.'"[11] Leon was Jimmy's younger half brother. Ben and
Ernie were the nicknames of Hendrix family friends Cornell Ben-
son and Ernestine Tobey, with whom Jimmy and Al had shared
lodgings in Seattle. Little did they realize how "so-so" Jimmy's con-

dition was. His acquaintances in Harlem that winter remembered him wearing a threadbare coat and having holes in the soles of his shoes. Jimmy, though, was no stranger to this condition. While he was in grade school, his dad had shown him how to use cardboard inserts to cover the holes in his shoes.

Days after sending that postcard Jimmy became a backup guitarist in saxophonist King Curtis's All-Stars. He admired Curtis's lead guitarist, Cornell Dupree, and bassist, Chuck Rainey, who, in turn, were impressed with the speed with which Jimmy learned new material. Hendrix appreciated having an opportunity to participate in King Curtis's sessions in Atlantic Studios, but he took umbrage at having to once again don a band uniform and move in lockstep with the rest of the backline. His time with King Curtis was short-lived. That May he rejoined Curtis Knight and the Squires for an audition at Club Cheetah, a newly opened discotheque on Fifty-Third and Broadway. As Knight recounted in *Jimi*, the Cheetah was considered "*the* club in New York City. It also paid the most money, so all the groups were trying to work there." After watching several other acts audition, the Squires took the stage. "We had Jimmy on lead guitar," Knight detailed. "I was playing rhythm and singing; we had an organist, bass and drums—and it was very together. We played the first song and they really dug it, and about halfway through the second number Jimmy started playing with his teeth, tongue, behind his back, between his legs. I was dancing as if my legs could fly. They stopped us right there in the middle of the song and said, 'You got the job!'"[12]

While Jimmy's eye-catching stage moves surprised the uninitiated, he was tapping into a long tradition, especially among African American blues musicians. During the 1920s, for instance, one of the Mississippi Delta's earliest bluesmen, Charley Patton, was renowned for his "clowning" with the guitar. As his contemporary Sam Chatmon remembered, "He be in there putting his guitar all between his legs, carry it behind his head, lay down on the floor, and never stopped picking!"[13] In more recent years T-Bone Walker, Buddy Guy, Guitar Slim, and several other well-known blues performers had similarly over-the-top stage moves. Jimmy had already mastered all of these moves, and he would soon innovate some new ones.

Despite the recollections of Curtis Knight and others, it's unlikely that Hendrix ever actually played guitar with his tongue. Randy Hansen, renowned for his ability to recreate Hendrix songs note for note, explained, "People say Jimi played with his tongue, but that's not true. The reason I know this is because I've tried it, and there's just no way you can do it. It would be like trying to play a guitar with a fresh strawberry or a piece of steak. It just doesn't work because it's limp. It's just meat, and you can't get an attack with it. It was all his teeth. There's a certain tone that comes out of the strings when you hit them with your teeth. Hendrix used to use his teeth for the solo part of 'Hey Joe' and for the ending of his live 'Purple Haze,' the part where everyone else stops and he keeps playing by himself. There were other times he'd do it too — he'd just play with his teeth when the mood struck him, like he did a lot of other things."[14]

With its wild décor, Club Cheetah allowed Jimmy to adopt a more vibrant way of dressing. Curtis Knight detailed, "The couches and wall décor were in a fabric that really looked like the coat of a cheetah. And there were lights and reflectors everywhere, making the whole place look like something from outer space. It was a gathering place for people of all ages, people who were into dancing and wearing way-out clothes. Jimmy and I thought we'd better get some of those way-out clothes ourselves. We went down to the Village and found some material that was almost the same as the décor of the club, and we designed ourselves shirts and jackets out of it. We added white bell-bottoms, and we looked like we were coming out of the walls."[15] During the Squires' residency at Club Cheetah, Jimmy, still playing Knight's Duo-Sonic, added a fuzz box to his signal chain.

At the same time Jimmy was camping it up at the Cheetah, the Rolling Stones were readying their 1966 U.S. summer tour. Keith Richards's girlfriend, twenty-year-old British fashion model Linda Keith, came to New York in advance of the band's arrival. In late May, at the tail end of a night on the town with her friends Roberta Goldstein and Mark Kauffman, she stopped by the Cheetah. "It was a huge, enormous place, like a ballroom," Linda remembered. "Very few people there. And just a regular band playing — not very well. I didn't take any interest in the band at all. And then suddenly I saw the guitar player, who was playing really quite discretely in the back row. And from that moment I just became completely involved. He was very naive. And he was very shy and nervous, and he didn't look at you when he spoke to you. And he came back to the apartment."[16] According to author Charles Cross, on the night Jimmy met Linda Keith, he was offered a hit of acid, still legal at the time. Hendrix reportedly answered, "No, I don't want any of that, but I'd love to try some of that LSD stuff."[17] Jimmy and Linda stayed up for hours, talking and listening to Bob Dylan's new album, *Blonde on Blonde*, and some of her blues singles. "Jimi idolized Dylan," Linda said. "He thought Dylan was the greatest."[18] As Jimmy played along on an unplugged guitar, Linda heard something few people in New York had paid any attention to: his tremendous potential as a musician. Jimmy later told a friend that during his initial acid trip, he looked into the mirror and thought he was Marilyn Monroe.

Jimmy and Linda met several times during the ensuing weeks. When Jimmy expressed a desire for a better guitar—especially a Fender Stratocaster like the ones played by Chicago bluesmen Buddy Guy and Otis Rush—Linda "loaned" him a new white Fender Stratocaster that Keith Richards had stowed in his hotel room. A lefty, Hendrix preferred guitars built for right-handers, believing that with their lower production runs, left-handed instruments couldn't have the same quality as the more common right-hand models. In addition to flipping the guitar over, Hendrix would reverse the nut and restring the instrument the standard way, with the skinniest strings closest to his toes. Although he would eventually accumulate many guitars, Jimmy would favor right-handed Stratocasters for the rest of his career.

Linda soon recognized that Jimmy had very different sides: "You only would have seen him being flashy and extroverted when he was playing. He was two different characters. When he was playing, he was super confident. He was in total control. His focus was immaculate. But when he wasn't playing, he was desperately insecure." More than anything else, Linda noticed, Jimmy was "concentrated on music. I never heard him talk about a sport. He didn't read the papers. He really had no interest for anything other than music and women. So Jimmy had two areas of expertise: he had his guitar playing, and then he had an intense sexuality. He was an entity unto himself. He was unique—his thought processes, his music, his verbalizations of things, his body language, his clothes.

'Right, good,' and he came down. He thought I was mad. He did not see what I was talking about. When he saw Jimi, he thought he was *nothing*."[24] Another friend who'd worked at *Billboard*, Seymour Stein, liked Hendrix's playing but said no when he saw the guitarist smash his instrument in an onstage fit of anger. Linda next brought the Rolling Stones, in town to play Forest Hills, to see the Blue Flames at Ondine's, a disco on the Upper East Side. Brian Jones and Bill Wyman were enthralled, Mick Jagger left unimpressed, and Keith Richards seemed mostly concerned with the nature of Linda's relationship with Jimmy.

In early August Jimmy's luck took a turn for the better when Linda Keith ran into Bryan "Chas" Chandler, the twenty-eight-year-old bassist for the Animals. Formed in Newcastle, England, the Animals had scored a number-one hit in the United States with their 1964 arrangement of the traditional tune "The House of the Rising Sun." By the summer of 1966 they had landed seven other singles in *Billboard*'s Top 40 chart. One of their best, "We Gotta Get Out of This Place," featured Chandler playing one of the era's most memorable bass lines. On the night Chas met Linda at Ondine's, he was well aware of reports that the Animals would be reorganizing upon their return to London. He told Linda of his desire to give up performing to become a record producer. He also mentioned that he'd recently heard Tim Rose's recording of "Hey Joe" and was so taken with the composition that he wanted to find an artist in England to cover the song. Linda encouraged him to make the pilgrimage to the Village to see Jimmy with the Blue Flames. A passage in Keith Richards's autobiography suggests that Linda may have tipped off Jimmy in advance of Chas's coming to see him perform: "She picked up a copy of a demo I had of Tim Rose singing a song called 'Hey Joe.' And took that round to Roberta Goldstein's, where Jimmy was, and played it to him. This is rock and roll history. So he got that song from me, apparently."[25]

"Hey Joe" told the harrowing tale of a man who buys a gun, murders his unfaithful wife, and tries to beat the hangman by skedaddling down to Mexico. Framed as a conversation, the lyrics give voice to the narrator, who asks Joe where he's going with that gun in his hand, and Joe, who answers. In an April 1967 interview with British journalist Chris Welch, Hendrix gave this take on the song: "'Hey Joe' is a traditional song and it's about one-hundred years old. Lots of people have done different arrangements of it, and Timmy Rose was the first to do it slowly. I like it played slowly. There are probably a thousand versions of it fast by the Byrds, Standells, Love, and others."[26] Various names have been given for the song's authorship, but the original copyright was filed by South Carolina folksinger Billy Roberts in 1962.

On the afternoon Chas Chandler showed up at Cafe Wha?, he was stunned by what he saw: "I thought musically Hendrix was the best guitarist I'd ever seen. He was playing with a pickup band. It was one of these coffee bar things that they had in Greenwich Village, where you get fifteen bucks to do a spot. And the first song Jimmy played that afternoon onstage was 'Hey Joe.' And he had it all. I just sat there and thought to myself, 'This is ridiculous. Why isn't someone signing this guy up? How come he's loose?'"[27] Then Jimi went into one of his favorite Bob Dylan songs. "As much as his version of 'Hey Joe' impressed me," Chandler continued, "what convinced me of his talent was another song he did that day, 'Like a Rolling Stone' by Bob Dylan. When Jimi sang the song, he did it with tremendous conviction, and the lyrics came right through to me."[28] The two men spoke for an hour. Jimmy told him about his background playing with Little Richard and the Isley Brothers and asked Chas about the amplifiers in England.

Chas brought up the subject of bringing Jimmy to England. "I tried not to get excited," Hendrix told Sharon Lawrence, "but I was thinking about the Animals' hit records, which I liked, and thinking that this *might* be a good connection. . . . Chas laid on the compliments in that thick accent of his. I mean, he *raved* till I was getting embarrassed; he was crazy about the slow version of 'Hey Joe.' He even seemed to like the way I sang it. I'd really never talked that long to anyone quite like him before, being English, hip to the blues, and all that."[29] Chandler concluded the conversation by saying that once he'd completed the Animals tour, he'd come back to New York to see if Hendrix wanted to accompany him to England. "Fair enough," Jimmy responded.

While Chandler toured stateside with the Animals, Hendrix continued to play around Greenwich Village. In early August blues performer John Hammond, son of the renowned Columbia Records producer, came into town to perform solo sets at the Gaslight. "One night between shows," Hammond recounted,

I went upstairs and my friend who was working at the Players Theatre on MacDougal Street right next to the Cafe Wha? came over and said, "John, there's this band playing downstairs that you've got to hear. This guy is doing songs off your old album, and he sounds better than you." So I thought I'd check this out. I went down there, and Hendrix was playing all these tunes off this album I'd done called *So Many Roads*, and he was playing the guitar parts better than Robbie Robertson had.

He was a really handsome black kid, playing with these guys who could barely keep the beat. They were terrible. Anyway, I went down there and introduced myself to him. He knew me and had my albums, and he was just knocked out that I was there. See, I had all these Muddy Waters and Howlin' Wolf tunes on the *So Many Roads* album, and he had gotten them from my record—at least this is what he told me. Jimmy James he called himself—Jimmy James and the Blue Flames. He was playing a Fender Stratocaster upside down and left-handed—one of those things that just boggles your mind. I just could not believe it. He was playing with his teeth and doing all those really slick techniques that I had seen in Chicago on the South Side on wild nights. But here was this guy doing it, and he was fantastic playing blues. He was incredibly facile. Anything he could hear, he could play. He was an amazing guy, on his own trip, and totally himself.[30]

When Hammond's booking at the Gaslight ended, he began rehearsing with the Blue Flames: "There was a guy in his band named Randy Wolfe, who was fantastic then playing slide guitar. I was just playing harmonica and singing because those guys were heavyweight electric guitar players. Jimmy did one solo number, a Bo Diddley tune—'I'm a Man,' I think. And he did it real good. We rehearsed and opened about two weeks after that at the Cafe Au Go Go. We worked out there for two weeks, and it was fantastic. Everybody—a who's who—came to hear us: Bob Dylan, the Animals all came in."[31]

Mike Bloomfield, who'd played electric guitar on Bob Dylan's *Highway 61 Revisited*, dropped in one night to see Hammond's young phenom. "The first time I saw Hendrix play, he was Jimmy James with the Blue Flames," Bloomfield remembered.

I was performing with Paul Butterfield, and I was the hot-shot guitarist on the block—I thought I was *it*. I'd never heard of Hendrix. Then someone said, "You got to see the guitar player with John Hammond." I went right across the street and saw him. Hendrix knew who I was, and that day, in front of my eyes, he burned me to death. I didn't even get my guitar out. H-bombs were going off, guided missiles were flying— I can't tell you the sounds he was getting out of his instrument. He was getting every sound I was ever to hear him get right there in that room with a Stratocaster, a Twin amp, a Maestro Fuzz-Tone, and that was all—he was doing it mainly through extreme volume. How he did this, I wish I understood. He just got right up in my face with that axe, and I didn't even want to pick up a guitar for the next year.

I was awed. I'd never heard anything like it. I didn't even know where he was coming from musically, because he wasn't playing any of his own tunes. He was doing things like "Like a Rolling Stone," but in the most unusual way. He wasn't a singer, he wasn't even particularly a player. That day, Jimmy Hendrix was laying things on me that were more sounds than they were licks. But I found, after hearing him two or three more times, that he was into pure melodic playing and lyricism as much as he was into sounds. In fact, he had melded them into a perfect blend.[32]

Hanging out together afterward, Hendrix told Bloomfield that he was frustrated with having to tour the chitlin circuit in the back-line of R&B acts. He also revealed that he'd never heard anyone else play in his particular style. "I remember going to his hotel room," Bloomfield recounted. "He had a little Kay amp against the wall, and he had his guitar out—immediately he was getting new sounds out of it. He *never* stopped playing. His guitar was the first thing he reached for when he woke up. We were bopping around New York once, and I said, 'Let's find some girls.' He said, 'That can wait, there's always time for that. Let's play, man.' He was the most compulsive player I've ever run into. That's why he was so good."[33]

Bloomfield, who had an encyclopedic knowledge of the blues and had played in Chicago clubs alongside giants such as Muddy

Waters and Howlin' Wolf, was impressed by the depth of Jimmy's knowledge of guitar players and styles. "Hendrix," he explained,

> was by far the greatest expert I've ever heard at playing rhythm and blues, the style of playing developed by Bobby Womack, Curtis Mayfield, Eric Gale, and others. I got the feeling there was no guitaring of any kind that he hadn't heard or studied, including steel guitar, Hawaiian, and dobro. In his playing I can really hear Curtis Mayfield, Wes Montgomery, Albert King, B. B. King, and Muddy Waters.
>
> Jimmy was the blackest guitarist I ever heard. His music was deeply rooted in pre-blues, the oldest musical forms, like field hollers and gospel melodies. From what I can garner, there was no form of black music that he hadn't listened to or studied, but he especially loved the real old black music forms, and they poured out in his playing. We often talked about Son House and the old blues guys. But what really did it to him was early Muddy Waters and John Lee Hooker records—that early electric music where the guitar was hugely amplified and boosted by the studio to give it the effect of more presence than it really had. He knew that stuff backwards—you can hear every old John Lee Hooker and Muddy Waters thing that ever was on that one long version of "Voodoo Chile."[34]

Hendrix had indeed heard a wide variety of music while growing up—gospel music at church, early rock and roll and R&B singles, swing music, show tunes, film and television soundtracks, and especially postwar blues. His father, a skilled and passionate jitterbug in his younger days, dabbled on the saxophone. When Jimmy first took up guitar around age fifteen, he'd mostly taught himself by playing along to records. "Jimmy would put my 45s on that turntable and play along," Al Hendrix remembered. "He'd try to copy what he heard, and he'd make up stuff too. He lived on the blues around the house. I had a lot of records by B. B. King and Louis Jordan and some of the downhome guys like Muddy Waters. I liked most of the blues guitar players and Chuck Berry. Jimmy was really excited by B. B. King and Chuck Berry. He was a fan of Albert King too, because he liked all them blues guitarists."[35]

Jimmy told Bloomfield of his fondness for rhythm guitar: "He was extremely interested in form—in a few seconds of playing, he'd let you know about the entire structure. That's why he liked rhythm guitar playing so much—the rhythm guitar could lay out the structure for the whole song. He would say, 'There is a world of lead guitar players, but the most essential thing to learn is the time, the rhythm.' He once told me he wanted to burn Clapton to death because he didn't play rhythm."[36] Although he'd scarcely have believed it at the time, Hendrix was just a few weeks away from having that opportunity—on Eric Clapton's home turf, no less.

During that summer in Greenwich Village, Jimmy showed a keen interest in learning as much as he could from other musicians. Bob Kulick witnessed this firsthand: "He was constantly at one club or another, either hanging out with the bands or picking up girls. Jimmy was a consummate musician who would jam with anybody anytime. When he watched other bands, he would even take notes. He'd pick up stuff from *everybody*—no matter how bad they were." But, Kulick insisted, Jimmy's playing never sounded derivative: "Jimmy totally had his own thing, and he was absolutely brilliant. There wasn't anybody around who could play like him. No one could even figure out what he was doing. . . . When Jimmy played behind his neck or did the dive-bomb trem [whammy bar] stuff, it knocked people out. Even the way he'd use his toggle switch—pushing the tone knob down on the bass pickup and flicking the toggle switch between the treble and bass positions to get that wah-wah effect—was totally unique."[37]

When the Animals tour ended, Chas Chandler returned to New York and found Jimmy at Cafe Wha?. He was relieved to learn that Jimmy had not signed any contracts since their previous meeting, and he restated his desire to take him to the United Kingdom. "I thought he would change the music face of England, if not the world," Chas said. "I knew he was going to be sensational in England."[38] Hendrix, still undecided, expressed concerns that England was already over-saturated with guitar players and that he didn't have much of a singing voice. He also asked Chandler if he knew Eric Clapton. Chandler assured him on all three points: Hendrix would surely do well in England, the issue of singing could be dealt with, and yes, he'd be happy to introduce him to Eric. Jimmy was swayed. After that conversation, he remembered, "I wasn't thinking about nothing but the idea of being in England. That's all

I was thinking about because I like to travel. One place bores me too long, so I have to try to see if I can get something together by moving somewhere else. And the idea of England just was the idea of England itself. I said, 'Wow,' you know. I'd never been there before."[39]

Chandler brought the Animals manager, Michael Jeffery, to the club. Their plan was to co-manage Hendrix: Chas would organize the group, produce the records, and handle other artistic matters, while Jeffery would be in charge of overseeing contractual and financial issues. Though Jimmy was cradling a guitar in his lap when they met, Jeffery expressed no interest in hearing him play. Instead, he focused his attention on Hendrix's appearance, which he apparently deemed photogenic, telling Chandler, "*He* could be the black Elvis!"[40] Asked about contracts he'd signed, Hendrix mentioned the papers he'd inked with Sue Records and PPX. "Not legal," Jeffery told him. "You had no representation of your own. Don't worry. I'll handle it."[41] Potential contract issues with Sue Records were quickly resolved with a single payment. In an oversight that he'd come to regret, Jeffery did not terminate Jimmy's agreement with Ed Chalpin and PPX. Chandler next took Jimmy to Leon Dicker, an attorney who represented both the Animals and Jeffery's Yameta Company Ltd., which had been set up earlier that year to shelter artists from being taxed in the United Kingdom for their overseas earnings. Sensing Chas's enthusiasm, Dicker agreed to assist them and advance them money to cover expenses.

When Jimmy inquired about taking his Greenwich Village group to England, Chandler said no: "There was an occasional blues solo from Randy, yes, but the rest was utter chaos. The bass player was a jerk and the drummer couldn't play. The way I looked at it was, 'Hey, you've been playing this and nobody's fucking signed you. What's the point in carrying on?'"[42] While Jimmy felt loyalty for Wolfe and the others, he recognized Chandler's offer as the break he'd long been seeking. "I can't tell you the number of times it hurt me to play the same notes, the same beat," he'd later say. "I wanted my own scene, making my own music. I always had a feeling that, if my mind was right, I'd get a break someday. It took a long time, playing a lot of dates that didn't pay very well, but I figured it was worth it. I don't think I could have stood another year of playing behind people. I'm glad Chas rescued me."[43] According to Jimi's future bandmate Mitch Mitchell, while Chas Chandler was still in New York, he came up with the idea of calling Hendrix's new band the "Experience." The other soon-to-be member of the group, Noel Redding, credited Jeffery for coming up with the name.

The final phase of preparation, finding Jimmy's birth certificate to secure his passport and visa, created significant hurdles. Hendrix was unaware that the name on his birth certificate in Seattle was "Johnny Allen Hendrix" rather than "James Marshall Hendrix," which his father had renamed him when he was three years old. After several attempts, Dicker finally secured the birth certificate and arranged Jimmy's passport. Another challenge arose when Hendrix was informed he'd have to get a smallpox vaccination. Throughout his life he was terrified of needles, and it took a lot of convincing to get him to sit still long enough for the shot. When it came to his overdue hotel bill, Hendrix was on his own. The management locked him out of his room and seized the stage clothing and handwritten song lyrics and poetry he'd stored there.

As soon as the passport for James Marshall Hendrix arrived, Chas announced that it was time to go. Before departure, Jimmy visited John Hammond to say goodbye: "Jimmy came to me and said, 'Look it, these guys have asked me to go over there, and they gave me a plane ticket and some money.' I said, 'Man, you got to go!' I knew there was no way he was going to be my guitar player. He was his own star."[44] Hendrix held Hammond in high regard, telling Sharon Lawrence, "He is one of the nicest human beings I have ever met. John is a *gentleman*, and he treated me like one too."[45] On his way out the door, Jimmy hit up Hammond's drummer for a $40 loan. This was all the money in his pocket when, on the evening of Friday, September 23, 1966, he settled into his seat on the Pan Am flight to London. His traveling companions were Chas Chandler and Terry McVay, road manager for the Animals' recent tour. Somewhere over the Atlantic, Jimmy agreed that he would now be known as "Jimi Hendrix."

2:September 1966

Swinging London

In this century, every decade has its city. . . . Today, it is London.
—*Time* magazine[1]

The flight landed at London's Heathrow Airport at 9:00 A.M. the following morning. Since Jimi didn't have a work permit, Terry McVay carried the white Stratocaster through the customs station. With no significant luggage, Jimi was detained and questioned. Chandler, an imposing former dock worker who, at six feet four inches, stood a half foot taller than his protégé, insisted that Jimi had legitimate cause to be in the United Kingdom. A lengthy argument ensued. "They didn't want to let me in," Jimi recalled. "They carried on like I was going to make all the money in England and take it back to the States."[2] Chas telephoned Tony Garland, a publicist who'd worked with the Animals, and implored him to come to the airport to help. Garland managed to convince the officers that as a soul singer and song composer, Jimi had come to England to collect royalties that he intended to spend in England. This seemed to jibe with Jimi's only having $40 on his person, so he was granted a seven-day non-work permit.

From the airport, Chas and Jimi went straight to the home of George Bruno "Zoot" Money and his wife, Ronnie, who lived in a terraced house on Gunterstone Road in Fulham. Since the early 1960s Zoot had fronted the popular Big Roll Band. The group's guitarist, Andy Summers, resided in the house at this time, but he has disavowed the oft-repeated story that he and Jimi jammed together that first day. But Jimi did give an impromptu performance. Im-

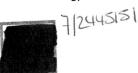

pressed, Ronnie ran to summon the hairdresser and part-time DJ who rented an upstairs flat, Kathy Etchingham, to see the newly arrived American guitarist. Kathy sleepily declined, but agreed to rendezvous with everyone later that day at the Scotch of St. James.

Chas and Jimi's next stop was the Hyde Park Towers, near Kensington Gardens in Bayswater. Constructed in the early 1800s as a private home, the four-story building had been converted into rooms with shared baths. Chas was already living there with his Swedish girlfriend Lotta Null. At the time the hotel was in serious disrepair, with dry rot rendering some rooms uninhabitable. Still, it was a step up from the lodgings Jimi had been accustomed to in New York City.

That evening Chas took Jimi to the Scotch of St. James, located near Piccadilly in the courtyard at 13 Mason's Yard. The small club was a favorite gathering spot of London's elite and trendy, where producers, journalists, and photographers could mingle with musicians, actors, and artists. With his Dylanesque Afro, white satin shirt with an oversize collar, and flared beige pants, Hendrix instantly drew attention. He asked if he could play a song or two on the tiny stage. This request caused Chandler concern, since a performance would violate Hendrix's just-issued tourist visa. Jimi sat down on a stool in a corner and went into an unaccompanied blues. The boisterous crowd fell silent and watched with rapt attention. Music journalist Keith Altham observed, "He was fantastic! My reaction—and Chas, of course, asked me what I thought afterward—was, 'The guy is brilliant, Chas, but he's so good he's kind of like a great jazz guitarist. He's just going to go right over the heads of the kids.'"[3]

As Jimi played, the Moneys and Kathy Etchingham arrived. At age twenty, Kathy already traveled in the same circles as the Animals, Beatles, Kinks, Moody Blues, and other London bands, and she'd had casual flings with Keith Moon, drummer for the Who, and Brian Jones. She was instantly intrigued. "Just as we settled down," Kathy wrote in her autobiography, *Through Gypsy Eyes*, "Chas stopped him and they came back to our table. Jimi was sitting with a dark-haired model girl but when she went to the Ladies he beckoned me over to sit with him and whispered in my ear. He kissed me on the ear and whispered, 'I think you're beautiful.' It was a corny line but there was something so sweet and innocent about the way he said it. I liked him immediately. I felt flustered by his flattery and tried to cover it up with casual conversation."[4]

Returning to the table, the model, identified by Kathy Etchingham as Linda Keith, said something dismissive about Kathy. Upon hearing this, Ronnie Money swore at Linda, who retaliated by pulling Ronnie's hair. According to Kathy,

> Ronnie picked up a bottle of whisky and smashed it down on the marble-topped table, sending splinters of glass flying in all directions and attracting all eyes in the club. Everything went horribly quiet. "Let go of my fucking hair," Ronnie snarled, every inch the ferocious Scottish fighter. She pushed the jagged end of the broken bottle up to the beautiful girl's exposed throat. "Jesus Christ," Chas looked panic-stricken as he turned to me, "get Jimi out of here for God's sake, Kathy, he's only on a visitor's visa. Take him back to the Hyde Park Towers. Quick, before someone calls the police." "Okay." I hustled Jimi out into Mason's Yard and onto the pavement. "Let's get a taxi," I said, turning round just in time to see him stepping straight in front of a cab, looking the wrong way. I pulled him back as the driver screeched to a halt, opened the cab door and bundled him in.... He seemed perplexed and rather shocked at this introduction to the London social scene.[5]

Kathy and Jimi got to know each other better over drinks at the Hyde Park Towers. After a few hours, he invited her up to his room and told her, "You're my girlfriend." Kathy wrote, "That night was a revelation to me. Jimi was far more sexually experienced and imaginative than any of the friends I'd been to bed with." The drama of Jimi's first twenty-four hours in London reached its crescendo the next morning, when they were awakened by someone coming into the room—Linda Keith. "Snatching up Jimi's guitar from its case, she swung it up as if about to bring it down on our heads," Kathy described. "'Wait, wait, wait!' Jimi protested as I dived under him for protection. 'Not the guitar.'" Stratocaster in hand, Linda stormed out of the hotel and sped off in a Jaguar. Jimi began to panic, telling Kathy that neither he nor Chas could afford to replace the guitar, and without it he might as well go home. A while later, Linda called Jimi. "She says I can't have the guitar until I get rid of you," Jimi told Kathy. "She's going to call in twenty minutes. You'll have to go." Later that afternoon Jimi called Kathy to let her know that he'd retrieved the guitar and the coast was clear. "That day," Kathy noted, "I moved out of Gunterstone Road into the Hyde Park Towers Hotel and Jimi and I became a couple."[6]

With the city's pop culture in full bloom, Jimi's arrival in "Swinging London," as the media dubbed it, could scarcely have been better-timed. Hundreds of small clubs in and around London provided venues for musicians. As Dave Mason of Traffic pointed out, bringing Jimi there when he did "was actually a very smart move on Chas's part. Unlike America, where you had a music scene in New York, a music scene in Nashville, a music scene in L.A., and a music scene in San Francisco, in England everybody finished up in one place—London."[7] Paul McCartney agreed: "There was this revolution happening in London in style, in clothes, in music, so we were all converging on London."[8] Soho's Carnaby Street and Chelsea's Kings Road had become the center of the newly emerging "musical and philosophical pop power."[9] This was the era of Twiggy, the mini skirt, and the pill. Recreational drugs were helping to inspire kaleidoscopic changes in fashion, art, films, and especially music. "The times," as Bob Dylan sang, "were a-changin.'" Keith Richards noticed it the moment the Stones returned from their American tour: "London was suddenly hippie-ville. I was already into that in America, but I wasn't expecting it when I came home to London. The scene had changed totally in a matter of weeks."[10]

Paul McCartney noted that Jimi's having Chas at his side brought instant benefits: "I think if Jimi had just arrived on his own with some manager who was just some guy, there wouldn't have been the 'in' that Jimi was afforded by Chas, because Chas knew all of us."[11] Jimi, for his part, "had enormous faith in Chas," Kathy said, "and he also knew that Chas was going to look after him. And that was very important for Jimi. He had to make sure that he was going to be in the hands of somebody who was going to take care of him. He needed looking after—and he always did. When he came to London, he needed looking after one hundred percent more."[12] With guidance from Chas and Kathy, Jimi rapidly blossomed in his new environment. "Very soon his reputation started to build," Kathy remembered, "and he was totally accepted into society here, the society that we had at that time—totally accepted. He was one of us."[13]

When venturing into the public, Jimi immediately stood out. For starters, outside of London and other large cities, there weren't many black people in the United Kingdom. The 1961 census estimated the black British population at 191,600—less than 1 percent of the total population. A decade later the figure had grown to just 400,000.[14] Having spent most of his life in a racially mixed section of Seattle, Jimi was accustomed to being surrounded by white people. Having been in the U.S. Army and toured the American chitlin circuit, though, he was keenly aware of racism and prejudice, although he seldom spoke of it in interviews.

There is considerable evidence that Jimi thought of himself multiethnic. His paternal grandmother, Zenora "Nora" Hendrix, was part Native American—Cherokee—as well as part African American and Irish. According to family lore, Jimi's paternal grandfather, Bertram Philander Ross Hendrix, was half white, his mother having been impregnated by a slave overseer. "To really understand Jimi," Al Hendrix claimed,

> you have to go back to his beginnings, to that blood running
> through his veins. Some of Jimi's ancestors were Indians
> and slaves. Jimi was fascinated by his Indian heritage, and
> my mother used to talk to him about it. Although she was
> never on a reservation, we did have Indian relics around the
> house when I was young, like an Indian peace pipe up on the
> mantel. I'm sure Jimi saw it while he was growing up. He was
> always interested in that sort of thing. As a kid, Jimi liked to
> dress himself up as much as he could, and he and his friends
> would play cowboys and Indians. Jimi was interested in his
> black ancestry as well, but that was somewhat different—no
> one wanted to play the slave! Having slave ancestors was a
> common thing among blacks. It was all in the past, and it was
> something we just had to live with. Jimi understood all that.[15]

For the most part London provided Hendrix a safe haven. He could walk hand-in-hand with Kathy without having to endure the stares and hassles an interracial couple would have faced in the United States. In smaller British towns, though, he was sometimes confronted with catcalls from passersby and backhanded compliments, such as when a fan in northern England told him, "Nigger boy, you have magic fingers."[16] Discussing this comment with

Sharon Lawrence, Jimi chose to take the high road: "I'm against labels of any kind except on pickle jars. I know that people are just people, whether they're green, yellow, black or white. I *am* colored, and I'm Indian, and I'm this, and I'm that. If someone says 'nigger' to me, as long as they mean it out of ignorance and not from cruelty, I generally don't think much about it."[17]

Any issues caused by the color of Jimi's skin were compounded by his long hair and penchant for wearing colorful and, in the eyes of some onlookers, gender-bending clothing. This would be more of an issue in working-class areas, where many young men still wore short hair and dressed like their fathers. "Wherever we went," Kathy wrote, "we could hear low mutters like, 'Is that a girl or what?' None of which bothered Jimi at all. Quite a few thought he was gay because of his appearance (although 'gayness' was still an unheard-of concept in all but the most sophisticated corners of the country), and the words 'pansy' and 'queer' could be heard here and there. Jimi probably didn't know what they meant, and if he did he certainly wasn't offended, being more confident of his sexuality than any man I had ever met."[18]

When it came to clothing, Jimi followed his own muse. "Right from the beginning," Kathy clarified, "he had a style of his own, wearing satin shirts with voluminous sleeves, army jackets, and bell bottoms with scarves tied around the legs long before anyone else. Even Brian Jones was still wearing suits when Jimi first arrived in London and it was only later that other musicians started wearing flowery clothes, feather boas, and jewelry. Jimi was original in his style."[19]

Jimi's fascination with dressing up probably began during childhood games of "cowboys and Indians" and kicked into high gear during the summer he spent with his grandmother Nora in Vancouver, Canada. During the 1910s, Nora and her sister, Belle Lamar, had sung and danced in a black vaudeville troupe. Family photos depicted Nora, whose face resembled Jimi's, dressed in sumptuous stage clothes. "While Jimi was staying in Vancouver," Al wrote, "he took to wearing a green cloth vest that was part of one of my mother's stage outfits. It had little tassels on it, like a Spanish dancer's vest. He used to wear that to school. Us kids used to fool around with my mother's old costume pieces when I was young, but we would never have thought of wearing them to school, but

Jimi liked that sort of thing. Of course, it stood out, because it wasn't something you'd ordinarily be wearing. That vest could have been the origin of his attraction to flamboyant clothes—I'll bet that's it, because he never got into any of Lucille's things when we were living together."[20] During his recent time in New York City, Jimi's attraction to flashy clothes had become more pronounced after his first white girlfriend, Carol Shiroky, introduced him to Trinidadian singer and limbo king Mike Quashie, who flaunted billowy shirts, colorful scarves, and costume jewelry.

While still in the first blush of romance, Jimi and Kathy discovered that although they'd grown up an ocean apart, in some ways they shared similar backgrounds. They'd both had challenging childhoods with at least one alcoholic parent. Both of their mothers had abandoned the family. Kathy had spent her earliest years in Derby, living in a working-class house without an indoor bathroom. After her mother left, she and her brother were sent to stay with relatives in Ireland. During her teens she was placed in Dublin's Holy Faith convent boarding school. Jimi had mostly grown up with his father and, on occasion, his younger brother Leon in a variety of rented rooms, apartments, and small houses around Seattle. When times got hard for Al, he shuttled his son to relatives and friends. "He'd had a very unhappy childhood," Kathy remembered. "He did talk about how he had no food, no shoes, hadn't got to have a change of clothes, had to go to other people's houses to be fed, how his dad used to punch him in the face and shave his hair, and how he would run away but had to go back because, of course, he had nowhere else to go. He didn't really consider that he had a family."[21]

Perhaps this sharing of their life stories inspired Jimi to pick up the telephone at 4:00 A.M. to make a collect call back home. In *My Son Jimi*, Al gave this version: "One day in late September 1966, our phone rang and the operator said 'London calling.' At first I was wondering who in the heck was calling me—I didn't know anybody over there. It was Jimi, and he was all excited as he told me, 'Dad, it looks like I'm on my way to the big time.' He went on to say he was in England, auditioning for a bass player and a drummer. 'I'm gonna call the group the Jimi Hendrix Experience,' he said, 'and I'm gonna have my name spelled J-i-m-i.'"[22] Kathy remembered the call differently: "Jimi said, 'Look, if you don't believe me, speak to my girlfriend.' So I got on the phone and said, 'Hello, Mr. Hendrix.' I spoke to him a few words, and he said, 'Look, my boy's in England? You tell my boy to write me. I'm not paying for no collect calls.'"[23] Six months later, interviewer Jan Waldrop asked Jimi about his dad. "I phoned him once, when I had just arrived in England," Jimi sadly confided. "I wanted to tell him what I had accomplished. He asked me who I had stolen the money from to go over to England."[24]

On September 28, Chas successfully obtained a work permit allowing Jimi to perform until year's end. That evening he took him to Les Cousins, a club Andy Matheou had opened in the basement of his parents' Greek restaurant.[25] Alexis Korner, a seminal figure in the British blues boom, was hosting a jam session there featuring American performers in town for the opening night of the fifth annual American Folk Blues Festival at the Royal Albert Hall. Chandler figured that Jimi, with his deep blues roots, would be a perfect fit for an audience that could help spread word of his arrival. Chris Welch noted, "There was a ready audience for what people thought was 'the source.' People wanted to see black artists in Britain because they were the inspiration for all our young musicians. People had grown up listening to B. B. King and Muddy Waters, Chuck Berry, and Bo Diddley. All of those great performers were really kind of revered. But when Jimi appeared, he seemed much younger, cooler, and hipper."[26]

The American Folk Blues Festivals had played an integral role in the early-1960s British blues boom, which found young musicians deriving influences from the sounds they'd picked up from American blues records and from watching visiting blues artists. Back home in America, as Jimi well knew, times were lean for African American blues performers, most of whom were relegated to playing the chitlin circuit. But in 1960s England, American blues artists were akin to royalty, as John Lee Hooker experienced during the first American Folk Blues Festival: "When I got to England in '62, it was like God just let Jesus go over there. That's all you could hear: 'John Lee Hooker!' Before I got to the concert hall—even if it was rainin'—the place be full with a line around the block."[27] The real thing, amped and cathartic, had arrived.

"Those shows had a really big impact," observed French producer/promoter Philippe Rault. "There was a bunch of English bands that put the fuse to the dynamite—like Alexis Korner and Cyril Davies—who really inspired all those groups like the Rolling Stones, but they were always the second-hand product. When those shows came over, there was a lot of attention, not only from the blues fans going to the shows, but from all of the English pop stars at the time. It was a major influence on spreading the blues in Europe at the time. That was a really pivotal period, 1962–1964. People were so starved for those shows because it was the real thing finally happening."[28] The Rolling Stones added Muddy Waters and Willie Dixon tunes to their repertoire. The Animals and Yardbirds adapted John Lee Hooker tunes. Eric Clapton formed his first band, the Roosters, to cover songs by Muddy Waters, Lightnin' Slim, Fats Domino, and T-Bone Walker. In Great Britain, albums by postwar bluesmen were highly sought after, as were small-label reissues of American country blues from the 1920s and 1930s. As he began earning money, Hendrix would assemble a formidable collection of blues albums.

The 1966 American Folk Blues Festival lineup featured singer Big Joe Turner; piano men Roosevelt Sykes and Little Brother Montgomery; Chicago mainstays Otis Rush, Junior Wells, and Jack Myers; Sippie Wallace, who'd first recorded in the early 1920s; and country blues artists Sleepy John Estes, Yank Rachell, and Robert Pete Williams. It's uncertain which musicians were present the night Jimi visited Les Cousins, but according to Andy Matheou, he did perform: "Alexis thought it would be good to get everyone together for an all-nighter with him topping the gig. That was the night Hendrix came in with Chas Chandler, his manager, and nobody had ever seen him before. This pale, quiet dude, and he just paid his money and walked in with no fuss. Later they asked him to play and he plugs in his white Fender and does all this stuff with his teeth and just blows everybody's mind."[29]

While Jimi Hendrix is often celebrated for his flash—the eardrum-ringing feedback, dive-bomb explosions, whammy and wah-wah, and ever-cool "electric prophet of the acid age" image— the music that he most closely identified with was the blues. This had been the soundtrack of his youth, and, as he'd prove on "Red House," "Bleeding Heart," "Hear My Train A Comin'," and other songs, he could easily hold his own alongside *any* bluesman. As Billy Cox, his closest friend and his bassist before and after the Experience, explained,

> You can call Jimi Hendrix whatever you like, but he was a blues master. That's what he was. A hell of a bluesman. You run that type of playing through a Fuzz Face and a loud amp, and what do you have? You have something that somebody may interpret as something else, but it's really nothing but the blues. Since he was so hot on the guitar, people said, "Wait a minute, we've never heard blues played like this," but that's what it was. His style also reflected his youth and social awareness, but just about everything Jimi and I recorded was blues. Everything was right from the soil, right from the depth of mankind. Blues was part of our being.[30]

As British audiences would soon discover, Jimi's approach to singing was flavored by the blues as well. "Jimi was singing like Muddy Waters," observed John McLaughlin. "Jimi had that thing, had the sound. It was almost part talking, part chanting. And he had the timbre, that sound that Muddy's voice had. So by the time he hit, people were just like, 'Wow, Jimi, beautiful!' Jimi had found his creative common. All the things by chance that were around him were absolutely ideal in that moment."[31]

Chas Chandler's first order of business was organizing a band to showcase Jimi's talent. First, he reached out to keyboardist Brian Auger, who was taken aback by Chandler's request. "What happened was I had just started the Brian Auger Trinity with Julie Driscoll," Auger said. "So I had already figured out exactly the direction I wanted to go, trying to make this kind of rock-jazz bridge. And shortly after that I got a call from Chas Chandler.... Chas said, 'Look. We've got this tremendous guitar player. I've just brought him over from New York, and I want him to front your band.' So I said, 'Well, that's all very nice, Chas, but A, I haven't heard the guy, and B, I have a guitar player. And I also have Julie Driscoll, and she fronts the band. So what are you expecting me to do? Just kind of fire these people? I'm certainly not really up to do that.' And the other thing was Mike Jeffery, man—I wanted absolutely nothing to do with this guy. The fact that he was offering me a situation which might lead to me being in the management pull of this guy, I went,

'No. Sorry, that's not gonna happen.'"[32] Instead, Auger suggested that Chandler bring Hendrix around for a jam session.

Chandler's next stop was a London club, the Birdland, where auditions were underway for the new Animals lineup. Here, Chandler figured, they might have luck recruiting musicians. Initially, Jimi wanted a nine-piece revue like Little Richard's. Chandler, though, convinced him to go with a smaller lineup, both to save money and to ensure that Jimi was the focus of attention. They briefly considered having a second guitarist and keyboardist, but Jimi decided against it. "I was thinking of the smallest piece possible with the hardest impact," he explained. "I figured that if you have a rhythm player it's going to slow down the whole thing because you have to show him exactly what you want. We did try the organ for about fifteen minutes, but it made us sound like just anybody."[33]

Responding to a "Musicians Wanted" notice he'd seen in *Melody Maker* announcing auditions for the New Animals, David Noel Redding, a twenty-year-old lead guitarist, made the journey from England's south coast to the Regent Street office listed in the ad. A spokesperson encouraged him to attend the Birdland auditions the following day. On Thursday, September 29, Noel auditioned with a couple of blues numbers, to little reaction. He had the distinct feeling that that Animals' lead guitar position had already been filled, but he was thrilled to be in the presence of pianist Mike O'Neill— "Nero" of the instrumental rock group Nero and the Gladiators— and drummer Aynsley Dunbar. Soon afterward, in walked Chas Chandler, whom Noel described in his autobiography as "bassist with the chart-topping Animals, TV star, and all-round god." Redding was less impressed with Chandler's companion, a tall, slender African American dressed in "a horrible tan raincoat and grotty black winkle-picker boots with zips! Awful!"[34]

Chandler asked Redding if he'd have a go at playing bass for his companion. Though he'd never played the instrument, Redding agreed. "Chas introduced me. Jimi, his name was, and he seemed quite pleasant and friendly. Jimi mumbled the chords of a song called 'Hey Joe' and we ran through it two or three times before briefly trying a couple of sequences in the same vein as 'Mercy, Mercy.' Jimi was amazed I remembered the chords so easily. But what's a blues progression when you've been in Germany learning new songs between sets? No one sang. It didn't seem like much of an audition. No talking, just this American guy playing nothing particularly special and the feeling that someone was planning a group."

When they set down their instruments, Noel invited Jimi to step out to a nearby pub called the Red Lion. As Jimi sipped his first taste of bitter ale, they chatted about music. Redding wondered if Jimi had ever seen Sam Cooke or Booker T. and the MG's: "He had! That improved him a lot in my estimation. Jimi commented on my hair, which I'd begun to grow long, even though it was curly like his own and therefore not trendy.... He said I must be groovy to have hair like that and as we walked back he asked if I would come up to the audition room the next day, as he hoped I'd be in a new group with him."[35] Noel agreed, with the provision that Chas provide him with ten shillings to cover his train fare.

That evening Chandler brought Jimi to sit in with the Brian Auger Trinity at Blaises, a small, trendy club in the basement of the Imperial Hotel. The place was packed. During the break Chas introduced Brian to Jimi. "He seemed like a really nice guy," Auger remembered. "I said, 'Okay, what would you want to play, Jim?' He said, 'Can you play this chord sequence?' He showed me the sequence. I said, 'Yeah, that's cool.' It was the sequence to 'Hey Joe.' Now, I didn't know 'Hey Joe.' I'd never played it. But the sequence was pretty easy. So I said, 'Fine, okay. Give us the tempo.'"[36] Jimi plugged his guitar in the Marshall amp belonging to Auger's guitarist, Vic Briggs. Hendrix, who'd never before seen a Marshall amp, immediately rolled the amp's dials to ten, much to amazement of its owner, who had yet to set the controls past five. Jimi, who typically set his amps on full power, preferred to use his guitar's volume knob to control his sound.

Unleashing a wall of feedback, Jimi segued into "Hey Joe." "Everyone did a kind of 'Oh, my God!'" Auger remembered. "Talk about double-take! It was like, 'Whoa!' [With] most of our guitar players, you could still kind of hear the people that they learned from, which was people like B. B. King, Freddie King, Albert King, Albert Collins, Howlin' Wolf. You know, they had all these things in their playing makeup still. Jimi Hendrix—now, I never heard anybody play like that. That was something else."[37] Other guitarists had already employed feedback in a minimal way—the opening note of the Beatles' 1964 recording of "I Feel Fine" provides a prime example—but as heard by clubgoers that night at Blaises, Jimi pioneered its use in an expansive and ultimately *musical* way. In addition, his manner of dress, the sinuous and sensuous way he moved, and the fact that he was playing his Stratocaster "upside-down" stood in stark contrast to most British rock guitarists, who tended to play standing still, looking down at their fretting hand.

French singing star Johnny Hallyday and his surrogate father/ manager, Lee Hallyday, witnessed this performance. "Johnny Hallyday was a French artist, a great, great performer and singer," Auger noted. "He was like the Elvis of France. He was that big. He'd have headlines in the paper every day."[38] As Jimi played, Chandler scored him his first paying gigs: "Lee said, 'Johnny's going out for his first French tour in five years. Have you got a band together for this guy? He could be a support act.' I said yes, even though I didn't—I only had the bass player fixed. Lee said that they started their tour in ten days' time and if we joined them in Nice we could do the whole tour. So we sat and did a deal that night."[39]

The following morning, Jeff Beck, already one of Britain's leading rock guitarists, received an unexpected a wake-up call.

Some girlfriend rang up and said, "You gotta hear this guy Jimi Hendrix." I went [*unenthused*], "Oh, really?" She said, "Yeah, I was at a club last night and he's unbelievable." That's all you want to hear first thing in the morning—someone's outrageous guitar playing. So I went along to see Hendrix at Blaises. Unbelievable! Great, great. It was like a bomb blowing up in the right place. I just went away from there thinking I've got to find something else to do. . . . He was a great source of inspiration—the fact that he was doing things so upfront and so wild. That's what I wanted to do, but being British and a victim of the class system and whatever—you know, these poxy old schools we used to go to—I couldn't do what he did.[40]

As Jimi had requested, Noel Redding returned to Birdland, only to find no one there. In a panic, he hurried to the Animals' office, ANIM Ltd., at 40 Gerrard Street. The first person he encountered, Mike Jeffery, told him, "It's okay. You got the audition. Move to London." Though overjoyed at being hired, Redding had misgivings about Jeffery—well-founded, it would turn out. Despite his bespectacled, student-like appearance, Jeffery carried a .32 Beretta in his shoulder holster and was rumored to have links to East End gangsters. He had no problem with people misspelling his name as "Jeffries" or "Jeffrey." He had many trappings of success—clubs in Newcastle and Majorca, a sumptuous £100-a-month London flat, and the money he'd made managing the Animals. He unwound by throwing knives into walls and wardrobes, and had a profound fear of flying. Redding wrote, "In moments of panic he'd nervously babble about working undercover for British Army Intelligence—real spine-chilling tales about attacking a secret Russian/Egyptian base during the Suez raid, or about being used as bait in Greece to lure three men in for the kill, or about being imprisoned and tortured in a Balkan castle, or about a fellow agent who was thrown back across the border with a glass tube broken in his penis. . . . I never knew what to make of him."[41] It was also well known that under Jeffery's management, the Animals' business affairs were in disarray. Nevertheless, the idea of starting his career anew alongside the bloke from America overcame his reservations about Jeffery.

By then Noel had been playing music, mostly on guitar, for about a dozen years. He'd given his first musical performance in primary school, playing "Tom Dooley" on a Jew's harp. "From then on I dreamed, first cautiously then flamboyantly, of being a *musician*," Noel wrote in his memoir.[42] His mother, who raised him as a single parent, ran a guesthouse in the small coastal village of Seabrook. While Margaret Redding was open to her middle child becoming a musician, she encouraged Noel to consider a career in architecture. While in grammar school Noel studied violin and taught himself mandolin from a book. Noticing his fascination for her classical guitar, a teacher who lived nearby let him try her instrument. "That was the end of the mandolin," Noel wrote. "I started pleading for a guitar for my birthday, but Mum thought it would be another flash-in-the-pan. As we were eternally hard up, the thought of £6.65 going for nothing was not appealing. And since my birthday was on Christmas Day, my dreams looked like they would be going unfulfilled."[43] Noel's mum came through, though, trading in the mandolin at the Helping Hand shop in Folkestone and emerging with an acoustic guitar. Within a week, the jubilant twelve-year-old was "driving her distracted" with two-chord vamps.

In 1958 Redding discovered rock and roll. His first entry into his Letts Schoolboy Diary simply read, "Rock and Roll is jolly good!" A schoolmate, Pete Kircher, had also just acquired a guitar. On Saturdays they'd meet at Noel's house to play skiffle, a folksy, bluesy, somewhat heavy-handed answer to America's folk boom. They also listened to the BBC's exciting new radio program, *Saturday Club*, showcasing up-and-coming bands. Noel became enthralled with the steady flow of new releases by Elvis Presley, Eddie Cochran, Buddy Holly, Gene Vincent, Chuck Berry, and others. During evenings he tuned in to Radio Luxembourg's broadcasts of American singles on programs such as *Rockin' to Dreamland*, *Record Hop*, and *Jamboree*. "This music changed my world," he wrote. "I totally loved American music!"[44] To earn money for a record player, Noel took on an early-morning paper route.

Other enduring influences came via concerts and TV broadcasts. In his autobiography, Redding recounted how in May 1959 he attended a memorable show by Billy Fury and Cliff Richard at the Folkestone Odeon. After the encore, he scaled the side of the building to the second-floor dressing room window to ask for their autographs, which he treasured throughout his life. He gave his first notable public performance on guitar at the Hythe Youth Club, playing a skiffle version of Lead Belly's "The Boll Weevil" and covers of Ricky Nelson and Laurie London hits. His first paid performance earned him two shillings and a cup of tea. "No stopping me now," he wrote. He spent the next summer selling ice cream from a bicycle cart, in hopes of earning enough to buy an electric guitar. That fall Noel's mother bought him his first amplifier, an eight-watt Grampion. Within a week he'd mounted a pickup onto his acoustic guitar and was playing amplified. At sixteen he obtained a Futurama solid-body guitar and dropped out of art school.

Redding played lead guitar in his earliest bands: the Strangers, from which he was evicted early on; the Lonely Ones, a cover band that recorded a few songs in 1963; and Neil Landon and the Burnettes, with whom he toured Scotland and Germany when he was seventeen. While in Germany, he began experimenting with drugs: "Inevitably, fatigue took over and we discovered helpful additives. For a 'straight' country there were lots of chemical drugs around, mostly stimulants. We got our pill education there. Generally, you could buy Captagon uppers very easily from club lavatory attendants. They helped offset the long hours and the amount of drink we consumed. Soon we were never without a supply."[45] During the fall of 1965 the Burnettes opened shows in England for the Hollies, the Ivy League, and the Nashville Teens. When the Burnettes disbanded, Noel resurrected the Lonely Ones. They obtained management, did session work for Engelbert Humperdinck, and recorded a pair of singles that sold poorly, but paying gigs were few and far between. Noel called it quits and returned home. "I confessed to Mum that I was completely down and she suggested one last try," he wrote.[46] This advice led him to answer the *Melody Maker* advertisement.

When Jimi invited Noel to join the band, Kathy Etchingham was less than enthusiastic about the choice, describing Redding as "an ordinary young man from Folkestone with no airs and graces. He just wanted to play guitar and get paid for it."[47] Unable to afford lodgings in London, Noel initially commuted back and forth from his mother's bungalow. The seventy-mile train journey took its toll, though, so he rented a single room in London with his friend Gerry Stickells, a skilled car mechanic who owned a van. During the days to come, Jimi and Noel would finalize the Experience lineup for the French tour and Stickells would become an essential member of their entourage.

3:October
1966

A Meeting of the Gods

Pictures have always fascinated me. I still sketch a lot, but now I've got to learn to paint pictures with my music. —Jimi Hendrix[1]

In American jazz and blues circles, there's an old variation of cat-and-mouse called "head-cutting," where a musician outperforms an unsuspecting competitor in front of an audience. The best practitioners tend to combine sublime musicianship with jaw-dropping stage moves—"showboating," as Stevie Ray Vaughan called it. With his uncanny ability to perform music he'd heard on the radio or records, the 1930s bluesman Robert Johnson, whose music Jimi admired, was expert in this area. Johnny Shines, who traveled with Johnson, described what would happen when they'd play for tips in Handy Park in Memphis: "Now, a guy over here have a big crowd, and we'd strike up over there and probably pull half his crowd or all of his crowd. If you pull all of his crowd, that's what we called 'head-cuttin'.' You know—we just cut his head!"[2] During the early 1950s, another of Jimi's musical heroes, Muddy Waters, specialized in cutting heads at "blues contests" around Chicago. As Muddy told it, "Little Walter, Jimmy Rogers, and myself, we would go around looking for bands that were playing. We called ourselves 'the Headhunters,' 'cause we'd go in and if we got the chance we were gonna burn 'em."[3] Although none of London's rock elites were as yet aware of it, Jimi Hendrix, intentionally or not, was already a master head-cutter, as Bloomfield had so recently experienced in Greenwich Village.

Less than a week after his arrival in London, Jimi Hendrix would get his chance to share the stage with England's foremost guitar star, a player so gifted that fans had taken to scrawling "Clapton Is God" on London's buildings and Underground walls. Following his celebrated stints in the Yardbirds and John Mayall's Bluesbreakers, Eric Clapton had in recent weeks unveiled rock's first power trio, Cream, with Jack Bruce on bass and Ginger Baker on drums. His intention, he'd told *Record Mirror* that August, was to expand his musical directions: "I'm tired of being called a specialist musician. People thought Cream was going to be a blues band, but it's not. It's a pop group, really."[4] Cream's October 1 performance at the Central London Polytechnic on Regent Street was highly anticipated. A few days before the gig, Chas Chandler remembered, "I bumped into Jack Bruce and Eric Clapton in a club called the Cromwellian. It was one of our watering holes then. I told them about Jimi. And they said, 'Well, bring him down to the Regent Polytechnic Saturday'—that was the very early days of Cream. They said, 'Bring him down and have him jam with us.'"[5]

On the night of the show, the Student Union was packed. "We were just getting ready to go on," Clapton recalled, "and Chas showed up with this young black guy who was very striking in every way—I mean, his appearance and his manner, which was to say, at the least, very, very shy. He was extremely shy, but at the same time quite kind of aware of himself. And he brought his own guitar. He was left-handed, for a start, and he played a normal Strat, so the whole thing was upside-down. So that was a little astonishing."[6] Talking backstage, Eric and Jimi discovered that they liked the same blues artists. The song he wanted to play, Jimi told Eric, was Howlin' Wolf's "Killing Floor." "I thought it was incredible that he would know how to play this," Clapton wrote in his autobiography, "as it was a tough one to get right."[7]

Two-thirds of the way through Cream's set, their special guest was called onstage. Jimi plugged his white Stratocaster into Bruce's bass amp and began playing chords. "Sashaying across the stage in some sort of mutant Chuck Berryesque duckwalk," as concert attendee Steve Barker described it, Jimi went straight into "Killing Floor."[8] Clapton, who'd immersed himself in American blues records and took great care in recreating the original guitar parts as authentically as he could, was utterly unprepared for what happened next. Hendrix, in essence, became like an updated version of Charlie Christian and other 1940s jazz luminaries who created bebop to break away from the strict structures of swing. Jimi pushed beyond his extensive background in blues and R&B to launch into a performance unlike anything the audience or members of Cream had ever experienced. "Eric's hands were on the guitar," Chandler recounted, "and they just dropped. He just stood there, looking at Jimi. He walked off the stage. I thought, 'Oh, dear, I knew this was gonna happen.'"[9] Chandler later took delight in telling people how, after Cream had concluded their set, he found Eric nervously smoking a cigarette in the dressing room. Eric looked up and said, "You didn't tell me how fucking good he was, did ya?" Kathy, who attended the performance, wrote that "at that time Jimi's playing was perfect because he was so fresh, so eager to prove himself, and totally sober."[10]

"Of course, Jimi played it exactly like it ought to be played," Clapton wrote,

> and he totally blew me away. When jamming with another band for the first time, most musicians will try to hold back, but Jimi just went for it. He played the guitar with his teeth, behind his head, lying on the floor, doing the splits, the whole business. It was amazing, and it was musically great, too, not just pyrotechnics. Even though I had already seen Buddy Guy and knew a lot of black players could do this kind of stuff, it's still pretty amazing when you're standing right next to it. The audience was completely gobsmacked by what they saw and heard, too. They loved it, and I loved it, too, but I remember thinking that here was a force to be reckoned with. It scared me, because he was clearly going to be a huge star, and just as we were finding our own speed, here was the real thing.[11]

"It was a very brave person who would do that," Jack Bruce said of Jimi's performance. "It was blues all the way, of course. He just played his ass off, basically. The first time I saw Eric, I thought, 'Wow. There's a master guitar player,' but Eric was a guitar player. Jimi was some sort of force of nature. It was like, 'wow!'—that kind of a thing. I know it had a tremendous effect on Eric."[12] Ginger Baker concurred: "Eric just stands there and plays. And then you've got this guy suddenly on his knees, playing with his teeth, and, you know, screwing his guitar onstage. I thought, 'God, what is this?!'"[13] In just a few minutes' time, Jimi Hendrix had head-cut Britain's reigning guitar deity.

Jimi, it turns out, already knew "Killing Floor" quite well. Howlin' Wolf had recorded his original version for Chess Records in August 1964 with Hubert Sumlin and Buddy Guy on electric guitars. On December 26, 1965, and January 22, 1966, Hendrix was taped playing the song with Curtis Knight at George's Club 20 in Hackensack, New Jersey. Aural evidence suggests that Hendrix sang the lead vocals on one of the two versions of "Killing Floor" recorded by Knight's band. The song would remain a staple in Jimi's concert repertoire for months to come.

Hendrix would later express regret for upstaging Clapton, telling Sharon Lawrence, "When I think back, it seems so pushy that I would have barged into someone else's show that way. I can hardly believe I treated Clapton—a hero of mine—with so little respect. I can still remember seeing him out of the corner of my eye, a glimpse of him watching me that night. I knew I was being rude. But at the time I had to get moving, so I did. You know that I love Eric Clapton."[14]

During the ensuing months, Jimi and Eric gradually forged a friendship based on their mutual admiration of each other's styles and shared influences. "As is the way with musicians," Clapton explained, "we just sort of dug up all our heroes and compared them. We actually thought the same. He liked Robert Johnson. He liked Freddie and B. B. King, and he liked Buddy Guy. He liked all the same people, and he just seemed to be conversant in all this. It was such a thrill for me, because it was all second-hand, in reality, for me. It was something that I learned from records. This guy had been amongst them and was one of them. . . . Most of what people [in London] had been used to was kind of dressed-up, watered-down soul music. And for someone like Jimi to come along was so powerful. I think it was simply that—that he was so powerful and so direct. It was what everyone had been waiting for."[15]

As he got to know Hendrix better, Clapton astutely observed that the image Jimi projected to others masked deeper feelings. "I think that is the curse of genius—that you are alone," Eric explained. "No one can understand the depths you go to when you reach down inside yourself to play or to express. You can't take anyone with you to those places. Sometimes you find things that are very scary. You have to survive that on your own, and that is a very lonely experi-ence. It's not something you choose, it's not something that you would necessarily go after. It's something you inherit with your gift—and he had it in aces. It did make him very lonely, even with other musicians of his caliber—and there weren't many. Perhaps there weren't any. I tried to get close to him, but there was always a kind of barrier that wasn't of his making, I'm sure. It's just that's the way it is when you're that great."[16]

During their initial rehearsals Jimi and Noel played without a drummer. "This is good," Noel wrote, "because we got to know each other a bit and learned to understand each other's guitar style without immediately having to incorporate a third musician. I was enjoying experimenting on bass. Never having played one before was very liberating in its way."[17] As Noel learned his way around Chandler's six-string Burns bass, the musicians ran through "Land of 1000 Dances," "In the Midnight Hour," "Everybody Needs Some-body to Love," "Respect," and "Johnny B. Goode." "We rehearsed casually," Noel said, "never resorting to 'This riff goes like this' or 'Play these notes.' When Jimi had a new idea, he gave the basic chord structure and tempo and within that framework we each found our own parts, and a song and arrangement emerged."[18] To facilitate string bends and better suit his voice, Jimi tuned his Stratocaster down a half step, making his strings, from low to high, Eb, Ab, Db, Gb, Bb, Eb. Redding followed suit. Unlike most bassists, who use bare fingers to pluck the strings, Noel usually played with a guitar pick—tortoiseshell plectrums at first, and later .88 mm plastic picks made in Germany. He preferred Rotosound wire-wound strings, praising their ability to deliver a "good, clear, trebly zing" even at high volume. Jimi favored a plastic, standard-shape, medium-gauge guitar pick and strung his guitar with Fender light-gauge strings that Chas bought for him at Sound City.

Due to the alignment of the Stratocaster's six-in-a-row tun-ing machines, flipping the guitar over and restringing it the stan-dard way changed the string tension across the guitar, making the low E string the longest string and the high E the shortest. Stevie Ray Vaughan, who came close to re-creating the classic Hendrix sound, explained how this rearrangement affects a Stratocaster's playability: "I have guitars where the necks are set up that way, and there is a difference. To me the bigger difference is the shape of the neck. I've got a left-handed neck on an old Strat that I have, and the main thing I notice about it is the neck feels different because it's shaped backwards. I didn't know about it until I put one on there. The neck feels different. The tension of the strings does work well that way. One thing that I noticed that's a lot different is where the wang bar is—if it's on the top or on the bottom. Whether I hold it with the same grip as if it was in the other place or not, it still feels different to me at the top. It seems more approachable or something."[19] By flipping over a right-handed Strat, Hendrix's "wang bar"—also known as a "tremolo arm," "whammy," and "vibrato bar"—was on top.

The most pressing issue facing Chandler was finding a drummer in time for the Hallyday tour. Aynsley Dunbar, John Banks of the Merseybeats, and others auditioned. Then, on October 4, learning that Mitch Mitchell was available, Chandler asked the nineteen-year-old to try out. In his book *Jimi Hendrix: Inside the Experience*, Mitchell described his first encounter with Jimi:

At the audition it was strange. I met this black guy with very, very wild hair, wearing this Burberry raincoat. He looked very straight, really, apart from the hair. We didn't talk much at first—you've got to remember this was an audition for me sandwiched in between two sessions. Jimi was very soft-spoken and gave the impression of being very gentle, almost shy. It was immediately apparent he was a good guitarist, but at that stage I was more knocked out that he could cover so many different styles as well. You name it, he could do it. I think we did "Have Mercy Baby" first. Jimi didn't really sing, more mumbled along to the music—Chas really had to coax it out of him. But we both clearly loved the same types of music.

So there we were in this tiny basement club, playing with these ridiculously small amps and for about two hours we ran through what we all knew—your Chuck Berry roots, Wilson Pickett, basically R&B stuff that everyone knows and accepts. Just feeling each other out. I didn't know then that Noel had only just picked up bass for the first time, apparently because he had the right haircut—but them's the breaks, you know? I remember throwing a few things at Hendrix. I really like

Curtis Mayfield and the Impressions, and I was astounded that he knew that style really, really fluently. He wasn't that flash as a guitarist on that occasion, it was more just going over rhythmic structures. I suppose we got through a lot of material in the two hours, but I got a little pissed off because I didn't really know how Jimi wanted me to play.... In fact, I'm not sure Jimi knew exactly what he wanted. That didn't come until we rehearsed properly the following week.[20]

John "Mitch" Mitchell was already known to the British public. A native Londoner, he had been to theatrical school, sung advertising jingles, and made his radio debut in the BBC's 1960 production of *Macbeth*. Under the name John Mitchell, he'd played the lead part in the 1958 TV series *Jennings at School* and went on to appear in a variety of television programs. By age fourteen he was more interested in drumming than acting. His part-time job in Jim Marshall's drum and guitar shop in Hanwell put him in contact with many musicians, which, in turn, led to his playing drums in a series of groups: Peter Nelson and the Travellers, featuring Vic Briggs on guitar; the Coronets, with whom he toured Germany; the Riot Squad; and, for the eighteen months leading up to the Hendrix audition, Georgie Fame and the Blue Flames, a position that required him to adhere to specific parts. He'd also compiled an impressive discography of studio work backing Petula Clark, Brenda Lee, Joe Mack, and others. As he explained in his autobiography, "I got a load of sessions because I was a rock drummer—a lot of the older guys or the jazz musicians couldn't cut it for pop stuff—even though I couldn't read."[21]

Mitchell credited his Fame bandmates for fueling his passion for jazz luminaries John Coltrane, Oliver Nelson, Thelonious Monk, Philly Joe Jones, Tony Williams, and especially Elvin Jones, whose polyrhythmic drumming style he especially admired. Just before the Hendrix audition, Mitchell found himself suddenly unemployed. As a *Melody Maker* headline put it, "Georgie Fame Snuffs Flames." From Jimi's perspective, the timing couldn't have been better: "Mitch Mitchell was the best out of about twenty drummers we heard. He used to play with Georgie Fame and the Blue Flames, and he's more of a classic drummer, more of a funky R&B–type

drummer. Mitch is a jazz addict and he keeps [going] on about this cat Elvin Jones all the time. He played me a record once by Elvin Jones and I said, 'Damn, that's you!'"[22]

Mitch, who until then had little more than a nodding acquaintance with Chas Chandler, was impressed that the former Animal would sell his basses to finance Jimi's band. "The second or third time we played," he wrote, "things started to stretch out considerably. That's when I started to feel it was a real chance, having come from such a structured unit as the Blue Flames, with horns and very tight arrangements, to come to something as loose as Hendrix. To have that much freedom was like being released from prison, and to have that much freedom was a most fortunate thing."[23]

The final choice for the drummer position came down to the flip of a coin. "Fortunately for us," Chandler said, "it turned up Mitch. I think we were very lucky there, because Mitch was the perfect man for the job. Noel played like the anchor in the band. He kept it steady. Jimi and Mitch then just opened up and just played off the seat of their pants. They could always come back to where Noel was, just keeping the whole thing together. It was a perfect fusion. It was very exciting."[24] In his diary, Noel cited October 6 as the date he was told Mitch was in the band.

During the initial rehearsals, Noel had difficulty navigating the six-string Burns bass, due to the strings being so close together. Chas suggested that he try his Gibson EB-2, a four-string semi-acoustic model. Noel found the Gibson's body too big and thought that the instrument lacked the powerful treble sound he was looking for, so Chandler loaned him a Danelectro Longhorn six-string guitar for the Hallyday tour. Eventually, Noel would settle on a four-string Fender Jazz Bass. During rehearsals, Mitch noticed, Noel's bass playing remained guitar-oriented. Chas tutored Noel on scales and walking patterns, and on occasion Jimi would show him the bass parts he wanted to hear.

For one rehearsal Procol Harum bassist David Knights was brought in and Noel moved to rhythm guitar. "But when David didn't fit in," Redding wrote, "Jimi admitted once and for all that he wanted freedom for the guitar himself, needed to be able to just let go without worrying about arrangements or treading on other soloists."[25] Like Jimi, Noel was taken with Mitch's playing: "His flashy style was perfect for us. With my Mick Green-inspired days as a skiffle-ready rock 'n' roll rhythm guitarist as the rock on which my bass style was built, Jimi and Mitch could—and would—be free to flip to either side of me. Sometimes it would feel like walking a tightrope between two cyclones."[26] This formula for group improvisation would prove especially exciting onstage.

The musical relationship that Jimi, Mitch, and Noel developed early on was similar to the approach used by John Coltrane when he and drummer Elvin Jones would engage in extended improvisations while bassist Jimmy Garrison provided the music's strong, steady pulse. In the Experience's trio setting, Noel's strongest musical asset was his innate ability to anchor the music with an impeccable groove. By simultaneously covering the rhythm and harmony, he freed Jimi and Mitch to go "out" as far as inspiration carried them. When the moment called for it, Noel could propel the music by playing slightly on top of the beat or swooping his hand up the instrument's neck. In 1966 London, the only other rock or pop band with a similar approach was Cream, which, like the Experience, combined musicians with backgrounds in jazz, blues, and rock.

During the Experience's formative stage, it was unclear who'd do the singing. "Nobody wanted to sing, not even at rehearsals," Noel wrote.

> Even though he'd been singing in New York, Jimi was still nervous about being in England and got terribly embarrassed about singing. Me too. I had a squeak, not a voice. Mitch's voice was more trained and relaxed because of his stage schooling, but wasn't what we needed, and besides, drummers weren't expected to sing. Our first gigs were virtually instrumentals with extremely minimal mumbles. Finally, we broke down Jimi's shyness and persuaded him to sing. We needed him to sing. His voice had a good fullness to it, and his American accent would certainly catch the English ear. At first he'd crank his guitar up really loud to cover his singing, but gradually he gained confidence and found the right balance between voice and guitar.[27]

Mitch's fiery side emerged early in the rehearsals. "We had no real songs as such," he explained. "On that subject, Hendrix and I actually ended up in a nose-to-nose confrontation on about the third rehearsal. Jimi said, 'Well, we've got some gigs coming up, let's do "Midnight Hour."' I, being a cocky little bastard at the time, said, 'Oh, fuck! Not this *again*. I've just come from doing "Midnight Hour" for two years. We've got a new band, can't we do better than this? Please?' I had nothing against the song—great, a classic—but that was my attitude. Because of this confrontation and the fact that I'd only agreed to the twenty quid for two weeks, I was branded by the management as 'The Troublemaker. This boy is no good for us.' Words were had behind my back—[but] not by Hendrix.... I think that because I spoke my mind, Jimi rooted for me. He thought we would work well together."[28] Kathy Etchingham expressed a different view, noting that "in the early days Jimi would become infuriated with Mitch's patronizing attitude. At one stage there was talk of sacking him and taking on Aynsley instead."[29]

As they prepared for the tour, the trio grew increasingly unhappy with playing through the sonically meek thirty-watt Burns amps Chandler had loaned them. "Gotta get rid of this stuff!" Jimi told his bandmates. According to accounts by Mitch and Noel, they deliberately sabotaged the Burns amps by throwing them down a flight of stairs. "Jimi wanted big Marshall amplifiers," Mitch wrote. "For a three-piece band, we thought, let's make it powerful."[30] Thus on October 8, Mitch took Jimi to meet his former employer, Jim Marshall, whose high-volume, namesake amplifiers were being used by Pete Townshend and several others. Jimi questioned Marshall at length about his amps. At first, Marshall remembered, "I thought he was just another one who wanted to have something for nothing. But he seemed to read what I was thinking and he said, almost in his next breath, 'Well, I don't want it for nothing. I wanna pay full price, but I want good service.' And that's what we gave him."[31] Their new equipment arrived three days later, just in time for the French tour.

On October 11, the eve of the Hallyday tour, Jimi, Mitch, and Noel met at the ANIM Ltd. office to sign a production deal with Chas Chandler and Michael Jeffery. Anxious to begin earning money, they did not have a lawyer review the document, and they were leery of asking questions that might convey a lack of trust with their new management. By signing, the musicians agreed to collectively work together as coequals in the "Jimi Hendrix Experience," serve as exclusive artists for Chandler and Jeffery for seven years, and grant their managers control of their recordings, song-writing, and publishing. Anyone who left the group would remain under contract and couldn't record with others without management's permission or grant any rights and licenses. The musicians also agreed not to get convicted, misbehave in public, or become ill.

In exchange, Jeffery and Chandler agreed to organize, pay for, and exploit the recordings. The contract granted Chandler and Jeffery rights to the name "Jimi Hendrix Experience," worldwide rights to song copyrights, all performance rights, and the right to assign any of these rights to someone else. For their efforts, Jeffery and Chandler would receive 20 percent of the band's income, as well as a share of the royalties and publishing. Buried among the legalese was the musicians' pay: a weekly salary of £15 and a shared 2.5 percent of the retail price of the vinyl recordings, calculated at 90 percent. This amount was halved for tapes and records sold in certain areas of the world. "The group would share as little as 0.31 percent in some cases," Redding wrote.[32] They were not given a copy of the documents they'd just signed.

"Charitably characterized," explains Lawrence Townsend, "this contract was opportunistic, greedy, exploitative ... but legal. Such a management relationship, grounded in plantation economics, was by no means an aberration back in the 1960s, and the practice continues to rear its ugly head to this day. The weekly musician payments were very low. These were later increased, but this was *after* they became big. It was bad enough that Hendrix and the band members were not encouraged to have their own lawyer review the contract before signing, especially where it's common, if not expected, that young musicians would and 'should' simply trust their professional manager. That they were never given copies of the contract is a telling detail of overreach that's by design and unapologetic."[33] In hindsight, Redding wished Chas Chandler had been the group's sole manager, but Chandler, too, was still signed to Jeffery. While he saw Jeffery as a "brilliant" agent/manager, Noel wrote that "his 'sheer confusion is best' policy haunted us. A real charming wheeler-dealer, he rarely let his left hand even know he had a right hand. However, he was well established and Chas's calling was creative management/production rather than business."[34]

At 7:00 A.M. on October 12, the Jimi Hendrix Experience and Chas Chandler boarded the plane for Paris. The day before, Chas had presented Jimi with a tailored two-piece blue mohair suit to wear for the shows. "Jimi hated it," Kathy remembered. As they awaited takeoff, Mitch watched with dismay as the luggage handlers carelessly tossed their brand-new stage gear—three Marshall amps, two speakers, two PA cabinets, three Shure microphones, and mike stands—into the luggage hold. After landing, Chandler helped the trio carry their equipment to an open-to-reporters rehearsal at the Paris Olympia. What a thrill it must have been for Jimi, who'd yet to perform in public with his band, to step onto the stage of this grand theater from the 1880s. *This* was a world apart from Southern dives and tiny Greenwich Village clubs. It was also an unlikely venue for test-driving their new amplification for the first time.

The next morning Jimi and the other musicians rode in a beat-up bus to the tour's opening performance, while Hallyday drove himself in a sports car. As they crossed the French countryside on the ninety-minute journey from Paris to Évreux, Mitch overcame the language barrier with one of Hallyday's French-speaking horn players by offering him an "illegal smoking substance." To calm their nerves before their gig that night, Jimi, Mitch, and Noel shared a homemade joint made of tobacco and hashish. Jimi Hendrix, it turned out, had difficulty rolling joints. "Jimi wasn't used to smoking in this way," Redding wrote, "and he always asked, 'Roll me one of those big English joints, Noel. I can't do it.' I don't think he ever sussed rolling those joints."[35] Kathy Etchingham noted this as well, calling rock's most dexterous guitarist "fumble-fingered" when it came to rolling joints.

On the evening of Thursday, October 13, 1966, the Jimi Hendrix Experience gave their debut performance at the Cinema Novelty in Évreux. Sharing the bill with the Blackbirds, Long Chris, and Johnny Hallyday, the trio were allotted fifteen minutes. Discovering a blown speaker, Noel had to play through the PA. They opened with "In the Midnight Hour," followed by "Have Mercy Baby," "Land of 1000 Dances," and "Hey Joe." Noel remembered that they were well-received, while Mitch found Jimi's performance a revelation: "Jimi was a quiet bloke—at least until he got onstage. It was on this first gig that we saw the whole other person, completely different from anything I'd seen before, even during rehearsals. I knew he played really tasty guitar, had the chops, but I didn't know about the showmanship that went with it. It was like, 'Whoosh! This man is really out-front!'... The showmanship—playing behind his head, with his teeth, etc.—was amazing. But even then it was obviously not just flashiness. He really did have the musicianship to go with it."[36]

Their performance garnered a tepid review in the local newspaper, *L'Eure Éclair*, which identified neither the name of the band nor Jimi himself. Described simply as "Hallyday's latest discovery," Jimi was described as a *"chanteur guitariste à la chevelure broussailleuse, mauvais cocktail de James Brown et de Chuck Berry, qui se contorsionne pendant un bon quart d'heure sur la scène en jouant également de la guitare avec les dents."*[37] This translates to "a singer-guitarist with bushy hair, a bad cocktail of James Brown and Chuck Berry who contorted onstage for a good quarter of an hour and sometimes played the guitar with his teeth."[38] Thirty years later, Évreux erected a plaque in the Chartraine shopping arcade commemorating the Jimi Hendrix Experience's first official concert.

The next morning the musicians embarked on the five-hour commute to Nancy, traveling through cold rain and congested traffic. After their arrival Noel introduced his bandmates to his drugs of choice, Captagon and Preludin. Normally prescribed to suppress the appetite and counter depression, nervousness, and narcolepsy, these drugs stimulated the central nervous system. Boosting the user's concentration and physical performance, they provided an overall feeling of well-being. "I rationed everyone to half a tablet," Noel wrote, "knowing that a whole one would keep us up all night. After that, before gigs it was 'Hey, Noel, got any of those tablets?'"[39]

That evening the Jimi Hendrix Experience played to an audience of 1,500 at Nancy's Cinéma le Rio. The next morning's edition of *L'Est Républicain* gave a rapturous description of Johnny Hallyday's performance, describing him first throwing his white tie into his adoring audience. His fans roared as his shirt buttons popped open. "Within fifteen minutes," continued the account, "his shirt is soaking wet. The next twenty minutes he finishes his set of songs bare-chested, using his muscles to mark the last bars. Johnny has the place turned upside down."[40] Jimi told Sharon Lawrence, "Johnny was very professional, one of the best-rehearsed entertainers I had ever seen. Chas and I watched every move he made, all his stage tricks. When and why he slowed the pace down. How and why he moved closer to the audience. He was never sloppy—ever. Johnny was very alert to the audience and to his band."[41] In another review of the Nancy show, the *Républicain Lorrain* renamed Jimi "Tommy Hemdrix," described him as "un noir," and mentioned that the guitarist showed a fine style by playing with his teeth.

The tour moved north to Villerupt, where the Experience played a six-song set at the Salle Des Fêtes. Once again, *L'Est Républicain* sent a reporter to cover the event. Translated into English, the account read: "Long Chris, who sees himself as a redeemer, was hissed at during his folk songs. It was too soft. By contrast, the whole audience became ecstatic when a certain Jimmy, an American resembling a Papuan, discovered in a suburb of London by Johnny, gave a remarkable exhibition on guitar. Not satisfied with playing the instrument behind his back, the 'virtuoso' also played with his teeth. Without doubt he had too much appetite the day before, in Nancy, since a string broke at the beginning of this performance."[42] In the parlance of the day, "Papuan" referred to Jimi's wild hair style rather than his skin color.[43] The notion that Hallyday had "discovered" Jimi Hendrix shows up in other contemporary accounts, but that credit clearly belongs to Linda Keith and Chas Chandler.

Jimi, Mitch, Noel, and Chas celebrated the concert by getting drunk together. Soon after their midnight departure for Paris, the bus ran out of fuel. "Was it cold!" Redding remembered. "Mitch grabbed Chas's raincoat for himself and went to sleep. Chas, Jimi, and I huddled together and tried to keep from freezing through the long, long night."[44] Luckily, they had the next day off. Feeling jittery about their Paris debut, they rehearsed at Olympia on the 17th. Afterward Jimi explored the sumptuous theater that had survived two world wars. He was delighted to learn that Bob Dylan had performed there five months earlier. After acclimating himself to the venue, he braved the chilly evening to roam Paris alone, taking in the grandeur of the Paris Opera and the Eiffel Tower, the nonstop hustle and bustle of people and cars, the scents and sounds. "Even me," he confided to Sharon Lawrence, "with my big imagination, had never imagined any place so beautiful—a city with so much history I wanted to know every single thing about what had happened there, the kings and queens and rebellions and how they built the city and what kind of people had lived there in the past.

I wished that I could stop time and explore all those fantastic buildings for weeks.... I loved every single thing about this city."[45]

On October 18, a capacity crowd filled the 2,000-seat Olympia to see the show billed as "Musicorama." The Brian Auger Trinity flew in to join the lineup. When it came time for the Experience's opening set, Mitch and Noel came onstage first, to cheers and applause. As an MC began his introduction, "Ladies and gentlemen, from Seattle, Washington," Jimi, backstage in the blue mohair suit, played a bluesy guitar run. When the announcer spoke his name, Jimi played the opening chords to "Killing Floor" as he walked onstage. He punctuated the band's energetic reading with two brief, perfectly placed solos and concluded the song with a beautiful trill. The crowd grew quiet as the trio segued into a slow version of "Hey Joe," Hendrix coloring his guitar tone with light distortion. Sweet and emotive, his voice displayed no trace of nervousness. He began the solo with his teeth. As the song concluded, Jimi played a two-note phrase that sounded like "thank you," to rapturous applause. With an offhand "Yeah, dig this right here," he plucked a dive-bomb sound on a single string, wavering the note with whammy. After a few seconds of guitar freak-out, he segued into the opening chords of "Wild Thing." His sexy vocals and solo, which he began with his teeth, caused another commotion. The audience roared their approval as the Experience left the stage.

"As it turned out," Noel wrote in his diary, "our three numbers went down a bomb," meaning, "very well." Auger concurred: "I watched Jimi play, and they absolutely loved him. I thought, 'Wow, this guy's going to be a huge star.'"[46] At the concert's end, Jimi, white Stratocaster in hand, joined the other acts for the encore. A French radio company made a direct-to-two-track recording of the Experience's three-song set, and these are the earliest known recordings of the Jimi Hendrix Experience. The Olympia versions of "Killing Floor" and "Hey Joe" came out decades later on MCA's *The Jimi Hendrix Experience* box set.

After the Olympia performance, the jubilant musicians celebrated backstage and then, as Noel wrote in his diary, "headed off to a big party in a posh downstairs nightclub and got drunker and more stoned, with uppers keeping us raving."[47] At 6:30 the next morning they realized they were running late and made a mad dash for the airport, grousing along the way about having to schlep their own gear. The group's debut tour earned their management 3,375 francs—at the time, about $700 in U.S. currency.

Upon their return to England, Chas Chandler set about arranging their first studio recording. Then and now, people typically assume that headlining musicians are financially well-off. But for Chandler and many others who'd "made it big" during the first wave of the British Invasion, this was untrue. Though the Animals had chart-topping international hits, American tours, and high-profile TV appearances, Chandler had little to show for it, other than a few nice instruments. Mike Jeffery had paid each of the members a weekly salary, and royalties had been miniscule. And now Chandler, already covering the lion's share of Jimi's living and equipment expenses, had to come up with the funds for studio sessions. Time was of the essence.

He booked a two-hour block at London's De Lane Lea Studios, located in the basement beneath a bank at 129 Kingsway. The tiny studio had a new Sound Techniques mixing board and the Animals had done most of their recordings there. In preparation, Chas and Jimi worked on perfecting "Hey Joe," with Jimi playing his Stratocaster unplugged or through a small Vox amplifier kept in their lodgings. Mitch and Noel were not invited to participate in deciding how the song would be arranged. "I wasn't concerned that Mitch or Noel might feel they weren't having enough—or any— say," Chandler said. "Their say was a bit of a nuisance, really. I didn't need the confusion. I had been touring and recording in a band for years, and I'd seen everything end as a compromise. Nobody ended up doing what they really wanted to do. I wasn't going to let that happen to Jimi."[48] As the Experience's debut session drew near, Jimi grew increasingly insecure about his singing. "Jimi was paranoid about his voice from the very first day I met him," Chandler remembered. "From my first day in the studio with him to my last, he would always want his voice buried, and I would want to place it more forward in the mix."[49]

On October 23, 1966, the Jimi Hendrix Experience made their first studio recording. With Chandler producing and Dave Siddle engineering, the trio began recording "Hey Joe" onto one-inch four-track tape. Jimi insisted on cranking up his Marshall twin stack to the point where items in the studio began to rattle. When Chandler told him to the lower the volume, Jimi responded, "If I can't play as loud as I want, I might as well go back to New York." Chandler, who'd earlier that day had met with immigration officials to secure Jimi's three-month passport extension, reached into his pocket, pulled out Jimi's passport and immigration papers, and tossed them onto the console. "Well, there you go. Piss off!" According to Chas, "He looked at them, started laughing, and said, 'All right, you called my bluff!' and that was it."[50] Rolling down his volume, Jimi dialed in a cleaner tone perfectly suited for the song's R&B feel. Curtis Mayfield's distinctive guitar style echoed in Hendrix's rhythm-and-lead style as they worked on capturing the basic track. "While we were working on it," Hendrix remembered, "I don't think we played it the same way twice."[51] After many takes, the trio produced a backing track that gained Chas's approval.

During the ensuing weeks Jimi recorded his "Hey Joe" lead vocal and guitar overdubs at a variety of London studios. "It was the first time I tried to sing on a record," he remembered. "I was too scared to sing. Chas made me sing serious."[52] *The Jimi Hendrix Experience* box set contains a pass Jimi made at Pye Studios with different background singers and an amusing false start where he laughingly said, "Oh, God damn! One more time. Hey, make the voice a little lower and the band a little louder, okay?" As the track continued playing, he picked up the first verse midway through. Mitch and Noel did not attend the "Hey Joe" vocal and guitar overdub sessions. "On those early overdub sessions that we did," Chas explained, "we just didn't bring Mitch and Noel in. It wasn't anything against them; it was just pragmatism. There was no point in bringing in anyone else if they weren't going to be doing anything. They would have been in the way. We didn't say it as such, but we knew that's how it was. Jimi would play me an idea for an overdub and if I thought it worked, it was, 'Let's go get this bloody thing done.' We didn't need to be arguing with Noel for ten minutes and Mitch for five. We *knew* what we wanted to do. We just couldn't afford the time."[53] Unbeknownst to Noel, at one of these sessions Chandler re-recorded the "Hey Joe" bass part, the only time he is known to have played on an Experience recording. The female voices on the released version were supplied by the Breakaways, a trio of seasoned session singers recently featured on several Petula Clark hits.

While many others had already recorded "Hey Joe," with his first complete recording for the Experience, Hendrix created the most enduring—and imitated—version of the song. For decades to come, mastering his "Hey Joe" guitar arrangement would be a rite of passage for up-and-coming players. But what to feature on the single's B side? Jimi suggested covering "Killing Floor," "Mercy, Mercy," or "Land of 1000 Dances." Chandler told him he'd need to write his own songs to make publishing royalties. That suited Jimi, who didn't feel "Hey Joe" accurately represented what he was capable of. "It's really a cowboy song," he'd later tell an interviewer. "We like it—that's why we recorded it. But it isn't really us."[54]

In London, Hendrix's transition from player to songwriter came quickly and naturally. After all, he'd been imaginative and creative all of his life. As a small child he'd communicated with an imagined friend called "Sessa." During his school years he enjoyed drawing and painting scenes of horses, dragons, race cars, knights in armor, sports events, musicians, and outer space. He dabbled in poetry—e. e. cummings was among his favorite writers—and pored over science fiction–themed comic books. "Before I can remember anything," he said in an interview with *Life* magazine, "I can remember music and stars and planets. I could go to sleep and write fifteen symphonies. I had very strange feelings that I was here for something and I was going to get a chance to be heard. I got the guitar together 'cause that was all I had. I used to be really lonely. A musician, if he's a messenger, is like a child who hasn't been handled too many times by man, hasn't had too many fingerprints across the brain. That's why music is so much heavier than anything you ever felt."[55]

He had attempted writing songs before, but the true flowering of Jimi Hendrix, composer, occurred after he'd move into Hyde Park Towers. As he explained to Sharon Lawrence, "Words paint pictures in my mind. Now I see that I knew next to nothing about songwriting until I got to London. I had ideas and phrases, but I was uneasy about how to make the words all hold together for an entire song. In England I learned dozens of new words and expressions every single day, which opened up my writing. Chas was supportive, even when he didn't know what I was rambling on about. He gave me confidence in my writing."[56] In another interview, Jimi offered insight into his creative process: "A lot of times I write words all over the place, on matchboxes or on napkins, and then sometimes music comes across to me just when I am sitting around doing nothing, and then the music makes me think of a few words I might have written. So I go back to those few words if I can find them and just get it together. Sometimes it all happens at the same time."[57]

Some of Hendrix's most sublime songs with the Experience began as poems scribbled into notebooks or onto hotel stationery. At home, Kathy recalled, "Jimi was always jotting down ideas on bits of paper, strumming his guitar as he did so. When we were together he would often spend ages sitting on the bed with the guitar, sometimes with amplifiers and sometimes unplugged so that only he could hear the sound."[58] A few early Hendrix songs, such as "Purple Haze," "Third Stone from the Sun," and "EXP," had themes and images related to science fiction and outer space. But for "Stone Free," his first official composition for the Experience, he focused on the more earthly concerns of a traveling musician. Jimi wrote the song in the Hyde Park Towers a day or two after the initial "Hey Joe" session. The song's opening lyrics referenced being in a different city every day of the week—an apt description of life on the chitlin circuit, or for that matter, the Experience's recent tour of France. Jimi made the song's overriding theme a cry for freedom: to dress the way one wants, to not be held down by lovers or expectations—in essence, the freedom to "do what I please."

While Jimi fine-tuned the song for his next recording session, his managers focused on lining up performances. Kathy Etchingham remembered that Mike Jeffery "started phoning people up that owned clubs and said, 'Look, we've got this boy—please, give him a chance. Let him play. We won't even charge. Just let him play.'"[59] Slowly but surely, the strategy worked. On October 25, the Jimi Hendrix Experience made their U.K. debut at the venue where Jimi had met Kathy a month earlier. "The Scotch of St. James was an original 'groove' club," Redding noted. "Chas must have been on his knees using up favours to get past the problem of 'Who? Never heard of 'em!' But our half-hour set with terrible sound went down well."[60] On the strength of this show, the Harold Davison Agency booked the Experience to play in Munich in November. During the ensuing weeks, the Experience would play at other small venues around London. Most evenings, Jimi, who loved to jam, made the rounds of clubs, welcoming opportunities to sit in with other bands.

In its October 29 issue, the influential British music magazine *Record Mirror* ran Richard Green's "Ex-Animal Adventures." This first English-language article about the Jimi Hendrix Experience managed to misspell Jimi's name three different ways, misstate his age, and attribute a racial stereotype to his manager. "Never one to let a good thing pass," it began, "Chas Chandler has signed and brought to this country a 20-year-old Negro called Jim Henrix [*sic*] who—among other things—plays the guitar with his teeth and is being hailed in some quarters as main contender for the title of 'the next big thing.' Chas first heard John [*sic*] playing in one of those myriad Greenwich Village clubs. It wasn't long before the ex-Animal had convinced the young man that the streets of London could be turned to gold for him. 'He looks like Dylan, he's got all that hair sticking all over the place,' Chas told me. 'He's coloured but he doesn't think like a coloured person. He's got a very good idea of what he wants to do.'" Green went on to speculate that "Jim's potential as a songwriter seems almost limitless. He has, apparently, written over two-hundred songs already and is always putting pen to paper when new ideas strike him." And, in a passage that likely raised eyebrows across London, Green quoted Chas as saying "He's better than Eric Clapton."[61]

4:November 1966

"The Best Guitarist in the World"

It was almost as if Jimi had been designed by a committee
to give the London hip-ourgeoise everything they wanted.
—Charles Shaar Murray[1]

On November 2, the Jimi Hendrix Experience completed "Stone Free" in a single session at De Lane Lea Studios. They recorded the basic track live as a three-piece and then added overdubs. Jimi began the performance with a whammied harmonic, then immediately set up a mesmerizing groove highlighting rhythm guitar, bass, and cowbell-driven percussion. After the second verse and chorus, Jimi exclaimed "Turn me loose, baby," and modulated for the solo. Unusual in both rock and jazz, this technique of changing keys for solos would become a hallmark of Jimi's playing with the Experience. Another example of his extraordinarily imaginative compositional approach occurred during the song's final eight seconds, when the band shifted tempo and Jimi created a psychedelic explosion of sound that rapidly fades away.

The Experience then took passes at two songs Jimi had recently written in the flat, "Can You See Me" and "Remember." This early version of "Can You See Me," which Hendrix described as a "song for teeny boppers," contained his scratch vocals, guitar solo, and the heavily vibratoed, skillfully panned whole-step string bend that instantly sets the song apart. Cast in the AAB form common to blues songs, the lyrics conveyed the perspective of someone confidently breaking up with a lover: "Can you hear me, baby, crying 'cause you put me down? If you can hear me doing that, you can hear a freight train coming from a thousand miles." Noel remembered that they recorded the song very quickly.

"Remember" conveyed an opposite perspective of relationships in an arrangement better suited to an R&B band than a power trio. With its bucolic images of a mockingbird, bluebirds, and honeybees, the lyrics found the singer longing for his baby to return and "make everybody as happy as can be." Jimi began the recording with a guitar figure reminiscent of his playing on singles with the Isley Brothers and Squires. He once again modulated for the solo and then returned to the song's original key to continue singing in a comfortable register. Deemed "too raggedy," this initial version of "Remember" was subsequently overhauled at Olympic Studios before its inclusion on the British pressing of *Are You Experienced*. Before departing, Chas and Jimi completed the final mix of "Stone Free" and made a copy to listen to at home. Musically adventurous, beautifully played, and unfettered by any obvious roots in blues or mainstream rock and roll, "Stone Free" marked an auspicious start for Jimi Hendrix, songwriter.

With tape in hand, Chandler began shopping for a record deal—a challenging task, it turned out. The A&R department at the Animals' label, EMI, refused to even listen to "Hey Joe" or "Stone Free." Hearing no "long-term potential," Dick Rowe, a rep at Decca, the label that had famously rejected the Beatles, likewise passed. Kathy Etchingham recalled that "the general feeling among the big record companies was that there wasn't an opening for a guitarist who looked as way-out as Jimi. Most of the big groups like Herman's Hermits and the Dave Clark Five had clean-cut images which everyone tried to emulate. Jimi didn't fit in with anything that was happening in the charts at the time. Chas's spirits never seemed to flag, no matter how many rejections he received."[2]

Fortuitously, Chandler ran into Kit Lambert and Chris Stamp, co-managers of the Who, one night while Jimi was jamming at the Scotch of St. James. Lambert and Stamp instantly saw his potential: "Kit practically knocked tables over to get across to talk to me," Chas remembered. "He said, 'I've just got to sign this guy.'" They indicated that they wanted to produce Jimi's records, but Chas told them that he was going to fulfill that role. "We looked at each other," Stamp recalled, "and said, 'Has he got a record label?' Of course, he didn't have a record label, so we immediately got into the machinations of creating a record label because of Jimi."[3] Before leaving the club, Lambert, Stamp, and Chandler sketched out a deal on a beer mat. Lambert and Stamp, who'd name their new label Track Records, agreed to pay a £1,000 advance for the Jimi Hendrix Experience and assured Chas that they'd be able to get the trio booked on the nationally broadcast *Ready Steady Go!* television program.

Back at Hyde Park Towers, Jimi began refining an ambitious composition he'd begun in Greenwich Village, the science-fiction-themed "Third Stone from the Sun." As Jimi explained to interviewer Klas Burling, "'Third Stone from the Sun' lasts about seven minutes, and it's an instrumental. These guys come from another planet, and 'third stone from the sun' is Earth. That's what it is—you know, they have Mercury, Venus, and then Earth. And they observe Earth for a while and they think the smartest animal on the whole Earth is chickens, hens. There's nothing else here to offer. They don't like people so much, so they just blow it up at the end. It has all these different sounds, but all of them are made from nothing but a guitar, bass, and drums, and then our slowed-down voices."[4]

Chandler, who kept dozens of science fiction novels in the flat, took credit for introducing Jimi to the genre. He described Jimi starting with George R. Stewart's post-apocalyptic classic, *Earth Abides*, and then reading the rest of the collection. "That's where 'Third Stone from the Sun' and 'Up from the Skies' came from," Chandler speculated.[5] In truth, though, Jimi's love of science fiction had begun much earlier. It likely began in grade school, when he took Leon to Saturday matinees to watch Buster Crabbe starring in *Flash Gordon* serials. "That's where Jimi got his name," Leon remembered. "We called him 'Buster' as a child—all his friends, everybody. After he saw that movie, he'd put a cape on, he'd go up on the roof and say, 'Leon, watch me!' So he jumped off the roof, flapping his arms, and *kaput*, hit the ground! ... That's why he got his name 'Buster,' because he was always emulating Buster Crabbe from *Flash Gordon*."[6] Leon's older brother would also use his voice to imitate the weird music and space-vehicle sound effects he heard in films like 1953's *The War of the Worlds*. Jimi's boyhood friend James Williams remembered that "he would go into these characterizations sometimes, and it would be hard to break him out of it."[7]

Another source of Jimi's interest in UFOs and the paranormal came from golden-age and silver-age comic books. "Jimi and I used to look at comic books and eat ice cream together," Al Hendrix recalled. "He read a lot of comic books, because I'd buy them. When Jimi bought his own comics, he'd read *Batman* and *Superman*. I liked those *Amazing Stories*–type comics with the rocket ships and people zapping each other with ray guns, so Jimi had plenty of reading material in that respect. Jimi was fascinated by spaceships. I used to read a lot of science fiction books and talk about saucers and such. On a good night Jimi and I would go outside once in a while and sit out there and look at the stars. Like a lot of kids, sometimes Jimi would look up at the sky and say, 'I'd like to be up there to see what's going on on another planet.' He also wondered what it was like traveling through space. Jimi and I would talk about how we'd like to meet an alien if some saucers floating around out there would beam us up."[8]

Soon after they began rooming together, Chas noticed something unusual about his protégé: his extraordinary dedication to his instrument. "He used to get up in the morning to go and fry himself a breakfast," Chandler described, "and he'd be frying bacon and eggs with the guitar on. That lad never had a guitar off less than eight hours every day, plus the gig at night. He'd take the guitar to the loo with him because he liked the sound of the echo in there. He'd sit in there for hours, just playing a Fender guitar—not plugged in—because he liked the sound coming off the tiles in the loo. He had a guitar on all the time, all the time. He was the best guitarist in the world because he wanted to be the best, and he was prepared to work at it."[9]

Those who'd lived with Hendrix before his arrival in Great Britain observed the same behavior. "Once he got that electric guitar," his dad wrote, "every day he would be plunking on it. He just worked at it and worked at it, practicing day and night. He played the guitar *every* day. He carried it around with him at all times."[10] Leon agreed: "He'd wake up in the morning with a guitar on his chest. So the first thing he'd do in his bedroom, before he'd brush his teeth or take a piss, he'd be playing licks. So it was inevitable that he would become a master and a maestro one day."[11] While Jimi was living in Nashville, his roommate Billy Cox recalled, "People nicknamed him Marbles, because he'd walk up the street playing an electric guitar. He'd play it in the show, and he'd play it coming back from the theater. I saw him put twenty-five years on the guitar in five years, because it was a constant, everyday occurrence with him. Some people thought he was crazy, because they couldn't understand why a man would constantly be playing the guitar all the time. But basically what he was doing was making this instrument an extension of his body."[12]

Jimi also displayed a remarkable ability to find musical potential in everyday sounds. Photographer Bruce Fleming, who shot the iconic *Are You Experienced* cover image seen on the European release, recalled that Jimi would "clink two glasses together and he'd start doing rhythm with them and then music, you know. He was a musician—a total musician. His inventiveness itself was quite extraordinary."[13]

Jimi's relationship with Kathy Etchingham deepened during their first weeks together. She was surprised to discover that he enjoyed eating at local Indian restaurants: "I was worried that everything on the menu was going to be too hot for him, but he didn't bat an eyelid. Jimi, I discovered, would eat anything, absolutely anything, except tuna or marmalade or anything I cooked."[14] With little money between them, the couple enjoyed sightseeing around London. "Whenever we went out for a walk," Kathy remembered, "Jimi used to stuff a dollar in his shoe for emergencies. 'A dollar won't do you any good over here,' I pointed out, but he just laughed. 'It makes me feel better. When you've been penniless you never forget it.'"[15] In a nod to voodoo beliefs and blues lore, Jimi also taped a lock of Kathy's hair into his shoe, so they would always be "in touch" with each other. As soon as he could afford to, Jimi bought board games—Monopoly, Scrabble, Twister, and his favorite, Risk. Their friend Graham Nash recalled that "Jimi was a great Risk player—and no slouch at Monopoly either!"[16] When he had a bit more money, Kathy recalled, Jimi bought himself a set of Scalextric slot cars: "We used to set it up on the lounge floor and race each other, his blue car and my red. If he thought I was winning, he would cheat by 'accidentally' disconnecting the track."[17] During his youth Hendrix had enjoyed attending car races in Seattle and had made many sketches of racing events, sports cars, and crashes.

In a charming account published on her website, Kathy described an adventure that took place in the Queensway ice rink near their lodgings: "Jimi was always game for a new experience. At the rink they had trouble finding a pair of boots big enough for Jimi's size eleven feet. They managed it eventually and he tucked his flares in and we set off. Within seconds of hitting the ice we were lying in an hysterical heap, weak with laughter. The other skaters just had to make their way round us as we rolled around trying to pull ourselves up on one another, only to lose our footing and come crashing down again. By the end of the session Jimi had got reasonably good and had actually managed to let go of the side and still stay upright, but every time I let go I went straight down again. . . . Jimi enjoyed himself so much that we went back several times and by the end he was pretty accomplished, whizzing round the rink, attracting everyone's stares with his hair waving in the breeze."[18]

Jimi enjoyed shopping for scarves, velvet pants, and other eye-catching clothing in London's trendy boutiques. One of his favorites, the newly opened I Was Lord Kitchener's Valet on Portobello Road, sold antique military jackets and other vintage chic. Eventually, Mitch Mitchell, recalled, "shops like Granny Takes a Trip, in the King's Road, used to make things up for Jimi."[19] Chas, normally tight-fisted with expenses, approved of expenditures that enhanced the Experience's image. "Chas was very conscious of the artistic necessities—a good 'look' and a catchy name," Noel wrote. "The fact that Jimi was black guaranteed him notice in England, even more so when he was playing next to two white guys. I can't think of any other mixed group in England at this point. Jimi wasn't tall, but when posed with us flanking him he photographed larger than life. The three of us looked really good together— symmetrical. Even onstage Jimi's left-handed technique against my right-handed one looked balanced. Jimi loved the English Carnaby Street fashions and in a few months we lost all vestiges of a traditional early-Sixties look. We began to realize how much we were itching to break out into something new. The possibilities excited me. We felt free."[20]

On November 8 the Jimi Hendrix Experience and Chas Chandler flew to Munich, Germany, in advance of their three-night stand at the Big Apple. Noel's roommate, Gerry Stickells, transported their gear by train. The venue, a small club frequented by U.S. military personnel, allowed the trio to rehearse new songs during the day.

Playing two forty-five-minute sets each night, the Experience drew ever-increasing crowds. On the second night Jimi accidentally smashed a guitar during the final song. In the process, he discovered what Noel termed "demolition feedback": "The crowd was going crazy and began to pull Jimi into the audience. He panicked, and to save his guitar he threw it onto the stage. It exploded into amazing sound in response to the impact. It startled Jimi, but the crowd went right over the top. New dimensions in sound, new dimensions in German audience freak-out."[21] Chandler noted that when Jimi saw that the guitar had cracked, "He just went barmy and smashed everything in sight. The German audience loved it, and we decided to keep it in as part of the act."[22] In time, guitar smashing—often the same guitar, glued back together—became a standard part of the set. Hendrix did not pioneer this attention-getter, though. The Who's Pete Townshend was already an old hand at smashing guitars.

Upon their return to London, Jimi accepted Brian Jones's invitation to attend a Rolling Stones recording session at the newly opened Olympic Studios facility on Church Road in Barnes. Built in 1908, the three-story brick building housing the studio had at various times served as a stage theater, motion picture cinema, and television studio. Olympic staff engineer Eddie Kramer, who beginning in 1967 would become Jimi's engineer of choice, explained that Olympic was "at the cutting edge of every studio in London. We were very innovative, and of course we had, I think, the best console in England and possibly the world at that time."[23] The Troggs' "Wild Thing" had been recorded on the facility's four-track recorder. Ironically, on the day Jimi visited Olympic, the Rolling Stones were recording "Ruby Tuesday"—a song, Keith Richards revealed in his autobiography, inspired by Linda Keith. "Basically," wrote Richards, "Linda is 'Ruby Tuesday.' After she left me, Linda was in a really bad way. Tuinals had given way to harder stuff. She went back to New York and took up further with Jimi Hendrix, who may have broken her heart, as she broke mine. Certainly, her friends say, she was very much in love with Jimi."[24]

Unable to afford Olympic Studios' hourly rate, the Experience continued to use facilities within their budget. Their next session, on November 18, brought them to Regent Sounds Studio A, primarily a facility for recording advertising jingles. Keith Richards, who'd recorded there with the Rolling Stones, described it as "just a little room full of egg boxes" with a two-track Grundig tape recorder mounted to the wall.[25] According to Mitch, nothing that they recorded there was used.

With no major gigs lined up, funds growing tighter by the day, and little help available from "Mike the Invisible Man(ager)" Jeffery, as Noel called him, Chas Chandler took a risk. Selling more instruments, he arranged for the Experience to give a lunchtime showcase at the Bag O'Nails, a 250-seat venue near Carnaby Street. He sent invitations to famous friends and a who's who of London's music journalists. The weather was perfect that day, and Chandler's strategy paid off. John Lennon, Paul McCartney, Eric Clapton, Jimmy Page, Donovan, and members of the Rolling Stones stood shoulder-to-shoulder with writers as the Experience blasted through "Like a Rolling Stone," "Everybody Needs Somebody to Love," "Johnny B. Goode," "Wild Thing," and "Hey Joe." "For only three people," Redding recalled, "the sheer volume was breathtaking." Some aghast witnesses fled the ear-ringing sonic assault, but the guitarists in the audience *loved* the show. John Lennon, the first to join them in the dressing room afterward, exclaimed, "Fucking grand, lads!" Paul McCartney, close behind, said, "James, you're a wonder!" Peter Jones, on assignment for *Record Mirror*, requested an interview. "We'd finally gotten the press's attention!" Noel enthused. Today, the Bag O'Nails displays a plaque that reads "The Jimi Hendrix Experience first played here on the 25th November 1966."

The Peter Jones interview took place in a pub near the *Record Mirror* office. Headlined "Mr. Phenomenon" in the December 10 issue, Jones's article began:

> Now hear this, and kindly hear it good! Are you one of the fans who think there's nothing much new happening on the pop scene? Right ... then we want to bring your attention to a new artist, a new star-in-the-making, who we predict is going to whirl round the business like a tornado. Name: Jimi Hendrix. Occupation: Guitarist-singer-composer—showman—dervish—original. His group, just three-strong: The Jimi Hendrix Experience.

Bill Harry and I dropped in at the Bag O'Nails club in Kingsley Street recently to hear the trio working out for the benefit of press and bookers. An astonished Harry muttered: "Is that full, big, blasting, swinging sound really being created by only three people?" It was, with the aid of a mountain of amplification equipment. Jimi was in full flight. Whirling like a demon, swirling his guitar every which way, this twenty-year-old (looking rather like James Brown) was quite amazing. Visually he grabs the eyeballs with his techniques of playing the guitar with his teeth, his elbow, rubbing it across the stage. But he also pleasurably hammers the eardrums with his expert playing. An astonishing technique, especially considering he started playing only five or six years ago. Sweatily exhausted, Jimi said afterwards: "I've only been in London three months— but Britain is really groovy. Just been working in Paris and Munich." In the trio: drummer Mitch Mitchell, a jazz fan, and rock 'n' roll addict Noel Redding on bass.

Jones asked Jimi to describe his music: "'We don't want to be classed in any category,' said Jimi. 'If it must have a tag, I'd like it to be called "free feeling." It's a mixture of rock, freak-out, blues and rave music ...' About that thing of playing the guitar with his teeth: he says it doesn't worry him. He doesn't feel anything. 'But I do have to brush my teeth three times a day.'"[26] The age was off by three years and Jimi had been playing for about eight years, but the article brought the Experience very welcome attention.

The day after the Bag O'Nails showcase, Kit Lambert took the group to IBC Studios to meet the Who. Pete Townshend, who'd yet to see Jimi play, was unimpressed: "Jimi sort of wandered in looking peculiar, just really peculiar, and Keith Moon was in a nasty mood and said, 'Who let that savage in here?' I mean he really did look pretty wild, and very scruffy. Anyway, he walked around for a bit and gave me a sort of lukewarm handshake.... I didn't know anything about his playing, and I never heard his music until I saw him first live."[27]

Seeing the Experience perform soon afterward, Pete Townshend, like other top-tier English rock guitarists, was profoundly impacted. For starters, his own patented stage moves—wind-milling his right arm to strum chords, leaping into the air, destroying guitars at set's end—seemed pale in comparison to Jimi's onstage attention-getters, some learned during his days with black R&B revues and others newly innovated. "Seeing Jimi perform *destroyed* me," Townshend told Matt Resnicoff.

Absolutely, completely destroyed me. It was horrifying because he took back black music. He came and stole it back. He made it very evident that's what he was doing. He'd been out on the road with people like Little Richard, had done that hard work, and then he'd come over to the U.K. And when he took his music back, he took a lot of the trimmings back too.

Slowly but surely Jimi became sure of himself. I'm talking about the first few weeks he was in London. You know, it was a new band, and they were just taking London by fucking storm! You can't believe it. You'd look around and the audience was just full of record company people and music business people. I suppose I went away and got very confused for a bit. I kind of groped around. I had a lot of spiritual problems. I felt that I hadn't the emotional equipment, really, the physical equipment, the natural psychic genius of somebody like Jimi. I realized that what I had was a bunch of gimmicks which he had come and taken away from me and attached them not only to the black R&B from whence they came, but also added a whole new dimension. I felt stripped, and I took refuge in my writing.

Townshend, like many others, also felt intimidated by the upfront nature of Jimi's sexuality, both onstage and off.

You have to remember that Jimi was astonishingly sexual. You could just sense this whole thing in the room where every woman would just go for him at a snap of a finger. There was a slightly prince-like quality about him, this kind of imp at work. I found him very charming, very easy, a very sweet guy. You know, I just kept hearing stories. One story that I heard— I think I might have been there—was the night he went up to Marianne Faithfull when she was there with Mick [Jagger] and said to her in her ear, "What are you doing with this asshole?" There were moments like that when he would be very, very attracted to somebody and felt that he would actually be able to get them, and he just couldn't resist trying. There were no boundaries, and that really scared me.[28]

The notion of Jimi being "astonishingly sexual" also hit home with Eric Clapton. The subject came up when *Rolling Stone* founder Jann Wenner interviewed Eric during Cream's first performances on the West Coast, mid-1967. Asked what he thought of Jimi, Clapton, using the then-common derogatory term "spade" to denote a black man, told Wenner:

> You know, English people have a very big thing towards a spade. They really love that magic thing, the sexual thing. They all fall for that sort of thing. Everybody and his brother in England still sort of think that spades have big dicks. And Jimi came over and exploited that to the limit. Everybody fell for it. I fell for it. . . . He had the whole combination in London. It was just what the market wanted, a psychedelic pop star who looked freaky. And they're also still hung up about spades and the blues thing was there. So Jimi walked in, put on all the gear, and made it straight away. It was a perfect formula. Underneath it all, he's got an incredible musical talent. He is really one of the finest musicians on the Western scene.[29]

After Jimi's in-studio meeting with the Who, the Experience opened for Eric Burdon and the reconfigured Animals at the Ricky-Tick in Hounslow, Middlesex. Mitch, who'd played there before with Georgie Fame, remembered the venue as "tiny, with a low ceiling. We were set up in a corner and had very little room to move. As I recall, the audience weren't exactly hostile, but they didn't know what to make of us. Most of our early gigs were like that. We were playing to audiences largely composed of mohair-suited mods and sort of proto-skinheads in boots and braces. They really didn't know how to take us—Jimi, especially—at all."[30] Unbeknownst to Jimi, Mitch, and Noel, within a few months not only would audiences know how to "take" their music, but fans would imitate their hairstyles and manner of dress.

On November 27, Jimi Hendrix, soon-to-be fashion icon, celebrated his twenty-fourth birthday.

5:December 1966

At Home with the Blues

We're not going to try and keep up with trends,
because we've got a chance to be our own trend.
—Jimi Hendrix[1]

On December 1, Michael Jeffery presented Jimi Hendrix a management agreement with Yameta Company Ltd. Unlike the production deal signed in October by all three members of the Jimi Hendrix Experience, this new contract focused exclusively on Jimi Hendrix as a "performer in all mediums." The document was prepared by solicitor John Hillman, who'd been instrumental in setting up Yameta. Hillman and Jeffery explained that Yameta would shelter Jimi's income from British and, eventually, American taxes and provide him long-term security. In essence, the four-year agreement stated that in exchange for promoting and furthering Jimi's career, Yameta would receive 40 percent of all gross payments, "excluding gross payments for recording and publishing. If Yameta terminated, Jeffery could claim Jimi for ten shillings."[2] The contract provided Jeffery other benefits as well. He suggested that his whopping 40 percent of Jimi's earnings—a stunning figure, even by entertainment business standards—would help cover "tour expenses." Without benefit of legal counsel or the knowledge of his co-manager Chas Chandler, Jimi signed. About six months later, Jeffery would amend the agreement to give Chas half of his 40 percent. Like the PPX contract, this document would seriously affect Jimi Hendrix and his estate for years to come.

Even if Hendrix himself had later challenged this and his earlier production agreement, it's unlikely he would have prevailed. Lawrence Townsend explains that in the 1960s, "few lawyers understood the workings of the music business, and even fewer judges. And sympathy for Hendrix by 'establishment' judges would be pretty much nonexistent. Also, as we know, even if the contract looks and smells unconscionable, it's sometimes easy to overlook the fact that it is a commercial contract between two adult business people. Contracts are almost never found void for unconscionability between business people, only between businesses and consumers. But the reason it's easy to overlook this is because artists—we love 'em—are adept at behaving like adorable children, and so we catch ourselves forgetting that the law sees it as a business-to-business contract."[3]

Kathy Etchingham, dissatisfied with the living quarters in the Hyde Park Towers, mentioned to Ringo Starr that she, Jimi, Chas, and Lotta Null were looking for somewhere more permanent. Starr, who had a flat at 34 Montagu Square, offered to sublet them the property for £30 a month. They accepted the offer, and on December 6 Chas, Jimi, Kathy, and Lotta moved to Montagu Square. "We were lucky to get it," Kathy wrote, "as Paul McCartney had just moved out of the flat before us. The neighbors weren't too happy about having musicians in the flat. Paul had been using it as a [demo] recording studio and I'm sure it wasn't very soundproof. The elderly lady who lived upstairs could be rather grumpy. She wouldn't let us have the keys to the communal gardens when the photographer wanted to take some photos of Jimi in the gardens."[4]

Just north of the Marble Arch, Montagu Square's brown brick houses dated to the Regency era. Originally a single residence, 34 Montagu Square had been converted to flats. The one leased by Ringo included the ground level and basement. Chas and Lotta claimed the first floor, with its sitting room, white-carpeted master bedroom, and adjoining bathroom with a pink sunken bath. Jimi and Kathy's basement digs had a dark-carpeted bedroom with wood-paneled walls and an old fireplace, as well as a bathroom, dressing room, and small kitchen shared by all four. Kathy described it as the best place she'd ever lived. A couple of weeks after they moved in, Jimi was photographed there by Petra Niemeier. Her shots reveal an unpretentious living quarters with a dark, green-gray carpet, tiny kitchen with an electric range and double-basin sink, a bedroom with a full-size bed, two rotary tele-phones on the floor, a well-worn couch and pair of chairs, a waste basket, and a throw pillow. The bedroom's mostly empty shelves contained a couple of dozen paperbacks, three small trophies, and a small bell.[5]

Jimi, who loved listening to music, began collecting albums. He enjoyed browsing the stacks at One Stop Records on South Molton. HMV on Oxford Street was a reliable source for classical LPs. While Jimi had extraordinarily wide-ranging musical tastes, his favorite genre was the blues. "People will argue with me," Kathy told James Rotondi, "but I tell you, that guy was a bluesman. That's where his heart really lay. Anybody who tells me he would have be-come a jazz musician—well, balls to them. The way Jimi was, if he was with a jazz musician, he liked jazz. If he was with a folk singer, he liked folk. But what he *really* liked, and what he really played at home, was blues."[6] During his initial months in London, Jimi purchased classic albums by postwar bluesmen Lightnin' Hopkins, Muddy Waters, Howlin' Wolf, John Lee Hooker, and Elmore James, as well as new releases such as Junior Wells's *It's My Life, Baby!*, featuring Buddy Guy, and John Mayall's *Blues Breakers* with Eric Clapton on guitar. He was drawn to anthologies of prewar blues as well, notably Robert Johnson's *King of the Delta Blues Singers*, Blind Blake's *Bootleg Rum Dum Blues*, and Lead Belly's *Take This Hammer*.

Among his first rock acquisitions were Bob Dylan's *Blonde on Blonde* and *Greatest Hits*, as well as the Byrds' *Fifth Dimension* and *Younger Than Yesterday*. Jimi especially treasured his Bill Cosby comedy albums, *I Started Out as a Child* and *Revenge*, which Kathy described as "Jimi's absolute favorites. He just loved them, and he'd play them for everyone who came by our flat."[7] During the ensuing three years, he would assemble a collection of nearly a hundred albums in a mind-boggling variety of genres. Did Jimi Hendrix take good care of his albums? Not a chance. For starters, he taped a nickel to his record player's arm to correct an imbalance. "He was terrible," Kathy remembered. "He never put the records back in the sleeves. They were all over the floor, and that's why they were all so damaged."[8]

Within a few days of the move to Montagu Square, Jimi was issued a permit allowing him to work in England for the next five weeks, the issue of *Record Mirror* with his first interview went on sale, and the Experience opened for John Mayall's Bluesbreakers at the Ram Jam Club on Brixton Road. According to Noel, the Experience "totally freaked the regulars at the Ram Jam—an all-reggae, black, smokers' pub—who had no idea what to make of us."[9]

The week beginning December 11 would prove to be one of the busiest and most productive of Jimi's career. On Sunday evening, looking resplendent in his recently purchased antique military jacket, he took Kathy to meet Little Richard, in town to perform at the Saville Theatre, where Beatles manager Brian Epstein staged Sunday performances. After the show, Jimi's former bandleader invited them to his room at the Rembrandt Hotel. Jimi asked Little Richard to pay him the $50 he still owed him. "You missed the bus, man" was all Little Richard would say. As they left without the money, Kathy asked what Little Richard had meant. "I overslept and missed the bus to the next gig, so he fired me," Jimi told her. "That was when I started putting a dollar in my shoe because the day I missed the bus I didn't have any money."[10]

Walking to the Cromwellian afterward, Jimi and Kathy were stopped by the police. Hendrix gave his most detailed account of this event during an interview with Alan Freeman:

Up comes this wagon with a blue light flashing and about five or six policemen jump out at me. They look into my face real close and severely and gather around. Then one of them points at my jacket and says, "That's British, isn't it?" So I said, "Yeah, I think it is." And they frowned and all that bit and they said, "You're not supposed to be wearing that. Men fought and died in that uniform. The guy's eyes were so bad he couldn't read the little print on the badges. So I said, "What, in the Veterinary Corps, 1898? Anyway, I *like* uniforms. I wore one long enough in the United States Army." They said, "What? What? You trying to get smart with us? Show us your passport." So we did all that bit too. I had to convince them that my accent was really American. Then they asked what group I was with and I said the Experience. So they made fun of that as well and made cracks about roving minstrels. After they made a few more funnies and when they had finally got their kicks they said they didn't want to see me in that gear any more, and they let me go. Just as I was walking away, one of them said, "Hey, you said you were in the Experience. What are you experiencing?" I said, "Harassment!" And I took off as quick as I could.[11]

On December 13, the Jimi Hendrix Experience taped "Hey Joe" at Studio 9 for the popular *Ready Steady Go!* show, three days ahead of its broadcast. In contrast to the BBC's *Top of the Pops*, which typically featured artists miming to their charting records, the independently produced *Ready Steady Go!* presented segments with live singing, even when prerecorded backing tracks were used. With only two major television channels broadcasting in England during this era, appearing on either of these music shows guaranteed performers a huge viewership. Honoring their agreement with Chandler, Chris Stamp and Kit Lambert had pulled the strings to fast-track the Experience onto the bill for the Friday-evening broadcast, which also featured the Merseybeats, the Troggs, the Escorts, Marc Bolan, and Yardbirds singer Keith Relf.

With his experiences as an actor, Mitch took the television appearance in stride, but Jimi and Noel became extremely nervous on the day of the taping. The group rehearsed in the morning, returned to the studio for a mid-afternoon run-through, and played at 7:00 P.M. "The hard part was staying sober all the boring day," Noel remembered.[12] Sometime between the run-through and performance, someone stole Redding's stage clothes, which necessitated a quick trip to a haberdashery for a pair of trousers and "a terribly conservative striped jumper." With cameras rolling, Jimi stretched out "Hey Joe" nearly a minute longer than the version they'd performed at the Paris Olympia. After playing with his white Stratocaster held behind his head, he capped the performance by soloing with his teeth.

Unhappy with the sound of the De Lane Lea recordings, Chas was advised by Kit Lambert to try CBS Studios, where the Who had recorded. Chandler was able to secure a three-hour block during the evening of the *Ready Steady Go!* taping. Arriving early, Mitch asked the studio's engineer, Mike Ross-Taylor, to individually mike each of his tom-toms for a fuller sound, a tactic that had worked well for him at a previous session. When Jimi's four Marshall cabinets were carried into the room, the engineer was stunned. He expressed uncertainty about how to mike such a powerful con-figuration. Jimi showed him how to position a Neumann multi-directional tube condenser microphone about eight feet from the cabinets. The technique worked, but Ross lamented that the sheer volume of Jimi's playing hurt his ears and caused objects in the room to rattle.

They began with a new Hendrix composition, "Foxey Lady." Jimi opened the track with an unusual sound—five seconds of distort-ing, finger-vibratoed notes punctuated by slight clickings. Neal Moser, a luthier familiar with Jimi's guitars, credited this sound to a modification Hendrix had made to his guitar: "One thing I noticed on some of Hendrix's guitars was a very small file cut on the 16th fret—just to the treble side of the G string. This was so that Jimi could rattle his third string back and forth across the notch for that little thing he did on 'Foxey Lady.'"[13] From there, Jimi turned up the distortion and segued into the granddaddy of all headbanger riffs, which lands on a dominant F7♯9 played with the passion of the procreant urge. The 7♯9 chord, which contains both the major and minor thirds, was fairly common in blues and R&B arrangements and had already appeared in rock songs—the Beatles' "Taxman," for instance. But in Hendrix's hands it took on a whole new feel, so much so that it's since become known as "the Hendrix chord." Dur-ing this initial take, Ross-Taylor was surprised to see Jimi tweaking his amp controls as he played. Jimi concluded the song by sliding the edge of his pick down his low-E string. With the "Foxey Lady" basic track on tape, Jimi overdubbed his lead vocal and second gui-tar part—a beautifully played solo with impeccable string bends—and Mitch and Noel spoke their one-word refrain of "foxy."

Pushing the musicians to accomplish as much as possible in the allotted time, Chandler had Jimi double the "Can You See Me" lead vocal they'd taped earlier that month and record the song's gui-tar break. In a space lasting just fourteen seconds, Jimi layered in a memorable and brilliantly primal solo. The Experience also took passes at two more Hendrix originals, "Love or Confusion" and "Third Stone from the Sun," which they'd revamp at later sessions. "We went through quite a lot of tape," Ross-Taylor remembered. "Chas was keen to keep everything, because he felt he could always edit the good bits together."[14]

The musicians spent the session's final fifteen minutes recording what was to become Jimi's signature blues song, "Red House." As Noel detailed, "Jimi said to us, 'This is a blues in B.' (B♭ because we were down half a tone.) There's no bass on this original recording, which was released on our Polydor LP *Are You Experienced*. I borrowed a terrible, awful, hollowbody electric guitar from someone at the studio because I liked to play along on rhythm to familiarize myself with the sequence. We ended up just recording it. First take, I think. My guitar's bass was tuned full up to make a good contrast to Jimi's."[15]

Witnesses described Hendrix playing a version of "Red House" in Greenwich Village with the Blue Flames, and he may have composed the song even earlier than that. Asked about its meaning, Billy Cox responded,

> As far as I know, "Red House" didn't have any significance in reference to a particular person or place or thing. It was just a blues number that Jimi put together. There are recurring blues themes that are constantly sung about—a red rooster, a red light, a red house, three o'clock in the morning, big-leg woman, big-hipped woman, mojo, hoodoo, root, the man, the two-timing woman, the two-timing man. And you got your low-down dirty blues and your regular blues, your uptown blues. Now, regular blues weren't that suggestive. Our parents wouldn't unplug their radio to B. B. King's "Sweet Little Angel." But if you brought into the house something like "Hoochie Coochie Man" or "Big Leg Woman" or even Jimi Hendrix's "Red House"—you know, "If my baby don't love me, I know her sister will"—that's low-down blues, man, where your morality is in jeopardy and you're subject to getting your radio [plug] pulled out or your record broken. Jimi's love of low-down blues was evident in "Red House." His other blues was kind of disguised, because he revolutionized blues. He took it to another level, and that was part of his uniqueness or greatness. And all of the changes he made were improvised.[16]

Jimi, Chas, and Noel reconvened at CBS Studios on Thursday, December 15. With Mitch Mitchell unable to attend, they worked on the rough mixes of "Foxey Lady," "Can You See Me," and "Third Stone from the Sun." Chandler, who'd failed to pay for the session two days earlier, got into an argument with studio co-owner Jake

Levy, who was unwilling to accommodate Chandler's request to wait until the album's release to receive payment. Their row escalated to the point where Chandler announced he'd never work in Levy's studio again and departed without the tapes they'd made. Levy subsequently refused to hand over the tapes until Chandler paid his bill in full about a week later. That was the last time the Experience used the facility.

On Friday, December 16, the Jimi Hendrix Experience's debut single, "Hey Joe" backed with "Stone Free," went on sale in the United Kingdom. Since Lambert and Stamp's new label, Track Records, was weeks away from being fully up-and-running, they'd made arrangements for Polydor, a German record company attempting to make its first inroads into the U.K. pop market, to release the seven-inch single. "We think Jimi's record is so good," Kit Lambert told *Melody Maker*, "we didn't want to hold it back until Track officially comes into being, so we've pre-released with Polydor Records."[17]

That evening music fans across the United Kingdom watched the Jimi Hendrix Experience perform their new single on *Ready Steady Go!* Among those tuned in was Roger Mayer, an assistant experimental sound engineer for the British Admiralty's Royal Naval Scientific Service. "I said, 'Damn, this guy's incredible!'" Mayer remembered. "He was the epitome of what any rock guitarist should be—we had no one of that caliber in England."[18] Mayer, who played guitar, had been experimenting with effects devices in his spare time. Some of his distortion units were already in use by his childhood friends Jeff Beck and Jimmy Page, as well as by Britain's leading studio guitarist, Big Jim Sullivan. Within a month, Mayer would be helping Jimi Hendrix shape his sound as well.

Charles Shaar Murray, who in the 1970s would emerge as one the United Kingdom's foremost music journalists, also vividly remembered that evening's broadcast of *Ready Steady Go!*:

It seemed to be what I had been waiting all my life to hear.
His music had a wayward adventurousness and sheer sensory
overload I loved in the loud, weird rock of those immediately
pre-psychedelic times, but it was weighted with the solid
humanity and emotional authenticity I'd found only in soul
music and the blues. Hendrix was hugely and quixotically

75

himself. He was everything the Townshends and Mayalls and Jaggers and Claptons had only pretended to be. At the same time he seemed contemporary and modern in a way that Muddy Waters, Howlin' Wolf, Bo Diddley, and Chuck Berry could never be; intense, direct and forthright where the Motown stars seemed glitzy and restrained; as nakedly spontaneous as Otis Redding and as colorfully surreal as the Beatles.[19]

After watching themselves on Chandler's television at Montagu Square, the band journeyed to Chislehurst Caves. Formerly Britain's largest air-raid shelter, this extensive series of tunnels created centuries earlier by chalk and flint miners included a subterranean music club. On the strength of the *Ready Steady Go!* broadcast, a packed house awaited the Experience, who were very well received. Nervous about carrying the band's fee in his pocket, Chas was startled after the show when a fan suddenly appeared in front of him. Mistaking him for a robber, he floored him with a single punch. The following day provided the Experience a welcome day of rest. On Sunday Chas threw a party in the Montagu Square flat in honor of his twenty-eighth birthday. Among the attendees were his former bandmates in the Animals—Eric Burdon and Alan Price—as well as Zoot Money, Andy Summers, Paul Williams, Brian Auger, and others. The party got a "bit out of hand," Kathy remembered, when their Christmas tree toppled over onto Bill Wyman and his girlfriend.

The Experience reconvened at De Lane Lea on Wednesday, December 21. They devoted most of the session to new takes of "Red House." Their first few passes were marred by missed notes, a sped-up tempo, and false starts. "Oh, Lord," Jimi said after one incomplete take, "see, one little thing throws me off." Then a voice from the control room suggested turning down the studio lights. "Oh, those lights!" Hendrix said. "That's what it was. Oh, Lord, no wonder!"[20] It worked, and the Experience completed the basic track on the next pass, with Jimi delivering a virtual masterclass in postwar blues soloing. Midway through the instrumental section, from around 2:32 to 2:57, a close echo was added to Jimi's guitar tone. This sound was briefly reactivated near the song's conclusion.

After final touches were added at Olympic Studios a few months later, this version of "Red House" was released in the United States on the 1969 *Smash Hits* album.

The Experience's much-anticipated appearance at Blaises immediately after the "Red House" session brought them a rave review in the New Year's Eve issue of *Melody Maker*. Chris Welch wrote, "Jimi Hendrix, a fantastic American guitarist, blew the minds of the star-packed crowd who went to see him at Blaises Club, London, on Wednesday. Among those in the audience were Pete Townshend, Roger Daltrey, John Entwistle, Chas Chandler, and Jeff Beck. They heard Jimi's trio blast through some beautiful sounds like 'Rock Me Baby,' 'Third Stone from the Sun,' 'Like a Rolling Stone,' 'Hey Joe,' and even an unusual version of the Troggs' 'Wild Thing.' Jimi has great stage presence and an exceptional guitar technique which involved playing with his teeth on occasions and no hands at all on others! Jimi looks like [he's] becoming one of the big club names of '67."[21]

The Experience's debut single quickly picked up momentum in the British press, with two stellar reviews coming out near Christmas Eve. An unidentified reviewer for *New Musical Express* wrote, "Here's a young man who could make a profound impression in the future. This ["Hey Joe"] is a raw, uninhibited treatment of a traditional number. It's in the insidious R&B pattern, with thundering drums, some spine-tingling guitar work, and a hypnotic slow beat. It's guttural, earthy, convincing, and authentic. Flip: Much the same remarks apply to this side ["Stone Free"], except it's faster-paced and more fancy-free. This is a disc for the connoisseurs."[22] *Record Mirror* proclaimed "Hey Joe" the "most genuinely soulful record ever made in Britain. Jimi has really inspired the other two musicians. Dig the way the bass comes through. The best record Polydor has issued. A 'must.' Flip is more urgent and equally soul-laden."[23]

As he spent his first Christmas in London, Jimi had much to be thankful for. In just three months he'd accomplished more musically than he had in all the years leading up to his departure in late September. He'd fronted his own band in England, France, and Germany; recorded several of his own compositions; attracted the support of the brightest stars in Britain's rock galaxy; and was gaining recognition in the British press. Noel, meanwhile, happily spent Christmas celebrating his twenty-first birthday with his family.

For their next live appearance, the Experience were booked to play northeast London's Upper Cut Club, co-owned by boxer Billy "Golden Boy" Walker and his brother Phil, on the day after Christmas. Housed in a former ice-skating rink, the cavernous venue, described in the *Stratford Express* as "a plush, big beat palace," was celebrating its opening week. Promoting the Monday events as "Boxing Day for All the Family," the Upper Cut's ad listed the Experience as the afternoon matinee attraction, for an admission price of five shillings for the gentlemen and three for the ladies. By contrast, admission to the Pretty Things' evening performance cost twelve shillings and ten shillings.[24]

While waiting in the dressing room for their 4:00 P.M. start, Jimi completed writing "Purple Haze." According to Chas Chandler, Hendrix had come up with the song's distinctive riff about ten days earlier. "That afternoon at the Upper Cut," Chandler recounted, "he started playing the riff in the dressing room. I said, 'Write the rest of it,' so he did."[25] Jimi began the song with tritones—the so-called "devil's interval" eschewed by medieval composers—and then centered the song around an E♭7♯9—again, the so-called "Hendrix chord."

The song's title, enigmatic lyrics, and background sounds caused many listeners, then and now, to assume that "Purple Haze" was written about LSD. However, the phrase "purple haze" was probably inspired by Philip José Farmer's short story "Night of Light—Day of Dreams," which ran in a 1957 issue of *Fantasy and Science Fiction*. As Jimi described, "I had this thing on my mind about a dream I once had that I was walking under the sea. It is linked to a story I read in a science fiction magazine about a purple death ray."[26] Farmer's story, which he expanded into the 1966 novella *Night of Light*, told of a distant planet where, once every seven years, the atmosphere was charged with a "purplish haze" that rearranges physical reality—in essence, causing those exposed to it to live their dreams while in a conscious state.

Written on a piece of lined yellow paper, the document sometimes cited as the original draft of Hendrix's lyrics may have instead been a poem that shared or inspired the song's title. Beneath his handwritten "Purple Haze" at the top of the page, Jimi wrote "Jesus Saves." The two verses—or stanzas, perhaps—scrawled beneath these headings bear little resemblance to the "Purple Haze" lyrics. Then again, given their six-syllable/eight-syllable structure, the document's opening two lines, "Purple haze, beyond insane / is it pleasure or is it pain" flow just as easily to the music as the recorded version's "Purple haze, all in my brain / Lately things they don't seem the same." In interviews, Jimi said that his original draft of the "Purple Haze" lyrics was several pages long. "The key to the meaning of the song," he explained, "lies in the line 'That girl put a spell on me.' The song just progressed from there. It's got nothing to do with drugs. It's about a guy. This girl turned this cat on, and he doesn't know if it's good or bad—that's all. He doesn't know if it's tomorrow or just the end of time, for instance. He likes this girl so much that he doesn't know what he's in—a sort of a daze, I suppose. That's what the song is all about."[27] Convinced of the composition's hit potential, over the next two weeks Chas would help Jimi refine and edit the lyrics and finalize the arrangement.

On December 29 the Experience performed for the second time on British television, sharing the bill with Wayne Fontana on the popular *Top of the Pops*, which aired on Thursday evenings. Since 1964 the program had typically featured Top-30 artists miming to their records as the audience danced around them in a setting designed to look like a discotheque. Due to union requirements, Noel and Mitch were reportedly asked to sync their playing to prerecorded tracks, while Hendrix sang the song live. Among those who regularly watched the show was teenaged Gordon Sumner, who, as Sting, would later form the Police with Andy Summers and go on to enjoy a very successful solo career. Nothing, Sting wrote in his memoir, could "have prepared me for the whirlwind, the tidal wave, the earthquake, the force of nature that was Jimi Hendrix. The Jimi Hendrix Experience appeared on *Top of the Pops* in December of 1966 and changed everything. Hendrix had transformed 'Hey Joe,' an old folk song, and propelled it by the elegant ferocity of his guitar playing into a sassy, bluesy vehicle of awesome power. His vocal was as sulky and offhand as it was passionate and openly sexual, and as the three-piece band stormed through the three-minute song, I imagined everyone in the whole country in front of their tellys, sitting bolt upright in their chairs: *Wow! What the fuck was that?*"[28]

Two days later, with no New Year's Eve performance scheduled, the Experience and their entourage traveled across the frozen English countryside to Folkestone, Noel Redding's home base on England's southeastern coast. Though Noel was the only member of the group he'd ever heard of, the owner of the Hillside Social Club agreed to pay them £50 to play a set. "It was a great night—amazing warmth and acceptance from the regular Folkestone crowd," Noel penned in his autobiography.

> But English licensing laws madly insisted on throwing you into the street just before midnight even on New Year's Eve, so we stopped at eleven-thirty and ran to the van. Gerry floored it and raced like a madman along the dark, marsh roads, but we didn't make it to Mum's till half-twelve. We, including Kathy Etchingham, who'd come down from London with Jimi, were dying to get sloppy and sentimental, sing "Auld Lang Syne," and drink to our New Year—our new life—with Mum and Gran. I loved sharing my family with Jimi. I knew he felt lonely and strange at times.
>
> First thing Jimi asked was, "May I stand in front of your fire?" He said he found it great to stand with his back to the warmth of the fire during the cold and damp English nights. Mum always felt that the words to "Fire" came from that night. Mum loved Jimi's reserved, polite, and shy manner. And Jimi took to Mum, later signing a photo to her with "From Your Son, Jimi." It's one of her most precious possessions. Jimi was like that. When asked to sign an autograph he usually tried to add a personal touch. When Jimi and Kathy retired, I donated my bed. I was too excited to sleep. Everything was starting to accelerate. We could feel our momentum building. I stayed up drinking-in 1967. A most amazing year it turned out to be.[29]

6:January
1967

"Wild Man of Borneo"

Jimi was always on the move—with his music, with his lyrics, with his art. He was always reaching, always searching, always looking for something else, something more, something higher.
—Leon Hendrix[1]

During their first performance of the new year, on January 3, the Experience played two extended sets at the Bromel Club, an hour southeast of London in Kent. Richard Green, on hand to cover the shows for *Record Mirror*, wrote that "Jimi's reputation had preceded him into Kent, and a large part of his audience had gone along to see exactly what tricks he did get up to. More and more often during his act, I was reminded of the early days of the Who, when Pete Townshend was at his most violent, except that Jimi takes it several stages further. He kisses the guitar, sits on it and treads on it. Quite apart from belting it with his elbow and caressing the amplifier with it." After the second set, Green asked Jimi if he relied on the "sex angle" for his performances. "No, not really," Jimi replied. "I guess there is some sex, but I don't plan anything. I just do what I feel at the time." When Green inquired about "gimmicks," Jimi said, "Gimmicks? Sure, but we don't work things out, though. We just let them happen."

Two months earlier Green had quoted Chandler as saying that Jimi played better than Eric Clapton. This time, he asked Jimi about it. "I've played with him and he's good," Hendrix answered. "It's difficult to compare us because our styles are so different. He plays the B. B. King type of thing. My main thing is the blues, but people like Elmore James and a few others the people here wouldn't know." Jimi's most revealing answer came when Richard Green mentioned that "Hey Joe" was quite different from the other songs they'd just played. "That record isn't us," Jimi told him. "The next one's gonna be different. We're working on an LP which will be mainly our own stuff." Headlined "Sex, Gimmicks, and Jimi," Green's article ran in January 14 issue of *Record Mirror*, alongside a photo of Jimi playing the guitar with his teeth. This time, the publication spelled both of his names correctly.[2]

The Experience's recently hired booking agent, Barry Dickins, arranged additional dates outside of London. On January 7 the musicians made the four-hour commute north to play the New Century Hall in Manchester. After their show, they returned to the hotel, changed clothes, and went club-hopping. "After about the third club," Mitch wrote, "we walked over to the car and suddenly Noel and I were grabbed and slung against the railings of the police station. We got slapped around a few times, and I was going, 'What the fuck's going on?' They were the police, but we didn't believe it at first. They were all in plain clothes. They took Hendrix's passport off of him, but left him alone as he was an American." During a search, an officer pulled a pill from Noel's wallet. As Redding tried to explain that it was a legal suppressant for cigarette cravings, the officer punched him in the face, knocking off his glasses. After that, Mitch wrote, "They searched the car but didn't find anything. It really shook us up, though. We went back to the hotel, phoned up Mike Jeffery, and managed to get through for once. Eventually two cops were thrown off the force because of it."[3]

The band pushed on to Sheffield, forty miles east, where the *Sheffield Star* ran an ad announcing "the new weirdo trio, Jimi Hendrick's Experience." Dave Manvell attended the Sunday show at the King Mojo Club and saved the club's "account card," which shows 416 paid admissions at five shillings for members, six for nonmembers. In a 2001 interview with *UniVibes*, Manvell credited Peter Stringfellow for booking the band, adding, "But it was touch and go whether the Jimi Hendrix Experience would play that evening in Sheffield.... Even before the gig started there were problems, as the Sheffield police had been tipped off about the night before in Manchester. The police in Sheffield at that time didn't quite know what to do when they received the tip-off from Manchester, so they sent in the fire brigade to check upon things! As Peter related it to me, two burly firemen came into the Mojo Club to see Jimi and said to him, 'Come on, blackie, where are the drugs?' To which Jimi replied, 'No drugs in here, man!' They looked around and could not find anything, so Peter told them to apologize to Jimi, which they did."

Manvell noted that Jimi performed his set with two Strato-casters—a sunburst and one with a blue finish. Before going into "Purple Haze," Jimi announced that the band would soon be recording the song. He introduced an instrumental segment as "the Blitz," a reference to Axis bombing raids of World War II. "It had wailing sirens and explosions, all generated by his guitar and amps," Marvell said. "And he did all the usual things, like playing behind his back, playing with his teeth, attacking the amps with his guitar, and bouncing the guitar on the stage. He used the blue Strat for the destructive bit. Musically, it was a real turning point in my life." Stepping down from the foot-high stage, Jimi asked Man-vell directions to the men's room: "I told him to follow me. As we stood together, Jimi asked me if he could get some 'stuff.' I told him to hang around at the club, as this was the usual place to buy. Of course, it was all very innocent in those days—usually uppers and downers, which had been taken from grannies' pill bottles."[4]

Though these early performances away from London pre-sented challenges for the band, Kathy Etchingham thought that they brought out the best in Jimi: "That's when I remember him at his very best—and his happiest. That was his best music ever, played for its own sake. None of those crazy expectations, no one hanging on."[5] Despite the hassles with the police, Mitch con-curred: "Strangely enough, our early out-of-town gigs, especially the northern ones, were really easy. The crowds were really recep-tive from the word go."[6]

In his journal entry for January 9, Noel noted that the "Hey Joe" single was "twenty-five in *NME*, fourteen in *Disc*, and twenty-six in *MM* charts."[7] Discrepancies such as these were common dur-ing the 1960s, when British record charts were manually compiled from sales figures reported by a scattering of "chart return" rec-ord stores. Aware of which shops were being sampled, savvy pro-moters and managers could send in buyers to game the system. Keith Altham confirmed that "Hey Joe" received such treatment, with Kathy Etchingham serving as a designated buyer: "Chas admitted that to me. In those days, people used to do that with artists initially, because if you didn't get into the charts, you didn't get played by the BBC, you couldn't get onto national radio play, so 'Hey Joe' was bought into the charts."[8]

Another source contributed to the record's rapid rise, as Harry Shapiro and Caesar Glebeek described in their excellent biography, *Jimi Hendrix: Electric Gypsy*: "Pirate radio stations operating at that time from ships anchored in the North Sea probably had as much impact on Jimi's early chart success as any manipulation of the statistics. These stations, together with Radio Luxembourg, which gave Jimi a great deal of air time, commanded huge teenage audiences and many Hendrix fans can thank DJs like Kenny Everett, Stuart Henry, and Emperor Rosko for their introduction to Jimi's incendiary music."[9] Rosko saw in Jimi "a dynamo, a monster onstage, a giant! What wasn't special about 'Hey Joe'? It sent chills up and down my spine. It was great, because he broke ground. Nobody had ever seen anybody play guitar with their teeth and go absolutely crazy. This guy just did magic."[10]

Chas, always on the lookout for promotional opportunities, scheduled numerous photo shoots and interviews. On Monday, January 9, for instance, the Experience participated in a zany photo shoot at the soon-to-be-opened 7½ Club. One shot depicted Jimi strumming on a push broom he'd converted into a faux one-string with a piece of twine, while Mitch held a ruler to a bent saw and Noel kept time, maracas-style, with a pair of mallets. In an interview with Keith Altham later that day, Jimi proved equally entertaining and not above adding an occasional embellishment. "Bored to death at sixteen," Hendrix told him, "I joined the Army Airborne. A little less than a year of screaming '*Ahhhhhhh!*' and '*I'm fallllliiing*' all the time, I squeezed my way out by breaking my ankle and hurting my back." Asked about his recruitment by the Isley Brothers, Jimi said, "One of the Isley Brothers heard me playing in a club and said he had a job open. Sleeping between them tall tenements was hell—rats running across your chest, cockroaches stealing your last candy bar—so I figured, 'Yeah, I'll gig.' But I got tired of playing in the key of F all the time and turned in my white mohair silk suit and patent leather shoes. A tour came through town with B. B. King, Sam Cooke, Chuck Jackson, Solomon Burke,

Jackie Wilson, and Hank Ballard. I learned an awful lot when I got a job guitar-picking behind all those names every night." Jimi briefly mentioned the Experience and then reportedly said, "Now I'm going to make certain I don't fluff it all up!"[11]

Away from public view, Jimi and Kathy's life together at 34 Montagu Square was not always peaceful. Chas and Lotta were sometimes taken aback by the volume of the arguments coming from the rooms downstairs. During one disagreement Kathy smashed her foot through the back of an acoustic guitar. Another one led to a broken sitting-room door. For Jimi and Kathy, though, heated arguments were nothing new. "Having rows never worried either of us much," Kathy wrote. "I guess we both had listened to them enough throughout our childhoods not to take them too seriously. We could be shouting and screaming one moment and forgetting about the whole thing the next. . . . Both of us operated on very short fuses, and neither of us was ever willing to climb down, so we could only end them by one or the other of us storming off—usually me."[12] At one point, Chandler and Jeffery called Jimi into the office and urged him to break up with Kathy. Hendrix told them to mind their own business. In truth, he was possessive of Kathy, and their most violent exchanges tended to occur when he felt jealous or suspicious of her.

An especially heated argument on January 10 inspired Jimi to write one of his most achingly beautiful songs. As Kathy described,

He was moaning about my cooking again and I felt I had put a lot of effort into whatever it was—mashed potatoes, probably. I didn't take kindly to being told they were disgusting, so I picked up the plate and smashed it on the floor. "Hell—what are you doing?" he screamed at me, so I picked up a few more plates and threw them around the room as well, yelling back at him. Eventually I turned on my heel and stalked out, crossing the street to find a cab. He followed, trying to persuade me to come back, but I refused to listen. I found a taxi and jumped in, and without letting Jimi hear I told the driver to take me to Angie and Eric [Burdon]'s place in Jermyn Street. When I returned the next day, having cooled down, I asked him what he had done while I was away. "I wrote a song," he said and handed me a piece of paper with "The Wind Cries Mary" written on it. Mary is my middle name, and the one he would use when he wanted to annoy me. I took the song and read it through. It was about the row we had just had, but I didn't feel the least bit appeased.[13]

Later that day, Mike Jeffery and Chas Chandler, "owners of the sole and exclusive services" of Jimi Hendrix, signed a three-year contract with Track Records. The contract's terms required four singles and two albums per year. Jimi, Mitch, and Noel were not involved. "Had we realized how our lives and creative efforts were being manipulated," Noel wrote, "the Experience might have ended right then. We hadn't an inkling of the multitude of contracts being signed.... Since our office was the Anim office, I'd been hanging out with Eric Burdon, Terry McVay, Tony Garland, and the office staff, who had seen the Animals' troubles go down. They tried to warn me to be careful, but I didn't really understand what they meant."[14]

In one of their most productive sessions, the Experience and Chas Chandler spent four hours that day at De Lane Lea, working again with Dave Siddle. They began with several takes of "Purple Haze." Mitch recollected that "Hendrix came in and kind of hummed us the riff and showed Noel the chords and the changes. I listened to it and went, 'Okay, let's do it.' We got it on the third take, as I recall."[15] A common misconception holds that Jimi alone played the tri-tones that begin the recording. As expert transcriber Jesse Gress detailed, "In fact, Redding holds down the alternating octave E roots on his A and G strings, while Hendrix shuttles between Fuzz-Faced low-to-high B♭ octaves (the ♭5). It's the combination of the two that creates the song's introductory *los diablos en musica*, or 'devil's interval.'"[16] Spirits ran high during the takes. During one early version, as Mitch and Noel chanted the words "Purple Haze" during the fade-out, Jimi suddenly sang "freak-out," broke into laughter, and added, "Mary had a little lamb" to more laughter. The accepted take would later be revamped at Olympic, where Jimi would recut his lead vocal and guitar solos.

The musicians moved on to Hendrix's storytelling "51st Anniversary." Set to an innovative pop structure with a shifting tempo, the lyrics juxtaposed idealized images of long-lasting marriages with blues-worthy images of relationships in disarray: "Yes, her mama's a louse / Daddy's down at the whiskey house." Jimi sung and spoke the lyrics, which conclude with the narrator announcing his desire to stay single. "The first part is just saying the good things about marriage, or maybe the usual things about marriage," Hendrix explained. "And the second part of the record tells about the parts of marriage which I've seen. I see both sides, but I just really want to witness the first side. All I'm doing in that two minutes is saying my own exact opinions of marriage. Marriage is okay for some people, but it's not for me. I don't like anything to tie me down."[17]

Chandler recalled Jimi composing "51st Anniversary" in a single evening: "That song is a good example of Jimi just sitting around the apartment singing and playing his guitar. I would sit across from him and say, 'That's good,' or 'No, change that to something like this.' These were pre-studio edits, if you like." On one of the unreleased takes, they experimented with multi-tracking Jimi's lead vocal. While "51st Anniversary" has no solo, considerable attention was paid to the guitar parts: "This is the first song where guitar overdubs played an important role," Chandler said. "There was quite a bit of overdubbing on that track, and it was the first time where we consciously thought of approaching the production that way. There were five guitar overdubs all linking in together to sound like one guitar."[18] During the second break-time section, Jimi spoke the lyrics and, beginning at the 2:25 mark, imitated the sound of someone inhaling a marijuana joint and speaking while attempting to hold in the smoke. He concluded the track with a repeated pull-off on his guitar. On the released version, Chas boosted a single track of Jimi's voice.

Dissatisfied with the "Third Stone from the Sun" recording from a month earlier, the band successfully recut the song's basic track, but failed in their attempts to make a finished master. Next up was "Fire." After determining which tempo worked best, they did seven live takes and were satisfied they had the basic track. Mitch's snare syncopations bolstered the up-tempo arrangement's improvisational feel, while Noel's chromatic walk-ups mirrored an approach commonly heard on American soul records. The glassy guitar sound in the opening suggests that Jimi had his Stratocaster set to the "notch" position, activating the neck and middle pickups. At the 1:09 mark, Jimi kicked on a fuzz box in time for the "Ah, move over, Rover" section. In subsequent sessions, he would overdub the lead vocals, guitar harmonies, and lead guitar, which modulates out of the original key and then returns in time for the second verse—a classic Hendrix move.

With twenty minutes remaining, Jimi wrapped up this historic session with "The Wind Cries Mary." Its lyrics, Chandler confirmed, were written "the night before at home. Mitch and Noel had never heard the song before. It was recorded—including five guitar overdubs—in twenty minutes, and that was all part of the session for 'Purple Haze.' We had the third single there and then."[19] Brian Delaney, a career guitarist who's played Hendrix covers since his youth, cites "The Wind Cries Mary" solo as "an extraordinary example of Jimi's skill with shifting tonalities. The vocal verse progression goes from C to B♭ to F, but when the solo begins, Jimi somewhat 'reverses' things, going from F to E♭ to B♭. The solo further builds when there is a move 'downward' to G, then up a minor third back to B♭, and then yet another minor third shift up to C♯, finally landing back at F. A mere mortal would typically play the best lines he could over the first three solo chords. Only Hendrix would construct a solo that not only builds drama, but also simultaneously creates the sonic and musical equivalent of a bird winging on thermals high in the upper atmosphere."[20]

Jimi later detailed that "The Wind Cries Mary" was recorded "in about two takes. I explained to Mitch and Noel what I had in mind, and we played it halfway through so Chas could get the balance. Then we played it through once. Six minutes later the song was ready to be mastered and pressed. We never do more than five or six takes in the studio—it's too expensive."[21] Asked to explicate his line about traffic lights turning blue, Jimi responded, "Well, 'The traffic lights turn a blue tomorrow,' that means, like, tomorrow everything's gonna be blue. Blue means feeling bad, you know. In other words, like, for instance, if you do your everyday things like go across the street or something like that, instead of the traffic lights being red and green, well, they're blue because in your mind. . . . It's just another story about a breakup, you know, just a girl and a boy breaking up, that's all."[22]

Kathy Etchingham provided further insight, explaining that after she'd shattered the plates, "Jimi got the broom, sweeping it up before Chas came back. He's saying that he's sweeping up the pages of yesterday's life—it's all over, it's finished. And then I ran out, up the stairs, and out of the apartment. He followed me, and I was standing underneath the traffic lights and I hailed a taxi. 'Traffic lights,' he says, 'turn a blue tomorrow.' 'Footsteps dressed in red' is because I had red hair at the time and was wearing red."[23] The line "After all the jacks are in their boxes," Kathy added, was inspired by the television's on-screen graphic after the day's programs had ended: "At the time, the BBC used to finish at 10:30 or 11:00, and the test card was a little girl putting her jack back in the box."[24]

In retrospect, spending only twenty minutes of studio time to complete such an exquisitely played, multi-tracked song is an extraordinary feat. But at this stage, this was business as usual for the Experience. Years later Chas reminisced, "It was great in the studio, especially in the early days, because it was so spontaneous. Everything was done in one or two takes. The *Are You Experienced* album—when you count up the hours, it was recorded and mixed in maybe sixty hours in the studio. *Axis: Bold as Love* was maybe eighty hours in the studio."[25]

In a testament to the musicians' stamina, that evening they played two sets at the Bag O'Nails. Eric Clapton, Paul McCartney, Ringo Starr, Brian Epstein, Bill Wyman, Lulu, Donovan, Georgie Fame, Geno Washington, Pete Townshend, and members of the Hollies, Small Faces, Moody Blues, and Animals were sighted among the onlookers. Reviewing the shows for *Disc and Music Echo*, Mike Ledgerwood wrote, "Jimi set the swinging London club scene alight last week with a stage act that left pop's top names on their feet shouting for more. . . . It was certainly a night to remember. Jimi did two spots of powerful, full-blooded blues, which produced some amazing sounds and guitar gymnastics. He looks set to become one of the brightest stars of '67."[26] Hendrix climaxed the performance on his knees, picking his guitar strings with his teeth. Afterward, Noel confessed to being "freaked out" by seeing so many celebrities, while Jimi calmly chatted backstage with Clapton and Townshend. Hendrix also met with Roger Mayer, the young electronics wizard who'd been awed by his playing on *Ready Steady Go!* They hit it off, and Mayer was invited to demo his devices at the Experience's upcoming return engagement at Chislehurst Caves. Another face in the crowd, Karl Ferris, would later score the enviable assignment of shooting the psychedelic band photo featured on the front cover of the U.S. release of *Are You Experienced*.

From Chas Chandler's perspective, everything was moving according to plan: "The Beatles and the Rolling Stones were the aristocracy of music at the time. And they very early on became big fans of Jimi. I remember Jagger turning around in an interview one day and saying, 'Why the hell are you interviewing me? You should be interviewing Jimi Hendrix.' Things like that made it happen so quickly."[27] Keith Altham, who would accompany Jimi on his return to America, credited Chandler for orchestrating Jimi's quick ascendency: "It was a very skillful PR campaign, to begin with. Chas worked very hard on it. He pushed the image and the photographs. It was necessary to get attention to Hendrix. It was a kind of savage image when you looked at it in photographs. When you actually met Jimi, of course, it was a slightly different kettle of rock altogether because he was this quiet, whispering, gentle character offstage."[28]

The Experience's next-day event at the Racing Car Show at the Olympia National Hall proved anticlimactic. Radio London requested that they mime their performance as the sound system blasted a recording of their new single. For Jimi, who took pride in never playing a song the same way twice, this was anathema: "The one thing I really hate is miming—it's so phony," he later told *New Musical Express*. "So far, the only thing I was asked to mime was a Radio London performance, and I felt guilty just standing there holding a guitar. If you want to scream and holler at a record, you can do that at home—I'm strictly a live performer."[29]

That evening the Experience celebrated the 7½ Club's grand opening with an hour-long set, with Mick Jagger, Marianne Faithfull, Pete Townshend, Eric Clapton, Anita Pallenberg, and Brian Epstein among the spectators. "I went down with Marianne," Mick Jagger recalled, "and he was just amazing. I mean, he was just amazing—blew me head off, completely. I just thought Jimi was a great guitar player. I thought he was the best and the most original, with a really original act."[30] During the next six days the Experience would give four more performances in the basement club, which Mitchell described as "another up-market Blaises kind of place, only smaller." French movie star Brigitte Bardot attended one of the performances.

An article in the January 12 issue of *Disc and Music Echo* contained one of the first instances of the racist "Wild Man of Borneo" stereotype being applied to Jimi Hendrix: "You'd be forgiven for mistaking him for the Wild Man of Borneo's understudy, with his outlandish appearance, flamboyant attire, and shock of jet-black, Dylan-type hair."[31] Rooted in century-old blackface minstrelsy, this "wild man" image of black people had survived through the decades via ads, toys and trinkets, live performances of white entertainers wearing blackface, and films. In Hal Roach's 1933 Our Gang comedy short *The Kid from Borneo*, for instance, the "wild man" sideshow character is depicted with dark skin, long and nappy hair, native garb, and a bone through his nose.

When word of Jimi's rising fame in London first reached his family in Seattle, the "Wild Man of Borneo" image was on full display. "When Jimi first went to England," Al remembered, "I didn't think he was going to be that successful, but then I started getting reports on him after he started playing as the Experience. There was a notice of him in some music magazines, and then one of my stepdaughters saw a picture of Jimi with a caption that said 'The Wild Man of Borneo.' When she first looked at the picture, she thought it was me for a minute. She said, 'What's Al doing in London?' Then she looked again and said, 'Ooh, that's Jimi Hendrix— "The Wild Man of Borneo" and "The New Sensation of London."'"[32]

During the 1920s minstrelsy-derived stereotypes had also been applied to Lonnie Johnson, the era's most advanced blues guitarist. Like Hendrix, Johnson was a musical visionary with unsurpassed technique. He, too, played in racially integrated settings and could easily hold his own alongside some of the most gifted musicians of his time—in Johnson's case, Louis Armstrong, Duke Ellington, and Eddie Lang. And, like Hendrix, Johnson was a soft-spoken, urbane man with a keen sense of fashion. To advertise his 78-rpm records, though, the OKeh company used some of the most racially insensitive images imaginable. A 1928 ad for Johnson's "Kansas City Blues," for instance, called him "boy" and depicted him as a minstrel-style dandy with oversized white lips, holding leashes connected to three well-dressed women trailing behind him. In other ads Johnson was paired with images of monkeys and baboons whose faces resembled his.

Why were minstrel images applied specifically to someone as

sophisticated as Lonnie Johnson? Music researcher Thom Loubet offers a compelling theory:

> Record company promoters were in the awkward position of pursuing black consumers while still promoting their deep-seated racist beliefs about the place and function of blacks and black music. The solution, of course, was to conjure up images of the past—a time when life was simple and African Americans worked as sharecroppers on farms in the South, rather than competing for factory jobs in the North. Thus, distinctly urban musical expressions were marketed in terms of minstrel tradition. The ads powerfully support the argument that the industry's marketing strategies grew, in part, out of a white fear of the rise of a black urban middle class. Lonnie was an especially large threat, and therefore the ads created for him were especially degrading.[33]

In Jimi's case, some residents in Great Britain saw his race and magnetic pull on women as a threat. After all, as Mitch observed, the Jimi Hendrix Experience "was the first band where you've got a young black guy in some position of power that white girls liked. It was a threat to the authority, you know. They just didn't like what was going down."[34] As far as his bandmates were concerned, though, the color of Jimi's skin made no difference. Asked what it was like playing with a "black guy," Noel told an interviewer, "I don't know. He's a guitar player, you know? We didn't consider him being black. I considered him being American."[35] The racial issues would become more acute when the Experience began touring America. There, Mitch noted, "The potential racial problems were magnified by people disliking not just Jimi for being black, per se, but because he was playing with two white boys. So we became aware of racial tensions pretty quickly. I have to say that there was never any problem *ever* within the band. . . . The bottom line, I think, for him was, 'I'm an artist. I don't care what your color is. If we work together well, that's all that matters.'"[36]

As January progressed, the Experience spent their weekends on the road. On Saturday, January 14, reggae singer Jimmy Cliff opened for them at Nottingham's Beachcomber Club, three hours north from London. Scrawled onto a page of Hyde Park Towers stationary, the Experience's set list ran as follows: "Can You See

Me," "Mercy, Mercy," "Like a Rolling Stone," "Rock Me Baby," "Third Stone from the Sun," "Foxey Lady," "Stone Free," "Hey Joe," and "Wild Thing."[37] The next afternoon the entourage piled into Gerry Stickells's van for the two-hour drive north to Yorkshire. In its advertisement for the evening concert, the Kirklevington Country Club claimed, "Jimmy is the rave of the London Scene. Clapton, Dylan, and James Brown rolled into one. Have you seen a guitarist play with his teeth? Don't miss this man. The most exciting colored artist from the U.S.A."[38]

The pattern of spending weekends traveling to and from gigs outside of London would continue for weeks to come. "Things changed fast," Noel noted, "and our days settled into a routine: up late, travel, gig, get pissed, crawl into bed between four and eight in the morning. Most of our days were spent in brain- and body-numbing travel covering every corner of England and much of the middle. Usually Stickells drove the van and we'd pack ourselves in with the gear. I'd squeeze in between the roof and equipment because there weren't enough seats.... We'd get back at some god-forsaken time of the morning and drag ourselves up to my place where we would sit, each in a corner with a beer and a hash joint, relaxing in silent thoughts we were often too tired to share."[39] Noel would sometimes play them one of his favorite records by the Kinks, Small Faces, or Byrds. Jimi, a natural-born mimic, especially enjoyed Noel's *The Best of the Goon Shows* albums, featuring the comedic sketches of Spike Milligan, Peter Sellers, and Harry Secombe.

Mitch Mitchell had fond memories of the musicians turning each other on to favorite artists. Before meeting Jimi, he'd heard of Muddy Waters, but his blues listening leaned toward jazzier singers such as King Pleasure and Mose Allison. He credited Jimi with turning him on to the country blues of Robert Johnson and other artists. "If it had been an English blues purist, like John Mayall, telling me all this," Mitch wrote, "I doubt I'd have listened. But being as it was Hendrix and he'd been through all that, I did. Also, he always did it in a very delicate way, just pointing out certain reference points."[40] Mitch, in turn, played Jimi his favorite Miles Davis, Roland Kirk, and John Coltrane LPs. "With Noel," Mitchell recalled, "it was usually, ''Ere, have you heard the new Small Faces record?' For all the years we were on the road, Noel had a Small

Faces album and a Byrds album and a portable record player. We always knew which hotel room *he* was in!"[41]

At their next studio call, at De Lane Lea on January 17, the Experience recorded two instrumental takes of "The Wind Cries Mary," but neither surpassed the original. That evening they played at the Tiles Club on Oxford Street. Afterward, they found themselves unable to come up with the £2.25 to cover their bar tab. Noel noted that he, Mitch, and Jimi were constantly "skint"—low on funds—during this time. After complaining to management, they were each given a £20 bonus and their weekly pay was raised from £15 to £25—an improvement, but barely enough to cover clothing, meals, and lodgings. "There were so many more expenses, especially the fancy and expensive stage clothes," Noel sighed. "Our accelerating popularity increased the numbers of hangers-on, and the pressure accelerated our drinking. It was difficult to leave anywhere without at least two girls on each arm. I was seeing about a dozen girls regularly. I think I spent most of January in bed."[42]

When it came to women, Jimi was obviously the band's most targeted conquest. But during the early months of 1967, when the word "groupie" first came into use, the scene in England was far more subdued than it would be in America during the Summer of Love and afterward. While living with Kathy during his initial stay in London, Jimi tended to be low-key and guarded about outside dalliances. Upon his return to America later in 1967, when his fame began to skyrocket, Jimi would partake more fully in what has become known as "the rock and roll lifestyle."

On January 18, the Experience journeyed to the BBC's Lime Grove Studios to promote their new single on *Top of the Pops*. Once again Hendrix sang the lyrics live, while he, Mitch, and Noel mimed to their prerecorded backing track. The following day Jimi did an interview with Mike Ledgerwood for *Disc and Music Echo*. With its short answers, "Jimi's Favorite Things" provided readers intriguing insights into an array of subjects. About his living quarters, Hendrix said, "I now share a flat with Chas Chandler. It used to belong to Ringo. In fact, they only took the drums away the other day. There's stereo all over the place, and a very kinky bathroom and lots of mirrors." Discussing food and drink, Jimi expressed his preference for spaghetti, strawberry shortcake with whipped cream, banana cream pie, soul food—"greens and rice"—and milk, scotch and Coke, rum and Coke, and American root beer. He confessed to smoking a pack of cigarettes every day and a half, adding, "If I didn't smoke I'd be fat as a pig. My nerves are very bad. I like tipped cigarettes mostly, alternating with menthol ones." Asked about cars, he replied, "With all these backward streets I don't think I could drive here. I had one back home but a girlfriend wrecked it. She ran it straight through a hamburger joint. After that I started to devote more time to my music than to girls."[43] According to Jimi's dad, this last part was likely an exaggeration: "Jimi never had a driver's license while he was living at home. I don't think Jimi ever had a driver's license. Jimi needed glasses for seeing distances and for driving. A friend once told me that when you got in the car with Jimi driving, you were taking your life in your hands."[44]

Turning to musical matters, Jimi opened up to Ledgerwood about his life's ambition: "To be known as having a particular sound. I'd like to be recognized for my music the same way as someone like Chuck Berry." Asked about his fears, he said, "You can't last forever. I hope I won't lose my gigs. I'd like to go from one gig straight onto another. If I write something about three or four in the morning, I can't wait to hear it played. It's even a drag to have to wait for the other cats to arrive. It's like being almost addicted to music. Music makes me high onstage, and that's the truth." To describe his views on marriage, Jimi used an image straight out of old-time blues lore: "With music there's no time for anything else—I'm already married to my music. You'd have to work a whole lot of voodoo on me to get me married. A girl tried once, crazy cat. She put a lock of her hair in the heel of my shoe. I had to go a doctor afterwards. You wouldn't think these sort of things happen, but I can tell you it's real scary when it does."

Questioned about his religious beliefs, Hendrix told Ledgerwood, "There are so many different beliefs that something must be phony. I used to go to Sunday school, but the only thing I believe in now is music." He listed "flashy people and flashy conversation" as his main dislikes, with conservative clothes following close behind: "I don't want to ever look at a tie again. I had enough of shiny suits and patent leather when I was with an R&B band. Clothes like that restrict your personality. You're just one of the other cats." His likes? "Thunderstorms. I like to watch the lightning, especially on the fields, and flowers when I'm on my own. Science fiction—it's about the only thing I read. I read anything I can on Bob Dylan, though."[45]

Jimi's ability to legally perform for pay in the United Kingdom was assured on January 20, when he was issued a six-month work permit. That afternoon he had another interview scheduled, with John King for *New Musical Express*. "The most obvious thing about Jimi Hendrix is that he's not pretty—neither is his raw, exciting brand of beat music," King wrote. "This has not stopped him from setting the pop scene on its ear." King noted that "Hey Joe" had climbed to number eight on the singles chart.[46] Before the Experience's Saturday performance at the Refectory in Golders Green, Chas had another interview scheduled. Hendrix showed his playful side to the interviewer for *Melody Maker*, explaining as his long-term ambition: "I want to be Marilyn Monroe's understudy. And I mean understudy. In about thirty-years' time, maybe." Asked about playing guitar with his teeth, Jimi responded, "I've never broken any, but I was thinking one time—for a freak-out, of course—of putting bits of paper in my mouth before the show and then spitting it out like all my teeth were dropping out."

Jimi was asked to define "freak-out," an expression first coined in 1965 to describe an overly intense drug experience. "Well, whatever the word means to you," Jimi offered, "add a few musical notes to that. Each to his own. I think for a new freak-out, people should get really high and dig a Mrs. Miller single on 33 rpm. Then they can talk about that for about two weeks until they're bored—then you look for something else. Musically, freak-out is something like playing the wrong notes. It's playing the opposite to what you think the notes should be. If you hit it with the right amount of feedback, it can come up very nice. It's like playing wrong notes seriously, dig? It's a lotta fun."

Jimi turned reverential during a segment about Bob Dylan, advising readers to go out and buy a book with Dylan's words in it. He spoke less enthusiastically about the Monkees—"dishwater!"—and British food: "Oh, God. Man, see English food ... it's difficult to explain. Mashed potatoes—that's all I can remember, mashed potatoes. And I ain't gonna say anything good about that!" He artfully dodged a question about "chicks," which the interviewer surely used to reference young women. "I think, naturally, of chicks on the farm! Real chicks, hens and roosters, and eggs—though I don't like them too much. I think I know what you're getting at, though! Farmland, horses, you know, little furry three-toed birds! Member of the bird family, you know, old chap!" What about love, Hendrix? "Right. I won't make a silly answer. Something I guess a mother rat has for her babies. Oh! Don't rats eat their babies? Well, I guess that's all love too, man."[47]

Reading through transcripts of Jimi's 1967 interviews, it becomes evident that he could be completely lucid when the mood struck. At other times he'd respond with non sequiturs and off-the-wall humor. Like many other musicians, he preferred to let his instrument do the talking. "I can't express myself in a conversation," he once confessed. "I can't explain myself like this or that sometimes, because it just doesn't come out like that. So when we're onstage, it's all a new world. That's your whole life."[48] Kathy Etchingham attributed at least some of Jimi's interview behavior—and music—to the recent influx of LSD in London: "As he got more into drugs, I would sit and listen to Jimi giving interviews, spouting the most ridiculous acid-inspired stuff which the journalists would soak up as if it were timeless wisdom. Like most acidheads he had visions and he wanted to create music to express what he saw. He would try to explain this to people, but it didn't make sense because it was not linked to reality in any way."[49]

In early 1967 psychedelic drugs were just coming into vogue in London. "Everyone was so, so involved with pot and stuff like that," Chris Stamp remembered. "And LSD was very important at the time. Everyone was either taking LSD or thinking about taking LSD. There were the people who hadn't taken it, and the people who had taken it, so to speak. That was an important drug. But the actual hard drugs weren't important at all, and they weren't really around very much at all. As you know, LSD is not the sort of drug that you get strung out on. It's not something one wants to take every day."[50] In time, Chas Chandler discovered that Jimi could handle the psychedelic drug experience far better than the average user. "I was never aware of how much dope they were putting down their throats," he said. "Jimi never seemed to be high or anything. I didn't find until after we'd completed *Axis: Bold as Love* that he had been taking acid, and this is a guy who was living in the same flat as me. You just couldn't tell with Jimi. He seemed to just cruise through anything that came along."[51]

In a testament to Chas's publicity skills, Jimi's recent interviews with *New Musical Express*, *Melody Maker*, and *Disc and Music Echo* all arrived on British newsstands during the same cycle. Meanwhile, the band played the Astoria in Oldham, Lancashire, on Sunday, January 22, and made their debut at London's prestigious Marquee Club on two nights later. The venue's weekly ad boasted of the "first appearance" of Jimi Hendrix in typeface that dwarfed the names of other acts appearing that week, including Pink Floyd and jazz luminaries Ben Webster and Blossom Dearie. The hype paid off: an estimated 1,400 fans queued up to see the Experience, breaking the Marquee's attendance record. The next evening the Experience performed in Norfolk at Orford Cellar, described by Noel as the "smallest, hottest place I've ever played in. Terrible sound."[52]

On Friday the Experience returned to Chislehurst Caves, playing to an audience of 2,000. Roger Mayer met with Jimi backstage. "I brought some of my experimental electronics that I had been fooling with," Mayer described. "Jimi played with them in the dressing room. One of the devices I showed Hendrix was the Octavia. It was developed just before my meeting with him, maybe a few months before. With it we could add forms of distortion and second harmonics. Basically, the Octavia is a frequency doubler with some additional frequency-shaping circuits within it. It contains envelope generating, amplitude modulation, and a lot of other things."[53] Quickly adapting Meyer's new sound-shaping technology, Jimi would use the Octavia during his upcoming sessions for "Purple Haze" and "Fire."

The Jimi Hendrix Experience devoted the final three days of January to making radio recordings and a "Hey Joe" promotional film. At the start of their January 30 performance for BBC Radio 1's *Pop North* program, the announcer introduced Jimi as "one of the greatest new sensations to hit the scene in a long, long time." The Experience began with "Hey Joe," Jimi's tone distorted by the sheer volume of his amplifiers. Thunderous applause followed their straight-forward reading. The trio followed with a high-energy arrangement of the blues standard "Rock Me Baby," Jimi's solo choruses displaying his command of string-bending. They wrapped up the performance with "Foxey Lady."

For the "Hey Joe" promotional film, Australian director Peter Clifton shot color footage of the Experience's January 29 performance at the Saville Theatre, with an additional segment, sans audience, filmed there two days later. The film's opening footage shows an impishly smiling Jimi heading to the Saville's backstage entrance in advance of the Experience opening for the Who. Before the concert, Tony Gale photographed Jimi posing with the Who's Roger Daltrey, Pete Townshend, and John Entwistle. Another of his shots captured Jimi happily reading a book of cartoon drawings called *It's a Mad Mad World*. "I got the impression of a slightly unsure but nice guy," Gale said of this encounter with Hendrix. "He was always smiling, happy, and relaxed, but unsure of how to pose in front of a camera."[54]

After the Koobas and the Thoughts warmed up the audience, the Experience came onstage. "What an Experience!" Chris Welch wrote in *Melody Maker*. "Jimi was hit by PA trouble, but the crowd were so keyed up they laughed sympathetically while Jimi searched for a mike that worked. He stormed through 'Like a Rolling Stone,' 'Can You See Me,' 'Hey Joe,' and the incredible 'Wild Thing,' ending in a freak-out of guitar biting, feedback and uproar. 'Follow that' was the feeling. Then came the Who—as wild and unpredictable as ever. They played their best for months. Gone were smoke bombs and amplifier smashing. In their place were good singing and playing."[55]

Eric Clapton brought Jack Bruce to the Saville performance, which he deemed "just blinding. I don't think Jack had really taken him in before. I knew what the guy was capable of from the minute I met him. It was the complete embodiment of the different aspects of rock and roll guitar rolled up into one. I could sense it coming off the guy. And when Jack did see it that night, after the gig he went home and came up with the riff for 'Sunshine of Your Love.' It was strictly a dedication to Jimi. And then we wrote a song on top of it."[56] Although he may have been unaware that he'd inspired Cream's highest-charting hit, Jimi added an instrumental version of "Sunshine of Your Love" to the Experience's concert repertoire.

The Saville performance also led to Jimi getting his first important notice in *Billboard*, the most respected music-business magazine in the United States. In a review headlined "Who & Hendrix an Upbeat Team in Saville Date," Mike Stafford wrote, "Brian Epstein's attempt to establish his Saville Theater into a pop showcase is having its ups and downs. But his teaming of the Who and the Jimi Hendrix act last Sunday (29) was definitely upbeat. The loudest screams of the evening went to the Hendrix group. Unknown to British fans weeks ago, Hendrix has built up a huge following in the London clubs since being brought over from New York by ex-Animal Caas [*sic*] Chandler. The audience shouted for more after his 'Wild Thing,' when he discarded a microphone and, leaning against the amplifier, played guitar with his foot. The Who deserved their place at the top of the bill, however. One of Britain's most creative groups, it has had many international hits."[57]

On the final day of January the Experience returned to the Saville, where Peter Clifton filmed them in color, sans sound, synching to the "Hey Joe" single. His white Stratocaster held up to his teeth, Jimi mimed the opening phrase and then quickly switched to playing the standard way. Noel, meanwhile, flat-picked the Gibson EB-2 bass Chas had loaned him. In the film's final frames, a mob of autograph seekers surround an elated Jimi.

Surrounded by promo posters, the month-old Experience plays Munich's Big Apple, November 1966. (INTERFOTO/Alamy Stock Photo)

Jimi in his Montagu Square flat, December 1966. (Photograph by Cyrus Andrews/Michael Ochs Archives/Getty Images)

Jimi, Noel, and Mitch backstage at *Top of the Pops*, December 29, 1966.
(Photographs by Harry Goodwin/BBC Photo Library)

Mitch, Jimi, and Noel, Bath Pavilion, February 20, 1967. (© Bath in Time, www.bathintime .co.uk)

Jimi holds court at Darlington's Imperial Hotel, February 2, 1967. (© Ian Wright/ National Portrait Gallery, London)

The Experience's March 2 performance at the Marquee was broadcast on *Beat-Club*. (Photograph by Bob Baker/Redferns/Getty Images)

Gered Mankowitz remembered that his March 8 photoshoot took place during a "particularly wonderful moment" in Jimi's life. (Photographs by Gered Mankowitz © Bowstir Ltd. 2018/mankowitz.com)

WALKER SURPRISES

WE were well and truly blitzed with "mini-happenings" on the Walker Brothers' Tour opening night, at Finsbury Park Astoria last Friday, when Jimi Hendrix literally set the scene alight after his guitar exploded in a sheet of flames at the end of his act.

The curtain fell and rose again on the Walkers' exciting act to reveal an Amazon-like fan mobbing Scott Engel and gallantly being rescued (or was it abetted?) by publicist Brian Sommerville.

Cat Stevens wore a stetson and gun holster to convince us all that "I'm Gonna Get Me A Gun" was just a little old cowboy song and nothing controversial, while Engelbert Humperdinck was smooth, suave and sophisticated and followed Hendrix rather like Dr. Jekyll following Mr. Hyde.

The Walkers proved to be supreme pop stars, giving us a sensible selection of "songs to scream to" (but what a pity no one takes time out to listen to Scott Engel's fine voice), including "Land Of A Thousand Dances," "Hold On I'm Coming," "What Now My Love," "The Sun Ain't Gonna Shine Anymore," "I Need You," and finishing with "Oop Oop A Doo."

Lovable "Leeds"—the Walkers' auxiliary drummer, gave us "Turn On Your Light" as his solo spot. He proved he still has his supporters

Cat Stevens looked good—in green Edwardian frock coat—sounded good, especially on "Matthew And Son" and "Here Comes My Baby."

An intelligent variation in numbers, in which he also performed "I Love My Dog," "If I Were A Carpenter," and "I'm Gonna Get Me A Gun" rounded off a first-class performance. To me Stevens was the surprise packet on the show.

Engelbert Humperdinck closed the first half and appeared the picture of sartorial elegance in a tuxedo, singing

By KEITH ALTHAM

a selection of songs more obviously suited to a cabaret audience.

This might have misfired had it not been for his professional approach and excellent stage manner. His best reaction was undoubtedly for his huge hit, "Release Me" and a fine vocal performance of "Summertime" well suited to his strong voice.

Other numbers were "Ain't That Good News," "Let Me Be Yours," "Midnight Hour," "Ten Guitars" and "Jambalaya."

The Jimi Hendrix Experience are a musical labyrinth—you either find your way into the solid wall of incredible sound, or you sit back and gasp at Hendrix' guitar antics and showmanship, wondering what it's all about.

The sounds are something new—you either dig it or you do not.

"Foxey Lady," "Can You See Me" and Jimi's two hits, "Hey Joe" and "Purple Haze," were the entire Hendrix programme.

Finale to Hendrix' act came about when his guitar burst into flames, by "accident" we are assured, and precipitated the entrance of a security officer who sprayed detergent from a canister all over compere Nick Jones.

The Californians' act was all but drowned by a posse of young "ladies" seated directly behind the reviewers.

The show was opened by the Quotations, who later provided brilliant backings for Cat Stevens and the Walkers.

Relaxing backstage on the opening night at Finsbury Park Astoria (l to r) JIMI HENDRIX, CAT STEVENS, GARY LEEDS and ENGELBERT HUMPERDINCK.

Keith Altham covered the opening night of the Walker Brothers tour in *New Musical Express*, April 8, 1967.

Following its U.K. release, "Purple Haze"/ "51st Anniversary" was issued by Polydor in Germany. (Courtesy of Jim Hawthorn, The Jimi Hendrix Record Guide, http://hendrix.guide .pagesperso-orange.fr /hendrix.htm)

Melody Maker's April 22 cover announced the upcoming release of "The Wind Cries Mary" single. (© TIME INC. (UK) Ltd.)

Track Records officially released *Are You Experienced* on May 12, 1967. (Courtesy of Jim Hawthorn, The Jimi Hendrix Record Guide, http://hendrix.guide.pagesperso-orange.fr/hendrix.htm)

Jimi, with hand-painted Stratocaster, climaxes his Monterey set, June 18, 1967. (Ed Caraeff/Iconic Images)

7:February 1967

Making a Media Darling

We'll do things our own way and make our own sound.
—Jimi Hendrix[1]

Credit where credit's due: without their management's unflagging pursuit of media coverage, the Jimi Hendrix Experience would not have had such a meteoric rise. Chas Chandler was the point man for most interviews, but on occasion Mike Jeffery became involved in arranging publicity as well.

Sometime during the first few days of February—the exact date is uncertain—Jimi gave an insightful interview to Steve Barker, who months earlier had seen him onstage with Cream. Hoping to place an article in his college newspaper, *The Polytechnic*, Steve had contacted Jeffery, who approved and set up the meeting. It's a testament to Jimi's affability and modesty that he would be willing to give such a wide-ranging and detailed interview to a novice journalist. Throughout their meeting, which lasted longer than the hour-long cassette Barker had brought with him, Hendrix was friendly and relaxed.

Noticing copies of Robert Johnson's *King of the Delta Blues Singers* and *Lenny Bruce Is Out Again* next to the stereo, Barker began by asking about the main influences on Jimi's music. "Well, I don't have any right now," Jimi told him. "I used to like Elmore James and early Muddy Waters and stuff like that—Robert Johnson and all those old cats." Asked if he felt any heritage from these bluesmen, Jimi responded, "No, 'cause I can't even sing! When I first started playing guitar it was way up in the Northwest, in Seattle,

Washington. They don't have too many of the real blues singers up there. When I really learned to play was down South. Then I went into the Army for about nine months, but I found a way to get out of that. When I came out I went down South and all the cats down there were playing blues, and this is when I really began to get interested in the scene."

They next explored Jimi's thoughts on the music scene in Great Britain. "From what I've seen, it's pretty good," Jimi offered. "I thought it could be a whole lot of cats who could play it but not really feel it. But I was surprised, especially when I heard Eric Clapton, man. It was ridiculous. I thought, 'God!' And every time we get together, that's all we talk about—playing music. I used to like Spencer Davis, but I heard that old Stevie's [Winwood] left them, and I think it's official about two days ago, or was it yesterday?" Barker followed up by asking about the "latest Beatles release," most likely a reference to the *Revolver* album. "I think it's good," Jimi said. "They're one group that you can't really put down because they're just too much. And it's so embarrassing, man, when America is sending over the Monkees—oh, God, that kills me! I'm so embarrassed that America could be so stupid as to make somebody like that. They could have at least done it with a group that has something to offer. They got groups in the States starving to death trying to get breaks and then these fairies come up." (Ironically, within six months of making this statement, Hendrix, thanks to Mike Jeffery, would find himself opening for the Monkees' American tour, a mismatched pairing that fizzled out after just eight shows.)

Steve Barker next asked Jimi if he'd ever met Bob Dylan.

I saw him one time, but both of us were stoned out of our minds. I remember it vaguely. It was at this place called the Kettle of Fish in the Village. We were both stoned there, and we just hung around laughing—yeah, we just laughed. People have always got to put him down. I really dig him, though. I like that *Highway 61 Revisited* album and especially "Just Like Tom Thumb's Blues"! He doesn't inspire me, actually, because I could never write the kind of words he does. But he's helped me out in trying to write about two or three words 'cause I got a thousand songs that will never be finished. I just lie around and write about two or three words, but now I have a little more confidence in trying to finish one.... I hear Dylan used to have a pad with him all the time to put down what he sees around him. I'd like to play some sessions behind Dylan. His group ought to be a little more creative.

The conversation shifted to the Experience. "How does the Experience get such fusion," Steve asked, "when you're basically a bluesman, Noel's a rock man, and Mitch a jazzman?" "I don't know!" Jimi replied. "Actually, this is more like a freestyle thing. We know what song we're gonna play and what key it's in and the chord sequences, and we just take it from there. And so far it hasn't bugged me in any way, like saying, 'Oh, no! There he goes playing that rock and roll bass pattern again.' Everybody's doing pretty cool. I guess it is experimenting just now. Maybe in about six or seven months or when our next album comes out we'll know more what we're doing. All the tracks on our first LP are going to be originals, but we might play Dylan's 'Like a Rolling Stone' on it."

Barker asked about the "auto-destruction" of the Who. Jimi, who'd yet to burn a guitar onstage, thought for a moment. "We don't really break anything onstage—only a few strings. Actually, we do anything we feel like. If we wanted to break something up, we would do it. There's a lot of times in the past I have felt like that too. But it isn't just for show, and I can't explain the feeling. It's just like you want to let loose and do exactly what you want if your parents weren't watching. I dig the Who—I like a lot of their songs! The Byrds are pretty good too, though I know you don't dig them over here. They're on a different kick. I like them." Asked his opinion of free jazz, Jimi responded, "I'd have to be in a certain mood if I could sit up and listen to it all day. I like Charles Mingus and this other cat who plays all the horns, Roland Kirk. I like very different jazz, not all this regular stuff. Most of it is blowing blues, and that's why I like freeform jazz—the groovy stuff instead of the old-time hits like when they get up there and play 'How High the Moon' for hours and hours. It gets to be a drag."

Jimi's answer to Barker's question about whether he ever read the British underground publication *International Times* took an interesting journey: "Oh, yeah! I think that's kind of groovy. They get almost too wrapped up with something, but it's really nice what they're doing. They have a paper like that in the Village, *The East Village Other*. The Village's Fugs are real crazy; they do things arranged from William Burroughs, songs about lesbians, and things like 'Freakin' Out with a Barrel of Tomatoes,' squashing them all between your armpits—euughh! You'd never believe it, man, those cats are downright vulgar. They tell these nasty, beautiful poems! The nastiest ones you could think of. Here's one thing I hate, man: When these cats say, 'Look at the band—they're playing psychedelic music!' and all they're really doing is flashing lights on them and playing 'Johnny B. Goode' with the wrong chords—it's terrible." At the interview's end, Jimi played Steve the Experience's recent recording of the "Purple Haze" basic track and invited him to attend the upcoming overdub session. "Of course, I was knocked out at the prospect and left in a great mood," Barker remembered. "But we met his then-manager Chas Chandler on the way, and he nixed my attendance. I left in moods swinging between elation and crestfallen."[2]

During their February travels outside of London, the Experience never knew quite what to expect. Noel Redding brought home this point in an article he penned for *Beat Instrumental* about the group's February 1 performance in the coastal town of South Shields. The venue was the New Cellar, a late-licensed bar promoted as "The £50,000 Disco Club." "About the only bad gig we've had so far was at South Shields," Redding wrote.

> We arrived a little late and we were in a bit of a rush. We were on the back of a revolving stage just getting tuned, ready to be swung round any minute. We had got these new 200-watt [Marshall] units and just as we were tuning, Jimi's amp blew up. He quickly plugged into mine and I looked round for something to borrow. In the end I had to make do with a tiny amp which the other group had been using—it must have been all of five watts. As we swung round, we opened up and the sound was terrible. My bass was just buzzing like mad. Gerry came up, gave me the P.A. amp, and put the vocals through this tiny thing. Of course, from then on we couldn't hear a word except in the breaks where we were singing and not playing, and even then we just heard a tiny whisper. As if that wasn't enough, at the end of the spot we were taken back round on

the revolving stage and as we went the audience grabbed us. I was hanging on to Jimi and he was hanging on to Mitch and we very nearly got crushed against the wall as we went round. It's quite a life working with Jimi, but I enjoy it.[3]

Playing at such a high volume increased the likelihood of amp failures and other equipment breakdowns. "We needed to be loud—and I mean deafening—to deliver our concept of a complete orchestra in three pieces," Redding explained. "We blew amps left, right, and center as we pumped up and up, trying to fill the whole hall and any gaps between us and the audience with sound. In order to hear me, Jimi liked one of my speakers on his side. I had no trouble hearing Jimi. Poor Mitch, who at times couldn't even hear us (no monitors) but could follow by watching the rhythm of my fingers, was left in the middle to beat his brains out electronically unassisted, trying to compete with hundreds of watts full up with nothing but sheer energy. The miking of drums was unheard of, and our electrical demands were already terrorizing clubs."[4]

On February 2, "Hey Joe" jumped to number seven on the charts. That evening's *Top of the Pops* rebroadcast the Experience's December performance of "Hey Joe." As it aired, the Experience were in Durham, getting ready to perform at the Blue Pad, an R&B club in the Imperial Hotel. Ian Wright, photographer for the local newspaper, the *Northern Echo*, witnessed the sound check: "They started, and it was a bloody racket. It was indescribable. After a few minutes they blew the fuses in the amps, then they blew the fuses in the lights. It all went black."[5] Soon afterward, Jimi gave a brief interview to Allene James, who covered the newspaper's music beat. "He was staying at the Imperial Hotel," she remembered, "and he had a white poodle on the bed. He could certainly play the guitar, but I thought he was quite unassuming. He was actually quite shy—he wasn't one of the many show-offs that I have interviewed in show business."[6] About two hundred people attended that evening's concert in the smoky ballroom.

Afterward Tony Carrington, lead guitarist of the Vipers, was having a drink with Jimi in the hotel bar, the Bolivar, when a roadie came in to report a missing Fender Stratocaster. "Hendrix didn't seem that bothered," Carrington remembered. "He was concerned about his white guitar, which was the best one. But it was his black one that had gone, and this was the one that was more or less used for show, to bang around the mike stand and the amps. . . . It had been used and abused and was not in a pristine condition. It did not even sound good. It was a dog as guitars go."[7] In a conflicting account, pub owner Kenny Beagle said that Hendrix "went down the Bolivar and was really kicking off about it, going berserk. People were trying to pacify him, but he was very volatile."[8] Upon leaving the venue, the band had to push their van through snow to jump-start its engine.

The next evening brought the Experience to the Ricky-Tick in Hounslow, Middlesex. Jimi climaxed the set by shoving the headstock of his Stratocaster, presumably the white one, through the club's low ceiling. This damaged two of the guitar's tuning machines, rendering the instrument temporarily unplayable. With the Experience's first session at Olympic Studios scheduled for later that night, Noel scrambled to borrow a Fender Telecaster he'd sold to Trevor Williams.[9]

Chandler, who wanted to refine the guitar sounds on the De Lane Lea takes of "Purple Haze," hoped the Experience would fare better at Olympic. The facility's large room could easily hold all of the band's gear and better accommodate the roaring volume at which Jimi liked to record. Even with "Hey Joe" climbing the charts, though, the Experience had initially been refused admission due to Chandler's lack of a credit history with the studio. Ultimately, Polydor opened an account there in Chandler's name and supplied the necessary funds. Chandler was anxious to get it done. "With 'Purple Haze,'" he explained, "Hendrix and I were striving for a sound and just kept going back in, two hours at a time, trying to achieve it. It wasn't like we were in there [in the studio] for days on end. We recorded it, and then Hendrix and I would be sitting at home, saying, 'Let's try that.' Then we would go in for an hour or two. However long it took to record that one specific idea, then that's how long we would book."[10]

In his insightful book *Ultimate Experience*, John McDermott explained how engineer Eddie Kramer changed the way the Experience made records: "The pre-Olympic recordings featured Redding's bass and Mitchell's drums recorded in mono on two of the tape's four available tracks. Kramer's approach was to record

Mitchell's drums in stereo on two tracks, reserving the two remaining tracks for bass and Hendrix's rhythm guitar. . . . Kramer and Chandler then took this tape to another four-track recorder, premixing the four tracks down to two in order to create an opening for two more tracks. These two tracks could then accommodate Hendrix's lead guitar, lead vocal, or any other overdub idea."[11] Jimi, Kramer soon saw, had a clear idea of the sounds he wanted to capture on tape: "Jimi was the master executioner in terms of, 'Okay, this is my idea. I know exactly how I want to play this, I know exactly how I want it to sound.' And I would just be there to interpret what he was doing."[12]

On Jimi's invitation, Roger Mayer attended the February 3 session. "There was not a lot of overdubbing on those cuts," Mayer remembered. "There were probably a maximum of three guitar tracks with vocals and backing vocals. We would go into the control room, and Jimi himself did some of the complex panning from left to right—the panoramic control. He was very instrumental in the creative sound of the mix."[13] Mayer brought along his Octavia for Jimi to use for the solo sections.

After cutting new lead vocals for "Purple Haze," Jimi proceeded to the guitar overdubs. With two of his Strats missing or out of action, it's possible that his iconic "Purple Haze" solos were recorded with a Telecaster. Since Redding and Trevor Williams both played right-handed, the borrowed Telecaster would almost surely have been strung in the standard way for a right-hander. If Jimi used this guitar—the absence of whammy in the overdubbed solos adds weight to this notion—there are several ways he could have done it. He could have removed the Tele's strings, flipped the nut, and restrung it in the manner to which he was accustomed. This would likely have been too time-consuming. A simpler method would have been to use a Phillips screwdriver to swap two of the tuning machines from the Telecaster to the damaged Stratocaster, since they were interchangeable. Audio evidence, though, suggests that Jimi may have done what virtually any other guitarist would have found unthinkable: simply leave the Tele strung as is, flip it over, and wail away the "wrong way," with the high strings on top.

Brian Delaney makes a compelling case for Jimi's having used the right-hand-strung Telecaster, explaining,

Jimi's first overdubbed solo, beginning at :48 seconds, sets up the next verse. The second overdub, at 1:08, is a repeat of the previous motif, but with Roger Mayer's Octavia effect kicked on—it builds from the previous motif, if only slightly. The third motif, the abstraction of the 'Purple Haze' riff, at 1:12, sets up Jimi for lift-off at 1:18, when he again kicks on the Octavia for the solo. The notes he plays when he says "Help me," from 1:12 to 1:18, are a punctuation. They are a *musical* part, but not necessarily a "guitaristic" part. A part like this is something you typically could only come up with in your mind, away from your guitar. Guitarists generally are stuck playing guitaristic things because their fingers and physicality have trained them to play a certain way on the instrument. But when you come up with a concept like Jimi's musical idea in this part, then you have to go to a guitar and say, "How do I execute this idea?" Then the final climax of the song and wailing ride-out have a distinctive downward-pull bend that you just can't get using a tremolo. You can hear this effect when Hubert Sumlin played between the vocals lines on Howlin' Wolf's "Goin' Down Slow," or on certain songs by Otis Rush, who strung his guitar the "wrong way," with the high strings skyward.

At the end of "Purple Haze," it's a siren's song, with the Octavia unrelenting and chaotic, and an occasional minor third overbend that is absolutely staggering—no one else was playing like this at the time. The ride-out could very well be the sound of a right-strung Telecaster on the lead pickup, having its treble string yanked downward toward the center of the fretboard in the upper octave with that Octavia. Both Strats and Teles of the era had tiny 7.25-inch radius fretboards that made bending problematic, but that never stopped Jimi. Jimi once said, "A Telecaster has two sounds—one good, one bad." He just used the treble pickup for the overdubs. Having owned an Octavia, I can honestly say that they don't track too well, so a hot Tele treble pickup would help the cause, compared to a somewhat anemic Strat treble pickup sound. The realization that Hendrix may have easily overdubbed these parts as a lefty with a right-handed guitar really speaks to his unbounded guitar abilities.[14]

There is strong anecdotal evidence that Jimi could pick up any guitar or electric bass and play it either way with equal finesse. Chas Chandler, for instance, saw Jimi sit in with a jazz trio, playing brilliantly on a flipped-over right-handed guitar that belonged to the trio's regular guitarist. James Gurley, whose band Big Brother and the Holding Company played shows with the Experience, insisted that "Jimi could play the guitar right-handed and left-handed. Either way! He could play right-handed guitar left handed, left-handed guitar right handed, right-handed guitar right handed, and left-handed guitar left handed. I could not tell any difference when I was listening to him play."[15] Andy Johns, who helped engineer the Experience's *Axis: Bold as Love* album, saw Jimi do this in the studio: "It didn't matter which way the strings went—he knew where the notes were. The guy was a genius! He was *extremely* clever."[16] Regardless of which guitar was used, the "Purple Haze" solo endures as a masterwork. "It freaked everybody out," Kramer remembered, "because it's one of the great, classic initial solos where psychedelia and blues are all rolled in together."[17] By session's end the sun had risen and Hendrix and Mayer had begun a lasting friendship.

A low-fidelity recording exists of the Experience's show at London's Flamingo Club the next day. Distorting from the band's needle-in-the-red volume, the reel-to-reel recording nevertheless offers insight into the Experience's club repertoire—two originals, six covers. The tape starts midway through a raving version of "Killing Floor." Ending with a feedback flourish, Jimi retuned his guitar and told the audience, "We'd like to continue on with a little tune, a very straight, Top-40, R&B rock and roll record, a little thing called 'Have Mercy'—'Have Mercy on Me, *Ba-by.*'" Hendrix's straight-ahead reading resurrected the rhythm-and-lead style he'd used with Curtis Knight. He announced the trio's next song as "'Can You See Me,' in the key of F♯" and injected a stunningly unfettered and ambitious solo between the verses. He dialed down his volume, double-checked his tuning, and went into a laid-backed "Like a Rolling Stone." The trio then bulldozed through a cover of B. B. King's "Rock Me Baby" powered by feedback, aching string bends, and a brilliant solo and finale.

In a nod to its opening line, Jimi introduced their cover of Muddy

Waters's "Rollin' Stone" as "Catfish Blues." Stretching the blues standard to eight minutes, Jimi easily displayed his mastery of the original's stop-time pacing and then rocketed into space, figuratively speaking, with a jaw-dropping extended solo highlighted by perfect string bends and machine-gunning chordal passages. Near its end, he took a page from Buddy Guy's playbook by bringing his sound down to a whisper and then roaring off once again. He played another fiery solo in "Stone Free" and then cooled down with "Hey Joe," playing the mid-section melody with his teeth. Jimi announced their final song as "the English anthem" and led Mitch and Noel into "Wild Thing." He quoted the Beatles' "Day Tripper" during the solo and likely "humped" his guitar against his Marshall amp to create the ending cacophony.

On the strength of shows such as this and their first single, the Experience kept up their momentum in the press. The new edition of *Melody Maker* prominently displayed Jimi on the front page. "It's Jumping Jimi!" ran the huge headline, with the subhead "Hendrix Leads Stones in Pop 50 Race." A black-and-white photo of Jimi performing with a pained expression on his face dominated the interior layout.

That weekend Noel returned home to Folkestone. Visiting Tofts, a club he'd played in his youth, he was greeted with a standing ovation and requests for autographs. Slowly but surely, though, the adulation and late nights were taking their toll on everyone in the band. "The unwinding," Noel explained,

> soon became a wind-up as more and more people gravitated
> towards our aura of success. We had party invites every night—
> more drinking, more smoking, and more pills for energy. Sleep
> was now reduced to two to six hours per night—*if* you went
> home, or home alone. The star treatment was overwhelming.
> No matter how much I'd dreamed about being a "star," I never
> appreciated what a mixed blessing it would be. I loved being
> recognized, but hated being unable to claim a bit of privacy
> when I needed it. And I needed it more and more.... The
> realization hits that your previous life has been demolished.
> Everything has changed. Even friends. Simple pleasures—
> a quiet pint and a chat, a good night's sleep—were gone. If
> I tried to go ice-skating, I'd be pulled apart by schoolgirls

(another lovely fantasy that's better in the head). If I went to a club, they'd announce my presence—applause, people rushing for autographs, free drinks, fucks. Getting a bag of chips became a production. My most wonderful dream was becoming the most nightmarish imposition.[18]

The relentless pace continued. On Monday, February 6, the Experience traveled south to Croydon for an appearance at the Star Hotel, where they played "Red House" during their set. The next day Noel, who'd been using a variety of borrowed basses, journeyed to Sound City, where he found the instrument of his dreams, a Fender Jazz bass. Since its price—"well over £200"—amounted to about two months of his take-home pay, Redding traded in one of his instruments and borrowed the rest of the money from Chas.

That evening the Experience returned to Olympic Studios for a session that ran past midnight. With Eddie Kramer engineering, they created room on the "Purple Haze" four-track master for Jimi's additional rhythm guitar and vocals, as well as Noel saying "ooh" and "ah." As always, special preparations had to be made for Jimi's vocal overdubs. As Kramer noted, Jimi "would never, ever, let anybody watch him putting vocals on. He was very shy about his voice. He thought he had the worst voice in the world. We used to put a line of screens up and stick him behind there, and he used to poke his head out and say, 'Alright now.'"[19] Chas described an unorthodox technique they used to add another dimension to the recording: "A lot of the background sound on 'Purple Haze' is actually a recording being fed back into the studio through earphones held around the microphone, moving them in and out to create a weird echo."[20]

Back at Olympic the next afternoon, they added more overdubs to "Purple Haze" and completed the song's final mix. The Experience then worked on "Fire," overdubbing Mitch's drums, doubling Noel's bass part from the De Lane Lea session, and adding Jimi's double-tracked guitar solo and Mitch and Noel's background vocals. Next up was "Foxey Lady." Jimi redid one of his guitar tracks, Mitch doubled his bass drum part, and Jimi's lead vocal and Noel's backing vocals were tweaked. By their tea-time finish, the final mix of "Foxey Lady" was completed. From there the Experience were off to a sold-out return engagement at the Bromel Club.

On Thursday, February 9, the Experience's *Pop North* radio broadcast aired and the band played the Locarno Ballroom in Bristol. A photograph taken at the event shows Jimi playing in front of a barricade to a packed floor and balcony. Nicholas Williams, covering the concert for the *Bristol Evening Post*, wrote that Jimi left concert-goers "reeling with the sound of his way-out guitar. Backed by a two-man group, he bombarded his audience with an unbelievable wall of sound, which he somehow coaxed from his electric guitar. He played it in the usual way. He played it under his arm, over his shoulder and between his legs. He scraped it on the stage floor and over the amplifiers—he even plucked the strings with his teeth. Something had to snap—and it did. He broke a string at the end of the show. But that's nothing unusual. 'I buy several sets a week,' said Hendrix."[21] At £260, this would be their highest-paying engagement in February.

After the Experience's next performance, at Newbury's Ricky-Tick the following day, a reporter for the *Plaza Bulletin* wrote,

> The Jimi Hendrix Experience roared and romped their way through an hour and a quarter's worth of music that shattered the senses both aurally and visually. Resplendent in red corduroy trousers and antique waistcoat, Jim proceeded to show just how many positions it was possible to play the guitar in, at the same time showing his very own professional skill, which must rate him as one of the most outstanding newcomers on the scene since Jeff Beck or Eric Clapton.... Throughout the evening, Jimi showed flashes of onstage humour for which he must be given full credit. "Hey Joe," current chart rider, was introduced as being written by Mickey Mouse; after a sudden frenzy of excitement in which he attacked his amplifier with his guitar (not a new idea, but somehow done refreshingly) he announced, "Anyone wanna buy an ole guitar? This one don't tune so well."
>
> The finish came suddenly, in an excess of violence. Mitch Mitchell attacked a cymbal stand and it broke into pieces, then distributed his drum kit round the stage and finally squirted the other two with a handy water pistol. The bass guitarist locked his guitar in its case and then kicked it about the stage. Jimi attacked his huge amplifier with his guitar, breaking

strings and nearly toppling the amplifier onto his hand. He then squatted on the guitar with both feet and rocked to and fro. Then the evening came to its conclusion in a storm of feedback, flying microphones and water pistols.[22]

At the band's Saturday performance in Cheltenham, for 350 fans at the Blue Moon, Noel debuted his new Fender Jazz Bass. During the interview segment of that day's *Saturday Club* broadcast, Brian Matthew asked Jimi if he saw any similarity in his music and Cream's. "No, not necessarily," Jimi said. "What we're trying to do is we're trying to get our own particular sound, like a freakish blues, this array almost, only with a little more feeling than what's been happening lately." As the Experience played "Stone Free," "Love or Confusion," "Hey Joe," and two takes of "Foxey Lady," the volume of their amps caused the studio's soundproof glass to shake. They then jumped back on the road for a Valentine's Day show at Gray's Club in Tilbury.

Jimi's February 15 interview for *Beat Instrumental* focused on his roots in American blues. Kevin Swift began his write-up by proclaiming that "he plays superb blues guitar, and what's more, he plays it from the heart, not from other artists' records. He is Jimi Hendrix, a very hot property in more than one sense, and he's come to Britain at just the right time. The scene was already set by the English bluesmen and visiting Americans, now we have the 'gen' [genuine] article, a young American blues star with a style that is born [*sic*] of deep 'feel,' hard work, and experience. If you belong to the school that believes you must suffer before you can play the blues, this bloke qualifies with no trouble at all."

Jimi described how, when first learning guitar in Seattle, he began on an acoustic strung for a right-hander, and then restrung it for a lefty. "Then I got tired of the guitar and put it away," he told Swift. "But when I heard Chuck Berry, it revived my interest." He briefly spoke of getting his first electric guitar, a Danelectro, and of joining the Army and playing around Nashville and Clarksville. On the subject of bluesmen, Jimi expressed his appreciation for Albert King and Albert Collins, then quickly added, "Well, I don't like to get hung up on any one guitarist, because I always feel kind of unfaithful when I move on to someone else. I should say my influences were B. B. King and Elmore James." For his closer, Swift asked why Jimi didn't choose two "blues-soaked men as drummer and bassist." Hendrix responded, "If I had two blues men with me we would have gone straight into one bag, the blues. That's not for me. This way we can do anything and develop our own music. We might do our arrangement of a Howlin' Wolf number followed straight away by 'Wild Thing,' or a Bobby Dylan number. We'll do things our own way and make our own sound."[23]

On February 16, a rare day off from playing, Jimi signed a boiler-plate publisher's agreement with Yameta Company Ltd. This document provides unassailable evidence of Jimi's ability to quickly compose songs. Whereas seven weeks earlier he had been hard-pressed to come up with an original B-side for "Hey Joe," the contract lists sixteen original Jimi Hendrix compositions: "In consideration of the sum of ONE (1) SHILLING on account of the royalties hereinafter made payable to the Composers by the Publishers (the receipt of which sum of ONE (1) SHILLING is hereby acknowledged) the Composers hereby assign to the Publisher THE FULL COPYRIGHT FOR ALL COUNTRIES in the musical compositions entitled 'The Wind Cries Mary,' 'Highway Chile,' 'Purple Haze,' '51st Anniversary,' 'Can You See Me,' 'Foxx Lady,' [sic] 'Manic Depression,' 'May This Be Love,' 'I Don't Live Today,' 'Fire,' 'Remember,' '3rd Stone from the Sun,' 'Are You Experienced,' 'Love or Confusion,' 'Red House,' 'Here He Comes.'"[24] And thus with a few strokes of a pen above a signature line that read "James Marshall Hendrix p/k/a Jimi Hendrix," Jimi Hendrix confirmed the transfer of control of many of his most beloved songs.

"What's remarkable about his publishing agreement," Lawrence Townsend writes, "is the sheer list of compositional gems, but I do not find anything legally significant. The one shilling is worth noting, but the compensation, of course, comes from the royalty amounts, which appeared to be in order. As I understand it, however, Chandler and Jeffery already controlled the titles, and this publishing agreement was most likely just a formality that the publisher required Jimi to sign. Although not recited in the agreement, the proceeds I'm sure, under separate agreement, were to be paid to the managers' account, assuring Jimi and the band would be lucky to see much or any of it."[25]

Financially, Mitch and Noel fared worse than Jimi. "Like most musicians," wrote Noel, "we hated to speak up, preferring instead to avoid any form of upset and concentrate on making music. We'd mumble and complain to each other and hustle on the side until we felt desperate enough for a confrontation. Slowly it began to sink in that unless we worked ourselves into a lather and complained, nothing would happen. Thinking of my earlier bands that had made less and taken home more, I started to write down the gig fee whenever I could discover it."[26] When their complaints grew loud enough, Jeffery raised their weekly salary to £30 apiece.

The next day Jimi, looking glum, posed alongside Mitch and Noel in front of a lion statue at Trafalgar Square. From there the Experience were off to an hour-long concert at the Ricky-Tick in the Thames Hotel in Windsor, Berkshire. A photo taken at the event shows fans standing so close to Jimi that they could touch the headstock of his guitar as he played. Offering more insights into the band's weekends on the road, Noel described their journey to Yorkshire for a performance in York University's Langwith College Dining Hall:

We had a photo session in London in the afternoon and we were late leaving. Gerry, our road manager, had already left with the gear and we were to follow in Mitch's car. We set off at 5:00 P.M. and belted off towards Nottingham but, after only a few miles, the generator went. We just about made it into Nottingham, left the car at a garage, and started to look round for something to get us to York, which was still a good hundred miles away.... Eventually we hired a car and about 9:45 P.M. we were on our way again. We turned up at midnight. Fortunately, we weren't due on until 1:00 A.M. The gear was all set up. We were cheesed off and tired, but the booking was okay. In fact, it was very, very good indeed.

People ask me if Jimi is hard to follow. I don't find him hard to keep up with at all. We have about the first two numbers arranged and after that it's just up to him and we follow. I used to play guitar myself and I watch him closely. On this particular night I was watching him so closely that I nearly had a bit of an accident. I just happened to look round and I saw that the top cabinet in my Marshall set-up had moved with the vibrations and was just about tottering on the edge of the other one. It would have fallen on my head if I hadn't turned round. Luckily there were no other hang-ups on this occasion. Jimi's always well prepared anyway. He always has two guitars plugged in, one he uses and the other he leaves at the side of the amp; he uses a fuzz box and has both guitars plugged into their own units.[27]

Stickells confirmed that during this time Jimi usually had two or three Arbiter Fuzz Faces on hand. These cheaply made, primitive fuzz boxes didn't last long, since Jimi tended to use his full weight to activate and deactivate them.

Finishing the concert at 2:00 A.M., Noel continued, the band returned to Nottingham and huddled in Stickell's van for several hours as they waited for the garage to open: "We were cold, miserable and tired. Eventually the guy came to open the garage. We got the car out and Gerry, who is a genius of a mechanic, fixed it all up. We left Nottingham around 10:00 A.M. We were making good time on the motorway when 'bang,' we had a blowout at 70 m.p.h.! We pulled over and as we didn't have a wheel brace, we just sat there. Eventually an AA man came along and helped us out and at 2:00 P.M. we were on our way again. The thing was that we had a gig that night at 6:00. I needn't tell you how tired we were. But at least it had been a good gig. They were flashing these color slides on the walls as we played and the whole thing was great."[28] In his diary, Noel noted that the venue had paid £150 for the Experience's performance.

During their next session, at De Lane Lea on Monday, February 20, the Experience taped several takes of "I Don't Live Today," one of Hendrix's darkest compositions. Like Robert Johnson's 1937 recordings of "Hell Hound on My Trail" and "Me and the Devil Blues," "I Don't Live Today" conjures the image of someone living on borrowed time: "No sun coming through my windows," sang Hendrix, "feel like I'm sitting at the bottom of a grave." Months later, he'd tell Steve Barker that the song was "dedicated to the American Indian and all minority depression groups."

Mitch began the basic track with robust tribal drumming. Hendrix reportedly used a hand-operated wah to shape the sound of two of his four guitar tracks. He fashioned another track with melodic feedback shaped by whammy. A classic example of Jimi's legato technique shows up in the first solo, beginning at 1:18. As Brian Delaney explains,

> A big part of Hendrix's style is his ability to play legato—to play fluidly. Aside from someone like Jeff Beck playing "Over Under Sideways Down" with the Yardbirds, you didn't really hear rock guitarists play legato until Jimi Hendrix. He had an extraordinary ability to sustain a guitar and create that flowing, floating sound, whereas most other guitarists at the time were playing very defined, choppy beats—the Dave Clark Five beat-band kind of thing. Hendrix shows up, and sure, his launching pad is the blues, but he takes it in an extreme way beyond the blues and plays legato with the use of things like Roger Mayer's effects. You can also hear this technique on "Purple Haze," the break in "Manic Depression," "Fire," and so many other tracks.[29]

On the released version, a strange guitar passage occurs between 2:09 and 2:22. "It almost sounds like they shut the tape machine off," Delaney details, "but I think what's probably happening here is that Jimi was holding the guitar on his lap, or most likely the studio floor, going for an effect. He could have created that section by simultaneously playing the bass string, flicking the selector switch, and pressing down the whammy bar with his fretting hand. Those subtle high notes in the background could be an open B string with the bar depressed all the way down. But he was not 'playing' the guitar in the traditional way—it was on the floor, or in a flat-on-its-back relationship. He would have had more leverage with the tremolo bar this way."[30] As a final touch, Jimi surrounded his spoken statement "There ain't no life nowhere" with a head-spinning soundscape.

At that evening's gig at the Pavilion in Bath, Jimi was photographed backstage holding a sunburst Stratocaster, likely a replacement for the one recently stolen. Josephine Bayne, covering the concert for the *Bath and Wilts Evening Chronicle*, described the scene as the Experience came onstage:

> Fans were stunned into silence. As Jimi Hendrix bellowed "Lord, have mercy" from his altar on the Pavilion stage at Bath last night, his worshippers gazed in silent adoration from

below. I echoed his sentiments as my ribs reverberated with the intolerable volume of electronic sound. His appearance was almost as awesome as the noise. His long, tousled hair fell about his face and over the collar of his gold-spangled jacket. ... The power of his delivery stunned the fans into silence and they were able to produce only conventional applause, punctuated by a few exhausted squeaks in place of screams.... Why he needs to create horrific wailing effects on his guitar and turn the amplifiers to full strength, I cannot imagine. His voice, when it can be heard, should be adequate to transmit his message. The personality that accompanies it is even more forceful. He has a new single due for release next month, which is apparently freakish. Perhaps someone should tell him that the "freakier than thou" competition is over and music is on the way back.[31]

In London the next day, Jimi, Mitch, and Noel collaborated on a piece for *New Musical Express*. The information they provided—short, separate responses beneath subject headings—suggests that they may have written the information on a questionnaire. Jimi began with a lighthearted response for his full name—"James Maurice Hendrix." The origin of his stage name, he revealed, was "88% from birth certificate, 12% from misspelling." He shaved three years off of his age, claiming November 27, 1945, as his birth date. He listed his height as 5′ 11″ and his weight as "11st 3lbs," or 157 pounds. On the subject of his parents he wrote only his father's middle name, "Allen." In addition to guitar, he listed piano, organ, drums, and bass as his instruments and described his musical education as "None, except radio and records, going to gigs to listen to the guitar players." He gave sixteen as the age at which he made his first amateur and professional appearances. The biggest break in his career: "Meeting Chas Chandler and forming group." Jimi named *Ready Steady Go!* as his first TV appearance. As his biggest musical influences, he listed blues, Elmore James, B. B. King, early Muddy Waters, and Bob Dylan. His occupation before show business? "Drop out (school that is)." His hobbies? "Reading science fiction, painting landscapes, daydreaming, MUSIC."

Hendrix listed "black, blue, certain shades of red, purple" as his favorite colors; strawberry shortcake and spaghetti as his favorite foods; and pineapple, orange juice, and chocolate milkshakes his preferred drinks. His favorite actors were a toss-up between Paul Newman and Natalie Wood. In the music section, he mentioned Cream, John Mayall, Spencer Davis, and Shotgun Express as his favorite bands/instrumentalists; Bob Dylan, Muddy Waters, and Mozart as his favorite composers; and the Beatles and Cream as his favorite groups. His miscellaneous likes were, in order, "music, hair, mountains, fields"; his dislikes were "marmalade, cold sheets." He named Tony Garland and Eric Clapton as his best friends, and described his own taste in music as "psychedelic, classical (own up), BLUES of course." Asked about his most thrilling experience, Jimi made a tongue-in-cheek reference to his days with the 101st Airborne: "Jumping out of a plane, jumping back in, getting thrown back out." He described his pets as "my two little furry-minded guitars." Jimi's most revealing answer came when asked about his personal ambition: "Have my own style of music. To see my mother and family again." Unbeknownst to readers, Lucille Jeter Hendrix had already been dead for nine years. Jimi wrapped it up with this revelation about his professional ambition: "To be a movie and caress the screen with my shining light."[32]

The Experience spent Wednesday afternoon, February 22, doing a live recording of "Hey Joe" for the BBC radio program *Parade of the Pops*. From there Jimi headed to the Speakeasy for a press reception for the group Soft Machine, celebrating the release of their first single. That evening the Experience concertized at the Roundhouse on Chalk Farm Road, where a smiling Jimi was photographed playing a dark Stratocaster. "Awful," Noel wrote of the gig. "Died a death. Horrible place. Jimi had his white guitar stolen."[33] Adding to their woes, they were paid only £100 of the agreed-upon £150 fee. The next day the Experience earned a respectable £189 for their sparsely attended evening performance at the Pier Pavilion in Worthing. For their Friday evening performance at Leicester College, a good gig marred by bad sound, they earned £75. During their Saturday concert at the Corn Exchange in Chelmsford, the Experience were recorded playing "Stone Free" and a no-frills "Like a Rolling Stone." From Chelmsford the Experience ventured to Southend-on-Sea for a Sunday-evening "Pop Festival" double-header at the Cliffs Pavilion. A group with the ungainly name of Dave Dee, Dozy, Beaky, Mick & Tich, who'd had three charting hits the previous year, received top billing over the Jimi Hendrix Experience and the Nashville Teens.

In an article in that weekend's *Record Mirror*, "Jimi Doesn't Think He's a Big Name Yet," Hendrix offered rare insights into his creative process: "At school I used to write poetry a lot. Then I was really happy, like in school. My poems were mostly about flowers and nature and people wearing robes. And then I used to paint a picture of, say, a really pretty mountain, then write about four lines of poetry about it. I don't hardly get a chance to paint now. The girl in the office bought me a paint box, but I haven't had a chance to buy paper. I like to paint different things, but I don't like to paint people.

"Up to now I've written about one hundred songs, but most of them are in those New York hotels I got thrown out of. When I go back I'm going to collect them from these hotel rooms where I missed the rent—I'm not ashamed to say that. I can't write no happy songs. 'Fotsy Lady' [*sic*] is about the only happy song I've written. Don't feel very happy when I start writing." Jimi also touched on the subject of his recordings: "We had one little record and I'm just wondering how the people are going to take the next one, because it's so different from 'Hey Joe.' I think everyone will think we've used different instruments, but it's still two guitars and drums. At one point the guitar sounds like a flute. I recorded it exactly as we do it onstage. Everything we do on record we can do onstage. If we had a disc with a violin on it, we'd hire a violin player to come onstage for that one number. Our third record will be even [more] different. They'd picked 'Loving Confusion' ["Love or Confusion"] to be our next single, but I had this thing on my mind about walking on the sea. Then I wrote 'Purple Haze.'"[34]

The new *Melody Maker* carried Paul McCartney's advance review of the "Purple Haze" single: "So, Jimi freaks out and sounds all the better for it. It's breaking out all over the place, you know. I thought it would be one of those things that people might keep down, but it's breaking through all over. You can't stop it. Hooray! Fingers Hendrix. An absolute ace on the guitar. This is yet another incredible record from the great Twinkle Teeth Hendrix!"[35] Luckily for Jimi, neither of McCartney's nicknames stuck.

Chas arranged for the group to meet with Bruce Fleming in his central London studio on Monday, February 27. The photographer's assignment was to capture an image suitable for an album cover. At the time, Fleming had never seen the Experience perform and had only heard a recording of "Hey Joe." Each musician chose his own outfit for the shoot. Jimi bedecked himself in dark pants, his favorite black shirt with roses, a brocaded dark vest, and dark cloak. Chas's instructions for the trio were simple: don't smile. Fleming began snapping. His favorite images were taken with the lens held low, looking up at Jimi, Mitch, and Noel. "What I wanted to get," he explained, "was an effect shot from the floor, looking up at Jimi so that the boys came out from under his cloak." Jimi impressed him as being "very caring" and a "very nice guy," asking him, "What can we do now? Where do you want me to stand?"[36] Fleming urged Polydor to use one of the edgier, down-low shots. The label ultimately chose a head-on image of Jimi standing with his cloaked arms outstretched over Noel and Mitch, who hadn't yet permed his hair to match Jimi and Noel's. Hendrix shared Fleming's disappointment with Polydor's decision.

8:March 1967

"The Black Bob Dylan"

It just gets me stoned out of my mind when I'm playing.
It's like a contact high between the music and me.
—Jimi Hendrix[1]

On March 1, Jimi Hendrix's name appeared for the first time in *Crawdaddy*, a popular American music magazine marketed to teenagers. In its "What Goes On" column, Hendrix was identified as a "twenty-two-year-old Seattle-born blues singer who has broken into the British music scene with fantastic success; his record of 'Hey Joe' is already #9 in England."[2] In the weeks to come, other mentions in American publications would help bring the Experience the recognition that would lead to their first American tour in June. Meanwhile, in a March 1 article headlined "Jimi Is Here to Stay" in the United Kingdom's *International Times*, Hendrix was quoted as saying, "Britain is our station now. We'll stay here till the end of June, then we'll see if we can get something going in America, and then we'll come back here. We'll be staying here off and on all the time."[3]

The Experience began the new month with a rehearsal at the Speakeasy and an afternoon session at De Lane Lea, where Jimi played "Like a Rolling Stone" on his sunburst Stratocaster. He and Chas wanted to feature the song on the Experience's debut album, but Noel had difficulty dialing in a good bass sound and Mitch had trouble keeping time. "It used to drive them nuts," Chas lamented, "because Mitch would either be winding up or slowing down. . . .

We wanted to record it, but we were never successful. I tried over and over to get it."[4]

The following day the Experience were filmed at a "private event" at the Marquee, for broadcast on the German television program *Beat-Club*. Dressed in dark pants and shirt, military jacket, and scarf, Jimi smiled shyly as he began "Hey Joe," gently playing a sunburst Stratocaster. This relaxed version stayed true to the released single. Essential viewing for anyone interested in Hendrix's guitar technique, a close-up of Jimi's face during the solo clearly shows him striking strings with his teeth. Near the song's end, another close-up reveals him loosely holding a standard pick between his thumb, forefinger, and middle finger. With the song's conclusion, the announcer briefly stepped into the frame to say, "Hey, fantastic sounds! Real psychedelic sounds from the Jimi Hendrix Experience. Well, the boys have got a new one out on the 17th of March, and this one's gonna really take the market by storm." With that, the trio went into "Purple Haze." Outstanding camera work showed Jimi's distinctive way of using just his fretting hand's index finger to apply vibrato to the song's main riff, a technique similar to B. B. King's trademark "hummingbird" vibrato. The film reveals the ease with which Jimi could segue from rhythm to lead, the extraordinary length of his fingers, and how he'd drape his thumb over the guitar's neck to fret bass notes. For the end solo, Jimi placed himself against his amp speakers and used his whammy to sculpt the ensuing feedback into a melodic passage. He then violently yanked the bar to create a freak-out feedback finale suitable for family viewing. Just under seven minutes, the superlative *Beat-Club* footage is widely available online.

The Experience then embarked on the first of two European jaunts scheduled that month. Traveling with Chas Chandler, Gerry Stickells, and Tony Garland, they landed in Paris on Friday, March 3. That evening Jimi paid a visit to the chic Chez Castel, a members-only establishment on the Left Bank. Instead of returning to his room at the Rue de Caumartin, he spent the night with new acquaintances at a hotel in the Latin Quarter. As morning broke over Paris, a panicked search for Jimi ensued. Calls were made to London, the airport, immigration authorities, and various hotels. After three hours, he was finally located. Chandler and

Garland took him on a quick tour of the Paris flea market and then shuttled him to the Europe 1 station for a radio interview.

That afternoon the Experience performed a forty-minute set at Le Cadran-Omnibus. Their concert that evening at the Law Society Graduation Ball at Panthéon-Assas University turned harrowing. "There was an oompah band on before us," Mitch described, "and they would not leave the stage. I remember one of our roadies, in a final act of desperation, pushing the trombonist's slide back into his mouth—blood and teeth everywhere. We finally set up and played a few numbers and for some reason this huge fight broke out. They were fighting everywhere—up and down the stairs, all over the place. It got completely out of hand, so we left the gear and got the hell out."[5]

The entourage traveled to Belgium for a Sunday concert in Mouscron, crossed back into France for a show in Loison-sous-Lens, and then circled back to spend the night in Brussels's Hotel Central. In his autobiography, Mitch wrote of this mini-tour: "Most places in Europe that we hit, we did broadcasts, even if it meant getting up at the crack of dawn and going out and miming to our latest record in a field while it was snowing. We used to think, 'What the hell are we doing this for,' but obviously it paid off in terms of publicity."[6] Chances are, this passage specifically refers to the Experience's film shoot on Monday, March 6. That morning, in the snow-dusted Zoniënwoud forest on the southeastern edge of Brussels, the Experience mimed "Hey Joe" and "Stone Free" for a Belgian TV show, *Vibrato*. A photo of the event shows Mitch seated behind his drum kit, Noel with his bass, and Jimi holding his unplugged sunburst Stratocaster.

Journalist Jan Waldrop, on hand to interview Jimi for *Humo* magazine, watched as a toothless old wood gatherer stood staring in disbelief at the appearance of Jimi in his military jacket and tight red corduroy pants. Using this image to begin an article entitled "Jimi Hendrix Shows His Teeth," Waldrop gave this cringe-worthy description of Hendrix: "The 'Black Bob Dylan,' as some call him, is a curiosity on its own. Jimi has an overwhelming amount of dark hair, which semi-carelessly waves around his head. He has a fantastic, almost picturesque, primitive head. His white-as-a-sheet teeth pierce as a battery of ready-to-fire field guns through his wide lips. Between his friendly dog eyes lies a nose like a trampled-down rubber hose. And if he feared in spite of all this he would remain unnoticed, Jimi wears cracking-red trousers and a fantastic military dress coat."

During a break in the filming, Waldrop asked Jimi about his life in Seattle. "I couldn't stick it at home," Jimi said. "I left school early. School wasn't for me. So according to my dad, I had to work. So I did that for a couple of weeks—for my dad. He had a not-all-that-well-running contracting firm and in me he saw a cheap laborer. I didn't see it that way. I had to carry stones and cement all day and he pocketed the money. At the age of fifteen [sic] I ran away after a blazing row with my dad. He hit me in the face and I ran away. Because I didn't have a cent in my pocket, I walked into the first recruiting office I saw and went into the Army." Asked his opinion of his time in the military, Jimi responded, "Horrible! A mess. The only thing which I liked was parachute jumping, but I wasn't all that good at it. After about half a year I made a terrible drop, broke my ankle and hurt my back. Just on time, because the Army was really getting on my nerves."

When Waldrop asked if Jimi disliked leading a "regular life," Hendrix responded, "Enormously. As soon as I've done something a few times or I stay somewhere a few weeks, I have enough of it! Then I *must* do something else or I walk with my head against the wall in misery." He returned to the misery theme, with major embellishments, when asked if he was successful in his early musical career in the States. "Not at all! For years I lived in misery and the biggest mess you could imagine. I slept wherever I could and stole my meals. I played in bars and on the streets and sometimes I made a few dollars. When things would become too boring, I would go with some friends and we would beat up a policeman. Within half an hour we would have a smashing row. Sometimes you would end up in jail, but the food would be great, so it wasn't that bad. Most of the police guys were bastards, but there were also some good ones. They didn't hit that hard as some others and you could eat better. But even that got boring."

Waldrop pressed Jimi to identify the kind of music he plays nowadays. "Blues, man," Hendrix said. "Blues. For me that's the only music there is. 'Hey Joe' is the blues version of a hundred-year-old cowboy song. Strictly speaking it isn't such a commercial song and I was amazed the number ended up so high in the charts. Our next single, 'Purple Haze,' is commercially even worse." So why release it? "Because we like it ourselves. I couldn't care less if the records sell or not. Making music is much more important." What about the money, Waldrop wondered. "I don't give a shit about that," Hendrix told him. "As long as I have enough money to eat and I can play what I want, I'm satisfied. I only hope to make enough money so that I can have a house built for my father. In the seven years I've been away from home I have never seen him. I phoned him once, when I had just arrived in England. I wanted to tell him what I had accomplished. He asked me who I had stolen the money from to go over to England."

As the interview wound down, Waldrop asked Jimi about his attraction to flashy attire. Jimi responded, "I have an enormous dislike for ordinary things and ordinary people. Folks with 'nice eyebrows' and things like that, those who dress so common." Asked to explain "what kind of a guy" he was, Jimi said, "Me? Well, I'm a quiet person. Usually I don't talk that much. What I have to say, I say with my guitar." As his final question, Waldrop asked Jimi's opinion about the filming they were currently doing for *Vibrato*. "Oh, is that the name of the program? Well, it is bloody cold outside and it's a disaster that we can't play live. I can't mime. I can't play a song the same way twice. I feel it differently every time." Called back to resume filming, Jimi gave Waldrop a firm handshake and Southern-drawled his farewell: "Now, y'all take it real easy, ya hear?"[7] The next day the Experience were required to mime again, doing "Hey Joe" and "Stone Free" for the Belgian TV program *Tienerklanken*. By late afternoon, they were aboard a return flight to London.

Around this time plans were being finalized by the Experience's agent, Dick Katz, for the trio to spend most of April on "The Walker Brothers Farewell Tour." Popular in America and Great Britain since the late 1950s, rock and roll package tours typically featured five or six acts who traveled together from town to town, playing two-per-day concerts in cinema theaters. The top two acts—those with an established fan base and/or high-charting records—would typically be allotted a half hour each, while the mid-level acts were given fifteen to twenty minutes. Opening acts were relegated to two or three songs. A few years earlier, the Beatles, Rolling Stones, and Animals had participated in package tours. By 1967 the audiences in provincial towns typically consisted of females in their early teens. From the start, it appears, Jimi had concerns about sharing billings with the Walker Brothers, Cat Stevens, and Engelbert Humperdinck.

Following a rare day off on March 8, Jimi, Mitch, and Noel resumed their heavy schedule. They began by posing for photographer Gered Mankowitz, whose studio was next door to the Scotch of St. James. In an interview with Brian Southall, Mankowitz remembered Jimi's disposition that day: "It was a particularly wonderful moment to have worked with him because I think he was very happy. This was a brief period when everything seemed to be coming together. The spotlight was on him, he wasn't in the backline anymore, and he was expressing himself in every possible way. He was much loved. He was really embraced by the music industry and he and the band were having a great time."[8]

After the Mankowitz shoot the Experience began on a four-day swing through England with an after-midnight performance at the Skyline Ballroom in Hull, Yorkshire. The Experience then traveled to Newcastle for two performances at Mike Jeffery's Club a-Go Go, where the Animals had done their residency. The queue for admission ran around the block. The trio played the early evening show in the Young Set, a smaller room designated for teenagers. This was the first time Sting saw Jimi play live. "The Jimi Hendrix Experience was an overwhelming, deafening wave of sound that obliterated analysis," the future headliner wrote. "I think I remember snatches of 'Hey Joe" and 'Foxey Lady,' but that event remains a blur of noise and breathtaking virtuosity, of Afro'd hair, wild clothes, and towers of Marshall amplifiers. It was also the first time I'd ever seen a black man. I remember Hendrix creating a hole in the plaster ceiling above the stage with the head of his guitar, and then it was over. I lay in my bed that night with my ears ringing and my world-view significantly altered."[9] The Experience played their second set in the club's Jazz Lounge.

The entourage rolled on to Leeds for a Saturday concert at the International Club. While there, Jimi wrote a letter of advice to a fan named Bil, who'd sent him a message: "Regardless of what people think about you, me or our group—just so long as you have your freedom of mind, freedom of speech and thought—Don't let nobody turn you off from your own thoughts and dreams. I am very interested in seeing you—I believe I would really love to talk to you

---

early teens. From the start, it appears, Jimi had concerns about sharing billings with the Walker Brothers, Cat Stevens, and Engelbert Humperdinck.

135

for a very long time. You seem *very* different from other girls who may write to us. . . . I believe your mind is really and truly together. But!!! Don't call yourself stupid anymore in LIFE. . . . This is your life—you must die by yourself, so for heaven's sake, live for yourself and no one else. . . . Love you forever, Jimi Hendrix."[10] Although they may have never met, Jimi remembered "Bil of some English town in England" in the dedication section of 1968's *Electric Lady-land* album.

Performing at the Gyro Club in Ilkley on Sunday night, the Experience were midway through their second song when police shut down the event. "Chaos After Police Break Up Crowded Pop Show" blared a headline in the next *Yorkshire Evening Post*. The article described what happened next: "There was chaos when police stopped a pop show last night. A door was ripped off its hinges, pictures were slashed and torn from their frames, electrical fittings and furniture were broken and the carpets were littered with broken glass at the Troutbeck Hotel, Ilkley. The Jimi Hendrix Experience were told to stop playing in the middle of their second number. Police told the audience of 800 that they would have to leave because the club was overcrowded. Jimi remarked, 'I wish they had let me play before emptying the club.'"[11] A follow-up story in the *Ilkley Gazette* absolved the Experience of any blame:

> A "spokesman for the Troutbeck" said he was surprised how
> 'quiet and orderly' the fans were and said limited damage
> had been caused simply because there were so many of
> them. A police officer confirmed this by telling the *Gazette*
> that no official complaints of vandalism had been received.
> He explained that officers were initially called to the hotel
> by residents because nearby roads were blocked by cars
> belonging to Hendrix fans. It was then discovered that the
> ballroom was seriously overcrowded and the decision taken
> to stop the concert in an attempt to reduce the audience to its
> legal limit of about 250. Chaos ensued and the concert did not
> resume.[12]

The Experience then embarked to Amsterdam for an appearance on the Dutch television show *Fanclub*. The disorganized event required them to sit around for hours awaiting their turn. In Noel's word, Jimi suffered from the "moodies" as the day wore on, which led to an unfortunate incident. "The equipment was the best ever," Hendrix described to Keith Altham a week later. "They said play as loud as you like, and we were really grooving when this little fairy comes running in and yells 'Stop! Stop! Stop!—the ceiling in the studio below is falling down.' And it was too—plaster and all."[13] After a heated exchange with the producer, Jimi left the studio in a huff. He made it to his late-afternoon press conference at the Hotel Schiller, then returned with the Experience for the *Fanclub* broadcast, where they were required to mime their recordings of "Hey Joe" and "Stone Free." Jimi, disgusted by the day's events, unwound that evening in the home of Dutch poet Simon Vinkenoog.

Returning to London the next morning, Jimi spoke to interviewers for German, Swedish, and Dutch publications in advance of the Experience's upcoming five-day tour. That evening the Experience attended a party hosted by Chris Stamp and Kit Lambert at the Speakeasy to celebrate new Track Records singles by the Experience, the Who, and John's Children. Jimi was photographed there alongside the Who and mingled with Simon and Garfunkel, Jean Shrimpton, Eric Clapton, and actors Terence Stamp and Michael Caine. A projector played promotional films of all three acts.

The following day, March 17, the "Purple Haze" / "51st Anniversary" single was officially released. The Experience flew to Hamburg that afternoon for a weekend series of concerts at the Star-Club, where five years earlier the Beatles had played extended engagements. While there, Mitch engaged in a bit of mischief. "We did the inevitable Star-Club in Hamburg," he wrote, "but not the six-shows-a-day routine. We just did a Friday-, Saturday-, and Sunday-night stint. We didn't have to do the whole matinee thing. The Star-Club was winding down a bit by then anyway. There was an Israeli band on who were doing the full six-weeks, five-shows-a-day deal. They were sort of a Beach Boys, harmony cover band. Anyway, it was their last night while we were there and during their final break we retuned their guitars up an octave. Obviously, they just rushed back, grabbed their guitars, bang, onstage. It was as though someone tightened their jockstraps."[14]

Before their two sets on Saturday night, the Experience played before a live audience at Studio 1, NDR Funkhaus, for broadcast on the *Twen Club* show. The trio's strong set consisted of "Foxey Lady," "Hey Joe," "Stone Free," "Fire," and "Purple Haze." Boosted to the front of the mix, Jimi's vocals were especially strong, as was Mitch's frenetic drumming on "Fire." Completing the Star-Club engagement on Sunday night, the group flew to Luxembourg on Monday for interviews with Radio Luxembourg, which had been spinning Experience records in heavy rotation.

Michael Jeffery, meanwhile, was in the United States negotiating an American distribution deal with Reprise Records. Founded by Frank Sinatra, the Warner Brothers subsidiary had mostly released records by Sinatra, his daughter Nancy, and his "Rat Pack" friends Dean Martin and Sammy Davis Jr. Signing the Jimi Hendrix Experience, Jeffery explained, would move them into new territory. Having read positive reports of Jimi's abilities, label president Mo Ostin asked Jack Nitzsche to get Mick Jagger's opinion. When Nitzsche reported back that Jagger deemed Hendrix the "most exciting" rocker in London, Ostin made his decision. The five-year contract he presented Jeffery reportedly provided a cash advance of $40,000, a guaranteed promotion budget of $20,000, and a 10 percent royalty of the retail list price—8 percent for the "artists" and two percent for Mike Jeffery and Yameta. As John McDermott clarified in *Jimi Hendrix: Setting the Record Straight*, "Warner Bros. had not signed Jimi Hendrix to Reprise Records, they signed Yameta Co. to provide 'master recordings, embodying the performance of Jimi Hendrix or the Jimi Hendrix Experience.' Neither Hendrix, Mitchell nor Redding ever signed the contract. They didn't have to, since they were already signed to exclusive recording, management, and publishing contracts with Yameta."[15] Jeffery and Chandler retained ownership of Hendrix's master recordings. McDermott confirmed that Jimi was paid $8,000 of the $40,000 advance, while a significant portion of the rest allowed Jeffery and Chandler to recoup money they'd spent on Jimi, Mitch, and Noel.

Upon the Experience's return to London, Hendrix and Chandler were forced to move from Montagu Square due to neighbors' complaints. Their new lease, for Apartment 9 in the modern building at 43 Upper Berkeley Street, was within walking distance of Montagu Square, enabling them to move their possessions without hiring a van. "Once again," Kathy wrote, "it was taken for granted that Chas and Lotta would have the best room and Jimi and I would get what was left. Managers were often thought of being the more senior in pop partnerships in those days. We stayed in that flat for about a year or so."[16] Swedish journalist Barbro Nordström described the new residence as "a large, elegant three-story flat, with red wall-to-wall carpets, a wooden kitchen, a living room with a fireplace, a stereo and wild oil paintings made by Chas early one New York morning. In the living room there is a TV set covered with books and records. Jimi leads a stressful life and if he relaxes, he doesn't do it in front of the TV."[17]

Keith Altham provided more details about the new living situation after interviewing Jimi there for *New Musical Express*. Chas Chandler, he wrote,

has developed a kind of split personality to cope with the new image. One moment will find him the good-natured ex-pop star wearing his Lord Kitchener uniform with gold braid, and the next immaculately attired in black suit and tie as Mr. Chandler, businessman—complaining resignedly about having to buy a £2,000 mixing tape-machine instead of the Lincoln Continental his heart desires. Both Chas and his protégé share a newly acquired apartment off Edgware Road, where, together with newly acquired publicist Chris Williams, I found myself last Friday surveying a room dominated by a psychedelic painting (bought by Chas while under the 'affluence of inkahol' in New York). It depicted a bleeding eye letting droplets fall on a naked woman. There was a brass scuttle from which projected a number of empty wine bottles— relics of some bygone happening—a book about vampires, the inevitable blind eye of the TV set, and an award for the Animals' best group record, "The House of the Rising Sun," on the mantelpiece, together with a model cannon. The rest of the Chandler war souvenirs collection is yet to be installed, and the floor was covered with LPs and singles from Solomon Burke to the Beatles.

As to Jimi's looks, Altham noted that "out of this world" is a "much applied phrase, but when it's applied to the extraordinary guitarist Jimi Hendrix, it's appropriate. Looking as incredible as anything conceived by science fiction writer Isaac Asimov, whose work he endlessly devours, Jimi is composing some numbers of equally unearthly inspiration." Switching his focus to the upcoming Walker Brothers tour, Altham described Jimi as "a musical perfectionist who does not expect everyone to understand, and believes even those who come only to stand and gawk may eventually catch on. On a tour which boasts contradictions in musical terms like Engelbert and Jimi, he has come to terms with himself. 'Most will come to see the Walkers,' said Jimi. 'Those who come to hear Engelbert sing "Release Me" may not dig me, but that's not tragic. We'll play for ourselves—we've done it before, where the audience stands about with their mouths open and you wait ten minutes before they clap.'" Before leaving, Altham spoke to Mitch Mitchell about his new high-heeled green suede boots. "Y'know what I'd really like to add to the act?" Mitch asked impishly. "I'd like to pour paraffin all over my drums while the guy from Premier is sitting in the audience. Then, at the end of the act, I'd set fire to 'em, and up they go in flames—just to see his face."[18]

That weekend the Experience played the Starlight Room in the Boston Gliderdrome in Lincolnshire, topping a lineup of five bands. Two unusual goings-on set this gig apart. The first was the appearance of an immaculately dressed elder gentleman, Stan Griggs, at the foot of the stage, his hair carefully slicked back, a baton in hand. As the Experience began to play, Griggs seemed to be "conducting" their music. It turned out that this local eccentric had been doing this routine since the 1940s, no matter who was onstage. The second unusual event had to do with the venue's revolving stage, which carried musicians through an archway when activated at the conclusion of their performance. The Experience's amplifiers were stacked too high to clear the arch, which caused them to come crashing down atop the musicians. Future Queen drummer Roger Taylor remembered the Gliderdrome performance as the loudest concert he'd ever attended.

On Sunday the band was off to Stockport, Cheshire, for a concert at the Tabernacle Club. Monday brought them to BBC Studio A in Lancashire for a lunchtime rehearsal and evening videotaping of "Purple Haze"—live vocals, studio backing tracks—for the *Dee Time* show. They were back in a BBC studio a day later, taping "Killing Floor," "Fire," and "Purple Haze," all set to a breakneck pace, for the April Fool's Day broadcast of *Saturday Club*. From there they journeyed forty miles northwest of London for their evening performance at the Assembly Hall in Aylesbury. By this time, Noel wrote, "It began to get crazy. We'd get ambushed and mauled going to gigs. Girls in the audience would scream our names louder than we could play our songs."[19]

With management's approval, ads and notices for upcoming gigs listed "Jimi Hendrix," without the "Experience" attached to his name. This, naturally, created what Noel described as "a resentful division. I began to feel we were being put down by our own management, even though we were playing well as a unit and working like slaves. It was also difficult to not take personally Chas's subtle reminders that my role was to be quietly supportive so as not to distract Jimi onstage. 'Why don't you just lay back and cool it, Noel. Just sway.' This actually made it difficult to relax because if the music took off, I felt restricted. I suppose Jimi was the same, but in reverse. If he felt like standing and playing seriously, the little voice in his head would go, 'Mad. Sexy. Wildman.' We began to vent our annoyance and resentment on each other. It was hard on Jimi, even though he was being groomed as a star. He began to feel the pressure of taking it all on his own and sometimes lost the light-hearted approach which was such a big part of his appeal." Chas's requirement that the band spend considerable time in the studio added to the building tension between the band and management. "We headed to the studio every free moment we had," Noel continued. "There, Chas and Jimi would quarrel over how high to mix the voice or how much volume distortion was acceptable."[20] True to form, the Experience spent the two days before the start of the Walker Brothers tour in studios.

They returned to De Lane Lea on March 29 to work on "Manic Depression." Chas's comment to Jimi that he sounded "manic depressive" during an interview had inspired the title. Before the session, Jimi had already worked out the song's enigmatic lyrics, main riff, and 3/4 time signature. Mitch displayed extraordinary stamina during the session, never letting up on his propulsive groove. "The challenge," observed John McDermott, "was to unify the song's intricate rhythm pattern, as Mitch Mitchell's revolving drum part buttressed Hendrix's driving guitar. Mitchell's performance on the song represented his finest studio effort to date, with his fondness for such jazz legends as Elvin Jones clearly apparent."[21] During the solo that begins at 1:17, Jimi modulated while Noel stayed in the original key, giving the section its very distinctive sound. The band also recorded an instrumental cover of Michel Polnareff's pop hit

"La Poupee qui fait non" (a.k.a. "No No No No"), with Jimi simply strumming clean-toned guitar chords on the basic track and over-dubbing scratch solos.

The Experience spent the next morning at the BBC's Lime Grove Studios, rehearsing for *Top of the Pops*. As the trio assembled on-stage that evening to perform "Purple Haze" with live vocals and the prerecorded backing track, a studio engineer accidentally played the backing track for another song, causing Jimi to quip, "I like the voice, man, but I don't know the words."[22] After the error was corrected, "Purple Haze" was successfully performed, with Jimi changing the line "'scuse me while I kiss the sky" to "'scuse me while I kiss this guy" as he pointed to one of his off-camera bandmates.

On the final day of March, the Jimi Hendrix Experience began its celebrated Walker Brothers package tour. The headlining Walker Brothers, were, in Noel's words, "England's biggest sex symbols." A trio of white, mop-top, unrelated Americans with choreographed stage moves, they had legions of teenage fans in Great Britain and had recently reached the British Top Ten with their singles "My Ship Is Coming In" and "The Sun Ain't Gonna Shine Anymore." The contract called for the Experience to be paid £100 per show.

For opening night, two shows were slated at the Finsbury Park Astoria, the first at 6:40 and the second at 10:10. Jimi showed up wearing a ruffled orange shirt and orange pants, clutching a sun-burst Stratocaster. Backstage, the Experience, Chas, and Keith Altham brainstormed about how to get the press's attention. "We were sitting in the dressing room," remembered Keith Altham, "and Chas said, 'How can I steal the show? How can I steal the publicity?' Because all the press were there that night. It was the first night. I said, 'You can't smash stuff up,' because the Who were doing that and the Move were smashing television sets onstage. And Jimi said, 'Maybe I could smash up an elephant.' I said, 'It's a shame you can't set fire to the guitar.' I knew it was a sold-state guitar. It wasn't going to burn. And there was a silence in the dress-ing room. And Chas looked at Gerry Stickells, the roadie, and said, 'Gerry, go out and get some lighter fuel.'"[23]

The Quotations played first. Screaming fans drowned out the second act, the surfy, Beach Boys–influenced Californians. The Jimi Hendrix Experience then took the stage, opening with "Foxey

Lady." They segued into "Can You See Me" and "Hey Joe," playing voluminously and with tremendous drive. During the "Purple Haze" finale, Jimi fell to his knees, laid his guitar on the stage, doused the instrument with lighter fluid, and struck a match. "Suddenly," Altham recalled, "*whoof*! He came up with the guitar, holding it above his head and whirled it around to begin with, which didn't impress the security guy too much, because it was a fire risk."[24] The flames leapt dangerously near the curtain. As the audience screamed, an enraged theater manager ran onstage with an extinguisher and doused the conflagration. Backstage, he vowed that the Experience would never again perform at the venue.

Tasked with following the Experience's headline-grabbing finale, Engelbert Humperdinck acquitted himself with aplomb, appearing, in Altham's words, "the picture of sartorial elegance in a tuxedo, singing a selection of songs more obviously suited to a cabaret audience." Altham likewise praised Cat Stevens—the "surprise packet on the show"—and credited the Walker Brothers as "supreme pop stars, giving us a sensible selection of 'songs to scream to.'"[25] But the night clearly belonged to Jimi Hendrix. As the Walker Brothers tour progressed, his stage antics would become front-page news.

9:April
1967

Hendrixmania

It's not an act, but a state of being at the time I'm doing it.
My music, my instrument, my sound, my body are all one
action with my mind. —Jimi Hendrix[1]

The much ballyhooed, month-long Walker Brothers package shows were publicized as the Jimi Hendrix Experience's "first British tour." Looking ahead to playing in the United States that summer, Jimi, Mitch, and Noel would refer to this as their "British farewell tour." Despite the obvious stylistic difference among the acts, the tour would prove that the Experience could thrive in larger venues. "This was our real turning point," Noel wrote. "We had to crack England now or never, as Jimi's work permit was running out. We paid for it. It was hell."[2]

On April Fool's Day the tour played the 1,800-seat Gaumont Cinema in Ipswich, Suffolk. Backstage Jimi and Gary Leeds, the Walker Brothers drummer, amused their fellow musicians with a "mini play" created by reciting lines from American comic books. Jimi's performance at the following evening's shows, at the Gaumont Cinema in Worchester, made it into the *Evening News*: "Most people had not really come to see Jimi Hendrix, but he left the audience breathless with the sheer force and volume that his three-man group pounded out. His left hand heavily bandaged from a burn he received doing his act on Friday, he opened with his hit 'Hey Joe' and then went into the similar 'Purple Haze.' A lengthy version of 'Like a Rolling Stone' followed before his act ended with the Troggs' 'Wild Thing.' Jimi battered his guitar against his amplifiers, and the drums fell down to close an act that is better suited to the clubs than the barrenness of a package show."[3]

After the Gaumont shows, Jimi was told to tone down his "vulgar" stage moves. As Chris Welch reported in *Melody Maker*, "Guitar star Jimi Hendrix, who jumped into the *MM* Pop 30 this week at #15 with 'Purple Haze,' was warned to 'clean up' his act on his tour with the Walker Brothers this week. . . . His manager Chas Chandler told the *MM* on Monday: 'After Jimi's performances on Saturday and Sunday night, I was told he has got to change his act. The tour organizers said he was too suggestive. I think this is a joke myself and there's not a chance of his changing his set.'"[4]

Musicians from the other bands noted that during their travels together, Jimi came across as quiet, polite, and given to mumbling except when talking about music. While much marijuana was consumed on the communal tour bus, Mitch noted that "there wasn't much interaction between the bands. Cat Stevens wouldn't travel on the coach after the first two days, because he thought we, the Experience, were loonies. God knows why. He eventually came back because he thought he was missing out, but we could have done without the companionship."[5]

During their first two-day break from the tour, the Experience returned to London for an April 3 marathon session at Olympic, with Eddie Kramer and George Chkiantz handling the engineering and Roger Mayer on hand to help with effects. The Experience began by cutting the basic track of "Highway Chile." The lyrics, which Jimi had written on the back of an envelope, could easily be viewed as autobiographical. They told of a drifter, guitar slung across his back, enduring scorned looks of passersby. Jimi sang, "He left home when he was seventeen. . . . Now you probably call him a tramp, but it goes a little deeper than that. . . . He's a highway chile." Jimi began his performance with a memorable descending passage produced by playing a fixed pitch on the high-E string while simultaneously hitting a lower pitch on the B string and rapidly bending up the note on the B string to match the note on the high E.

A half century after its recording, "Highway Chile," like other Hendrix tracks recorded during this era, retains its freshness in a way that's similar to how Charlie Christian's pioneering efforts on the electric guitar in the late 1930s also remain fresh and vital.

"Part of this," points out Brian Delaney, "is due to the recording's simplicity. A track like 'Highway Chile' is not over-produced. It's honest and bare-bones. Even with the parts that are overdubbed, it's people playing together in a room. It's not 'machine music' like so much of today's pop music, which is extremely dependent on machinery."[6] After the song's release as the B-side of "The Wind Cries Mary," Chandler occasionally had to correct British journalists and record company execs who mispronounced the song's title as "Highway Chili."

Another song they worked on, "May This Be Love," was originally titled "Waterfall." His volume dialed down on the guitar to suit the song's ballad feel, Jimi opened the track with an unusual slide guitar passage played in his normal tuning. Ever the innovator, Mitch began his part with a rolling beat on his rack toms and enhanced his cymbal sound by placing a Ching Ring around the bell of his hi-hat to add a tambourine-like "ching." Eddie Kramer recorded the drums in mono, compressing the sound of the toms. Through skillful panning during the main body of the song, Kramer remembered, "Jimi was able to create an effect which sounded backward. This multiple imaging was enhanced during the mixing process by simultaneously panning the rhythm and lead guitar."[7] The innovative guitar passage that begins at 1:55 displays a textbook example of Jimi's legato playing. With delays and repeats enhancing his tone and his fretting hand doing most of the work, Jimi created a sound and feel akin to notes bowed on a traditional Chinese erhu.

The Experience next recorded a romping two-minute instrumental with wall-to-wall guitar, listed simply as "Title #3." Expertly played, the track remained a studio outtake. Then they began and finished recording "Title #4," which would be renamed "Are You Experienced?" Mitch set the pace for the basic track, drumming a processional rhythm while Jimi strummed rhythm. After several attempts, they completed the basic track. After room was made for guitar overdubs, Hendrix stunned the engineers with his ability to rapidly create a backward rhythm track. "When he recorded that," Roger Mayer remembered, "that pretty much amazed everyone. He said, 'Right. We're gonna record the track backwards.' And I said, 'Oh?' Jimi said, 'Yeah, just turn the tape over.' He majorly had that one worked out.... When it came to mixing and recording techniques, especially when it came to layering his own solos and punching in—absolute master at it."[8]

To prepare for this moment, Jimi had spent hours alone with his reel-to-reel tape recorder, carefully studying the special effects that could be created by recording sound onto magnetic tape and then physically reversing the tape so that the sound is heard in reverse. The technique dated back to the 1950s, when musique concrète innovators had experimented with reverse tape effects. More recently, the Beatles and their producer, George Martin, had used backwards taping to create psychedelic effects on 1966's "I'm Only Sleeping" and "Tomorrow Never Knows," from *Revolver*, as well as on their recently released "Strawberry Fields Forever," which was high in the U.K. singles charts on the day the Experience recorded "Are You Experienced?" As a final touch, Jimi added another overdub: "That's Jimi playing the octaves on the wonderful, old, out-of-tune upright piano at Olympic," Kramer explained. "That piano sound, reminiscent of a bell tolling, was an essential part of the basic track."[9] In an interview two months after the session, Jimi described the track as "an imaginary freeform song, where you just use your mind, where you just imagine with your mind."[10]

Returning to Olympic the following day, Jimi did overdubs for "Are You Experienced?" and "Highway Chile," and the trio recut sections of "Third Stone from the Sun." Roger Mayer remembered that for the latter, the goal was to attain a "different sense of movement. That's what we were into. We were into making sounds that transported people.... Jimi was very, very much into science fiction, so our kind of mental model was that the guitar should appear like the guy was on the floating disc in front of you and then suddenly zooming away or moving away and coming toward you. We were trying to paint a moving picture of sound."[11] Jimi crafted the beautiful, full-sounding passage starting at 0:42 with lovely Wes Montgomery–style octaves, most likely playing with his index finger on the lower string and ring finger on the upper octave. In a technique similar to what the Beatles used to create sitar-like sounds on "Norwegian Wood," Jimi achieved the song's Oriental-sounding effect, 1:20–1:27, by playing his G string against the open B and high-E strings. Picking up the tempo at the 2:30 mark, the song began its sonic journey simulating space travel. Portions of Jimi's massive sound in the remaining section were caused by harmonics reshaped by the fuzz box.

For "Love or Confusion," Jimi ran his signal through one of Roger Mayer's custom fuzz boxes. In the opening phrase, he can be heard clicking his pickup selector switch. He shaped the track's feedback by gently rocking his Stratocaster's tremolo arm. Overall, the recording proved especially challenging. "It involved the linking of the panning effect to Jimi's rhythm guitar," Eddie Kramer revealed. "The panning was then timed to the bending of the guitar note."[12] At Jimi's request, his voice was placed in the background of the mix. The Experience concluded the recording portion of the session with a spirited pass at "Here He Comes" (a.k.a. "Lover Man"), complete with basic track and guitar solo, and then moved on to mixing.

The next day the Experience were back onstage, playing two shows at the Odeon Theatre in Leeds. They garnered negative mentions in both local newspapers. The *Yorkshire Evening Post* noted that "the Jimi Hendrix Experience had gimmicks galore (including split trousers) but did not impress," while the reviewer for the *Yorkshire Post* quipped, "The Jimi Hendrix Experience was one I would prefer not to repeat." From Leeds, the entourage crossed into Scotland for a performance at the Glasgow Odeon. Jimi consented to a backstage interview with Donald Bruce for the *Daily Record*. In his opener, Bruce dwelled on Jimi's looks and accent:

> Talking to Jimi Hendrix about him and his Experience is, in itself, quite an experience. For one thing, Jimi is scarcely likely to qualify for a best-looking bloke competition. For another thing he's from the West Coast (no, not Largs, lady, Seattle), and that's like listening to someone who mixes Scotch with a bit of German, a lot of American and a wee tottie French. He doesn't talk. He drawls "ah, ya know, well, ya see, it's this way, ah don't know, yeah, I guess so, well, it's hard to say." And so on.
>
> What can't be contradicted is that the Jimi Hendrix Experience (Jimi and two others) in Glasgow last night on the Walker Brothers show have made the biggest impact in the shortest possible time on the pop scene since maybe the Walker Brothers themselves. Jimi has only been in Britain since last September. But in that time he has been described

by Mr. Brian Epstein (no mug) as "the greatest talent since the Rolling Stones," and, more practically, he has had one record ("Hey Joe") in the top five, with his present one, "Purple Haze," racing crazily to the top. So why should Jimi worry if he looks like a wild-eyed revolutionary from the Caribbean and that he talks with the shut-eye still in his big mouth?

Moving on to "Purple Haze," Bruce wrote, "Certainly, its brooding, threatening beat will find its natural home in dark cafés and thumping juke boxes, or in dimly lit clubs where jungle rhythms find an irresistible affinity. And for those who worry about these things, purple haze is what happens to a young man when the drug of love overcomes him. Or as Jimi puts it: 'He likes this girl so much that he doesn't know what he's in, ya know. A sort of daze, ah suppose. That's what the song is all about.'"[13]

Around this time Engelbert Humperdinck's guitarist left the tour. Noel, who'd played sessions with the singer, was hired as his replacement. "But I couldn't join his band onstage," Noel wrote, "so there I sat, all alone in the darkened wings, just a long lead trailing out to the amp onstage. I wonder if anyone in the audience ever guessed where the lead guitar was coming from? For this honor, I received two quid a night. It felt like I was being bounced back and forth in a time warp. Their set couldn't have been more of a contrast to ours."[14] At least he was able to play guitar. That month Humperdinck's "Release Me," indeed a far cry from anything ever played by the Experience, would become the number-three single in the U.K. charts, while "Purple Haze" would climb to number eleven.[15]

The Walker Brothers tour next appeared at the ABC Cinema in Carlisle. Jimi skipped a pre-show press event at the theater, claiming that the ankle he'd injured in the Army Airborne was swollen. After the Experience's performances at the ABC, Lorraine Walsh, reporter for the *Carlisle and Cumberland Journal*, verified that Jimi was, as Chas predicted, keeping his stage moves intact. The audience didn't seem to mind one bit:

> Soon the chants of "Jimi, Jimi" drowned the compere's voice and the curtain lifted to screams of ecstasy from the Cumbrian fans. One young girl ran down the main aisle and managed to vault over the orchestra pit into Jimi's own arms. A Carlisle Corporation bouncer named Ginger Watson gently escorted

her off stage and the Lonsdale ABC echoed to the haunting sound of "Hey Joe," Jimi's opening number. In the following numbers only "Purple Haze" was distinguishable in the screams and cries of delight from the 2,000 fans. Jimi did a good impression of making love to his guitar onstage and then proceeded to pluck the strings with his teeth. At this stage, uppity St. John's Ambulance Brigade were busy reviving young girls who had either fainted or become hysterical. As the curtain came down twenty-one-year-old Nick Jones tried to keep his composure and prepare the audience to greet Engelbert Humperdinck, only to be drowned out by the continuing screams for Jimi.[16]

On Saturday, April 8, the tour arrived in Derbyshire, where Kathy Etchingham had spent her childhood. The next issue of *Disc and Music Echo* reported that during the first show at the ABC theater Jimi injured his foot while stomping on his fuzz box. After receiving four stitches, he played his second set. In an article headlined "Release Me from This Noisy Mob," a reviewer for the *Derbyshire Times* wrote, "Jimi Hendrix and the Experience is one Experience I would rather forget. This volatile performer, who manages to look remarkably like a Negress on occasions, was completely unintelligible."[17] Jimi later told Kathy that he was dismayed to see a Derbyshire pub named "The Black Boy."

The last stop on this leg of the tour took the musicians to the Empire Theatre in Liverpool, hometown of the Beatles. "By now," Noel wrote,

the crowds were making it tough to escape the theatre. In Liverpool we had to wait nervously backstage while someone found a cabbie willing to force his way through the mob to collect us. Dying for a pint, we headed for the sanctuary of the nearby pub, pursued all the way. The screaming fans surrounded the premises, hammering on the fancy glass doors while inside the clientele began to realize who we were and move in on us aggressively. The manager pushed us, frantically protesting and genuinely terrified, out into the mob. We could only hold on to each other and run, praying for our lives. By the time we found a taxi who would take us, we had been stripped of everything loose, our pockets emptied so we couldn't even pay the cabbie. It was getting too frightening to be fun.[18]

With a one-day break from touring, the Experience retreated to London. On the afternoon of April 10, they did a radio broadcast at the BBC Playhouse Theatre, performing "Purple Haze" and "Foxey Lady" for the *Monday Monday* show. They spent the evening at Olympic, finishing vocal overdubs for "Third Stone from the Sun." The session's highpoint came when Hendrix voiced the words of a spacecraft pilot communicating with a Star Fleet commander, vocalized by Chas Chandler. Anthologized in *The Jimi Hendrix Experience* box set, the unedited version of this zany exchange features false starts, laughter, and Jimi using his voice to create spaceship sounds. Near the end, Jimi, speaking in his natural voice, says, "And you'll never hear surf music again," after which he slyly adds, "Sounds like a lie to me." Amid much laughter, they were able to complete the exchange in five takes. In the final mix Eddie Kramer highlighted Mitch's cymbals and the spaceship noises Jimi created with his voice. These recordings were enhanced by playing them back through headphones being moved around a microphone. For the final master, Kramer panned all four tracks.

Before returning to the tour, Jimi sat for an interview with Chris Welch, who published the results as "Who Says Jimi Hendrix Can't Sing? (He Does!)" in *Melody Maker*. Welch's opener described the setting: "I met Jimi at his bright and airy apartment at the top of a modern block near Marble Arch. He was listening excitedly to acetates of tracks from his forthcoming LP. He smoked endless cigarettes and crouched on a low stool, dressed in flowery, violently colored shirt and trousers in a sparsely furnished room. The screen of a TV set was covered in soot and hadn't been used in weeks. The hi-fi equipment was bright and new and in constant use. 'I can't read a note of music,' grinned Jimi, fingering the burnt-out wreck of his guitar which burst into flames on the opening night of his tour with the Walker Brothers."

Asked his impressions of the Walker Brothers tour, Jimi revealed that some of their sets had been intentionally sabotaged. "The bosses of the tour are giving us hell," he said.

> The organizers don't give us a chance to tune up before we go onstage. They say we are obscene and vulgar, but we play our

act as we have always played it everywhere else, and there have never been complaints before. We refuse to change our act, and the result is my amplifier sometimes gets cut off at the funniest times. I wonder why? But I don't let them hang me up. I play to the people and I don't think our actions are obscene. We just get excited by the music and carried away.... It's really funny playing for this tour. I don't know if it's like it on all tours, but just before I go on I turn around and find a guitar string is broken, or I find my guitar is all out of tune after I just tuned it. I kinda don't know what to say about that. They just don't give a damn about us. But they are not going to get rid of us unless we are officially thrown off the tour.

Asked when he's happiest playing music, Jimi revealed, "I like playing clubs, but I don't want to play them for the rest of my life. We are satisfied with what we are doing at the moment, because it's playing the way we feel. I just want to make the music acceptable. It's freeform. I wish I could sing really nice, but I know I can't sing. I just feel the words out. I just try all right to hit a pretty note, but it's hard. I'm more of an entertainer and performer than a singer."[19] Noel noted in his diary that other "petty things" had transpired during their sets, such as the house lights coming on mid-set.

The Walker Brothers tour trudged on, with six one-nighters in a row. They performed at the Granada, a movie theater in Bedford, on Tuesday the 11th. An account of the event in the *Woburn Reporter* gives insight into the type of audience drawn to the shows: "The Granada was packed out. Some of the mums were there, some of the young 'uns too, but for the most they were teenage girls with tonsils at the ready for a thorough and continuous screaming. And scream they did, right from the Quotations (Walker Brothers backing group) through the Californians, who had trouble with their amplifying equipment in the first show, and going quite mad when three hirsute and weirdly dressed characters came on. I am referring to the Jimi Hendrix Experience. They began with 'Hey Joe.' Jimi showed that he really can play the guitar with his teeth, and they ended with their new record 'Purple Haze.'"[20]

After appearing at the Gaumont in Wolverhampton, the Californians' hometown, the tour came to Bolton, where pandemonium awaited the headliners. "Screaming Teenage Girls Raid Stage," claimed a headline in Saturday's *Bolton Evening News*. The article reported that "hysterical girls fought savagely with attendants protecting the stage when the Walker Brothers starred in a pop concert in Bolton last night. Several managed to battle past the ring of security men and staff at the Odeon Theatre and get onstage, where lead singer Scott Walker had to be rescued when they clung desperately to him as he sang. In sensational scenes during their first-house performance, dozens of screaming and weeping girls were carried or dragged to the door and thrown out. Many more had to be treated by St. John's Ambulance Brigade workers after they had fainted. When the Walkers came onstage the screams reached fever pitch and hundreds of fans surged forward to the stage and threw embroidered cushion, scarves, handkerchiefs and an autograph book on the stage."[21] Four female fans went a step further, writing "please" 70,000 times on their petition to meet the Walker Brothers. Their ploy, reported the newspaper, didn't work. The Experience, by contrast, received a less enthusiastic reception. Noel wrote that Jimi was "in bad form. He messed through only three or four numbers. If you play Bolton and don't deliver, you don't hang around after the show. We were advised to take the next train to Blackpool."[22]

In a scene reminiscent of the Beatles' film *A Hard Day's Night*, passionate fans awaited the Experience's arrival at Blackpool's Odeon. "In Blackpool," Jimi told *Disc and Music Echo*, "the police slipped Mitch and Noel in through side doors and took me around the block five times before helping me in."[23] After the concert, reported the *Scottish Daily Press*, "a Blackpool hotel turned him [Hendrix] away, denying that any booking had been made. But in the same city, a thousand screaming fans took a sizeable chunk out of his luxuriant hairstyle when they pursued him after the show."[24] At a local club, Jimi, Mitch, and Noel ran into Jayne Mansfield. "This cheered us up," Noel wrote, "until she left with Engelbert. We took a couple of pills and headed to the hotel. But we couldn't remember which one the tour was booked into, and no other hotel would take us. At five in the morning we gave up and crashed in a B&B. Next day we discovered everyone else just around the corner. Was it the banana skins we'd smoked?"[25]

The Experience spent the ensuing two-day break in London. On Monday, April 17, they appeared on the BBC's *Late Night Line-Up*, a program devoted to discussions of the arts. After an enigmatic introduction—"We end our lineup not with a psychedelic experience, but it is, at least, the sort of music associated with such happenings"—the band played "Manic Depression," with Jimi going full-psychedelic during the solo. Back at the flat, Jimi gave an interview to Hugh Nolan for *Disc and Music Echo*. The journalist was taken aback by Jimi's quiet demeanor, noting that "the ferocious Mr. Hendrix, so wild onstage with his attacking guitar work and singing, is very much quieter and more easygoing at home than you'd have a right to expect."

In the most intriguing part of the conversation, Nolan asked Jimi what it meant to "be black in a white man's country" and whether England was so different from America. "Soon as I arrived over here I shared a flat with Chas and immediately complaints started to pour in," Jimi told him.

> We used to get complaints about loud, late parties when we were out of town on a gig! Come back the next morning and hear all the complaints. Chas got real mad about it. I didn't let it bug me very much. Sometimes some kids will shout something at you while you're waiting for a taxi on the corner. Otherwise it's okay—everything's fine. I guess I don't worry much about that whole scene anymore. Man, I'd even play South Africa as long as there wasn't any physical violence. And if they tried to get at me in other ways, I just wouldn't take much of it. Anyway, they can only call you names. I just don't give a damn—as long as I have beautiful England to come back to! There's so much I want to do. I want to get color into music— I'd like to play a note and have it come out in color. In fact, I've got an electrician [Roger Mayer] working on a machine to do that right now.[26]

Nolan headlined his article "For Jimi Hendrix, Colour Means His Shade of Music."

Jimi, Mitch, and Noel rejoined the Walker Brothers for the most grueling leg of the tour—ten one-nighters, two shows per day, over an eleven-day period. They began on April 19 at the Odeon in Birmingham. Two months after the event, *Fabulous 208* published

June Southworth's a morning-in-the-life account of Jimi's departure from Birmingham.

> The day began for Jimi Hendrix in a rough-and-tumble exit from a modest hotel to the theatre in Birmingham where the coach was about to leave for Lincoln. Jimi sank into a place halfway down the coach. He tried to appear ordinary, as disbelieving faces surveyed him from a nearby building site. Since he was dressed in a fur-trimmed jacket from the Crimean War and resembled a lion and his tamer all rolled into one, this was a somewhat difficult exercise. Behind him, Mitch and Noel, newly emerged from a visit to the joke shop, occasionally let off smoke bombs and disappeared behind a purple haze. A normal day for the Jimi Hendrix Experience. On the journey, Jimi thoughtfully chewed matchsticks and fiddled with a red rubber nose from which a can-can dancer's shapely leg spasmodically kicked. But mostly he looked through the window and let ideas run wild in his mind. These are the precious moments when an artiste has time to think. There was the inevitable stop at the motorway café, the weary search for a hotel when the coach arrived, the inspection of the new dressing room. Then the long, long hours at the theatre until it was time to creep onstage.[27]

At this stage of the tour, staying backstage had become a necessity that, in turn, led to boredom and conflict. "Since we could no longer go out and cool off between shows," Noel wrote, "we had no option but to sit around in dressing rooms with nothing to do but get smashed. . . . Just what was one supposed to do, sitting on a wooden bench, breathing stale air in an eight-by-ten-foot windowless box with wall-to-wall hangers-on? You *might* have one horrid toilet and/or basin with a *cold* tap (dripping). You'd certainly have peeling paint speckled with graffiti and who knows what else, cracked concrete floors with antique cigarette butts, and a ceiling cascading with condensation."[28] On the flip side, Noel observed, the rhapsodic reaction to some of their shows seemed to buoy Jimi's self-perception: "Between our popularity and the Walker Brothers, the tour sold out. It began to dawn on Jimi that he *could* be personally successful, that his dreams *could* come true, and that boosted his confidence tremendously. Our egos grew and sometimes clashed. But our conflicts, mostly over women, were short-lived. After I went home with a girl he fancied, Jimi freaked and hit *her*. Next day, all was forgotten—except by the poor girl, I guess."[29]

Before performing at the Lincolnshire ABC on the 20th, Jimi sat for a photo session in the hotel gardens and gave a brief interview to a representative of the *Lincolnshire Echo*. "A great guy on and off stage," the write-up began, "Jimi Hendrix was in a very bouncy mood. His opening remark was: 'I'm gonna put a curse on everyone so that all their babies are born naked.' A remark which he obviously thought had some deep significance. He was wearing turquoise trousers and an old-fashioned military jacket trimmed with silver braid and fur. 'When I was six my grandmother gave me a Spanish jacket covered with baubles, and ever since I have loved "freaky" clothes,' he explained. He described his clothes as 'freak and funky' and his wild music as 'a touch of blues, jazz and rock.' He also agreed that some of his music is psychedelic—no real beat and a sound in which the imagination of the audience plays a large part."[30]

A more conservative reviewer for the *Lincolnshire Chronicle* deemed the Experience's stage show inappropriate for the ABC audience: "I wasn't impressed with the performance of singer Jimi Hendrix.... His movements were far too suggestive for an audience mostly in the fourteen-to-eighteen age group. I didn't like his music either, although the sound he made, taken from his movements, had some girls in hysterics."[31] June Southworth added that after the Experience concluded their "primitive, strange, earthy" set, "a score of girls rushed the stage. The Experience fled to their smoky dressing-room and collapsed. And soon it was over. Another day, another show, another coach to catch."[32] That coach took them to Newcastle-Upon-Tyne for shows at the City Hall, followed by weekend concerts at the Manchester Odeon and the Hanley Gaumont.

On the evening of Tuesday, April 25, Jimi, Chas, and Eddie Kramer met at Olympic to make stereo and mono mixes of eight tracks designated for their debut album, *Are You Experienced*. Chandler needed these mixes for his meeting the next morning with Horst Schmaltze, A&R director for Polydor. This would be the first time anyone at the label would hear the result of all their work. Chas nervously awaited Schmaltze's reaction as he spun the lacquer disc cut just hours earlier. The exec listened to both sides in silence and then sat quietly for a few moments. Finally he said, "This is brilliant. This is the greatest thing I've ever heard!"[33] Schmaltze agreed to have Polydor provide additional funding for Track Records. In the months to come, he would dedicate himself to ensuring that the Jimi Hendrix Experience would be well promoted and marketed.

Relieved, the Experience commuted to Colston Hall in Bristol. Once again, a local reviewer declared the Experience a mismatch for the rest of the bill: "The Jimi Hendrix Experience were completely out of place on this particular package show. Hendrix played well with the guitar behind his back, better with his teeth, and was a maestro playing straight. The group's music was weird, exciting and inventive, but it was too way out for the Walker fans. Cat Stevens was also on the bill. His tiny voice couldn't be heard, but he jerked and jiggled away merrily—and everyone seemed perfectly happy."[34]

The final five dates with the Walker Brothers carried the musicians from South Wales to London. They played the Capitol Cinema in Cardiff, the ABC in Aldershot, and the Adelphi in Slough, where 3,000 excited fans voiced enthusiastic support. Once again, local reviewers did not come away converts. "Mr. Hendrix and his two cohorts brought a deafened audience the 'new music' otherwise known as psychedelic," reported the *Slough Observer* reviewer, "and if there was one note of music in it, I couldn't find it."[35] A writer for the *Slough Express* acknowledged the Experience's popularity, but was more drawn to their outfits than their musical output: "Personally I did not like the amplifier worshipping, playing the guitar under the thigh and behind the back, throwing oneself on the floor. I liked their clothes, flowered shirts, shocking pink scarves, striped blazers and bouffant hair."[36] On Saturday concert-goers milled around the stage entrance at Bournemouth's Winter Gardens as Jimi pulled up in Roger Mayer's white MG midget sports car. They made it safely inside, but after the concert Mayer discovered that fans had ripped off his windshield wipers and scrawled "I love Jimi" in lipstick all over his car. He and Jimi drove to a gas station, where they cleaned lipstick off the windshield and then drove on to the Speakeasy.

On Sunday, April 30, the final Walker Brothers concerts were held at the Granada in Tooting. Mitch celebrated the event by pranking Cat Stevens, whom he deemed "a real snot." As Stevens performed "I'm Gonna Get Me a Gun" during the final matinee, Mitch wrote, "I placed this mechanical robot, which I had bought, onstage. Its chest opened up and all these little machine guns started blazing away. He tried to kick it offstage, but this thing refused to die. He didn't take the joke too well. Anyway, I retrieved it and put it onstage for the Walkers, when Scott was singing 'My Ship Is Coming In.' He took it a lot better."[37]

That weekend's edition of *Disc and Music Echo* ran Penny Valentine's advance review of "The Wind Cries Mary," which Chas Chandler had rushed to release: "As popular as Jimi Hendrix is, it seems odd to suddenly issue another record so quickly after his last—as good even though it is. But ours not to reason why, and certainly the record is superb. Let us look at the record in the light of Hendrix becoming something of legend in his field. He wrote the song himself and sings it clearly and strongly, sounding oddly like Dylan. It is very slow and more gentle than past efforts. His guitar sounds prettier, the ugly lurching has gone. It is a very careful record and one rather to listen to with satisfaction than to jump about raving to. It is a record of understatement. As such it may not have immediate commercial success, but as such it is a good indication of how this man is going to expand musically. Out next Friday."[38] Chas defended his strategy: "This disc is different to everything else around, and such a complete contrast to the kind of record that people might expect from Jimi that we believe that it will not compete in any way with 'Purple Haze.' We see no reason why both discs should not feature simultaneously in the charts without harming each other's sales."[39]

10:May 1967

"The Group They Love to Hate"

I could really get myself together over there. There wasn't so many hang-ups as there was in America—you know, mental hang-ups.
—Jimi Hendrix[1]

On May 1, Reprise Records issued the Jimi Hendrix Experience's debut single in the United States—"Hey Joe," backed with "51st Anniversary." On the same day, the new issue of *Beat Instrumental* announced that the Experience's debut album, consisting of Jimi Hendrix compositions, would be released by month's end.

During his three-day respite from performing concerts, Jimi spent his afternoons giving interviews and his evening making the rounds of clubs, looking for opportunities to jam. One of the reporters he spoke with, Ann Nightingale, opened her article in the *Sunday Mirror*, a large-circulation tabloid weekly, with unabashedly racist imagery:

> You might think that Jimi Hendrix would appear menacingly swinging from tree-tops, brandishing a spear, and yelling blood-curdling cries of "Aargh!" For Jimi, who makes Mick Jagger look as respectable as Edward Heath and as genial as David Frost, could pass for a Hottentot on the rampage, looks as if his foot-long hair has been petrified by a thousand shock waves, and is given to playing the guitar with his teeth.
>
> When the Jimi Hendrix Experience made its first appearance in Britain a few months ago, he was immediately

dubbed "the Wild Man of Borneo," and the group was referred to as "an unfortunate experience." And yet his first record, "Hey Joe," went straight into the Top 10; his second disc, "Purple Haze," is currently number six, and this week his new disc, "The Wind Cries Mary" (Track), should provide him with two records simultaneously in the Top 10. Moan. Later this month, the wild sounds from his first LP, *Are You Experienced*, should have parents moaning for the quieter days of the Rolling Stones. The Jimi Hendrix Experience has, it seems, filled a very necessary gap in becoming the Group They Love to Hate. Mums and dads started to like the top pop names, but they are almost guaranteed not to dig Mr. Hendrix.

Yet Jimi Hendrix is no snarling jungle primitive. Though the gold-braided military jacket over the black satin shirt could be taken as incongruous, Jimi off-stage behaves with a quiet polite charm that's almost olde worlde. He stands up when you enter a room, lights all your cigarettes, and says: "Do go on" if he thinks he might be interrupting you. That "ugly" image, however, doesn't worry him in the slightest. And he says: "Some of the fans think I'm cuddly, and as long as people buy my records I'll be happy." He could be laughing all the way to the bank.[2]

Barbro Nordström, who met with Jimi at his Upper Berkeley flat on May 2 to do an interview for Sweden's *Bildjournalen*, also initially focused on Jimi's appearance—his "green fur-trimmed jacket from Tsarist Russia with golden braids and cords, a yellow shirt, a green-red-yellow scarf, brown trousers, swaying hair, a bony milk-chocolate-skinned face, a snub nose, broad lips, black eyes. At first you think only about his hair, standing in clouds around his head." Her first question: Does Hendrix comb his hair? "No," Jimi responded, "I brush it. A comb would probably get caught." As to his outfit du jour, Jimi explained, "These are my stage clothes. I like colors." Nordström described Jimi's stage presence as "a small volcanic eruption. His guitar playing is intense, diabolical, ferocious. Sometimes he plays guitar lying down on the floor. The amplified sound is enormously overdriven.... The sounds he makes with his guitar are fantastic, sometimes devilish, nerve-shattering tones, and at other times harmonically pleasing melodies. Jimi is rated as one of the best guitar players in England.... He gets completely immersed in everything he performs. He IS what he sings. Because singing is what he does, despite him claiming the opposite. Jimi plays explosively, looks explosive, but in private he is so quiet and considerate that you believe he is a split personality."[3]

Hendrix also collaborated with Keith Altham on "Question Time with Jimi Hendrix" for *New Musical Express*. Altham's intro credited Jimi with "beginning to emerge from behind that skillfully placed publicity screen of early days when success was too fragile to toss in the air and see what came down. His retorts are more spontaneous and there is a 'Jaggered edge' to some, which indicates a not unreasonable impatience with those misguided people who think he is more of a freak attraction than a gifted musician." Then Altham, too, gave Jimi's appearance an unflattering assessment: "He is in fact an extraordinarily talented guitarist with a strikingly ugly appearance trying quite sincerely to produce songs and sounds which are reflective of today—his music—'NOW' music."

When Altham asked him to assess the Walker Brothers tour, Jimi responded,

> The tour was good experience, but our billing position was all wrong. I was setting the stage on fire for everyone else, following those pretty people like the Quotations and the Californians. I think we deserved to close the first half—that Engel-flumplefuff hadn't any stage presence. He never got anything going. Stopped it all stone dead. But it was a gas, in spite of the hassles. I really learned a lot about British audiences, because every night we had two more to meet and after every show Chas and I would discuss how everything went down and ways to improve. It was a good tour, though— one guy jumped about twenty feet from a box in the theatre at Luton onto the stage just to shake hands with us. We'd step outside the stage door where the teeny boppers were and think, "Oh, they won't bother about us" and get torn apart!

Questioned about the changes he'd made to his set, Jimi explained, "I realized you can't fight the whole world at once, but we only brought in numbers that have some life of their own. We did Dylan's 'Like a Rolling Stone' and 'Wild Thing'—you can get inside the composer's mind on those things—but we're not going in for any of this 'Midnight Hour' kick—no 'gotta, gotta, gotta,' because we don't have ta, have ta, have ta!" Altham aimed his follow-up question at Jimi's looks, inquiring if he was concerned that his "unusual appearance" causes people to look at him rather than listen to him. Jimi responded, "Before I go onstage my road manager says to me, 'Jimi, you scruffy looking git, you're not going on looking like that tonight, are you?' And I say: 'As soon as I've put out this cigarette—I'm fully dressed.' This is how I like it. I feel comfortable like this." What about would-be Jimi Hendrix imitators lifting some of his patented moves? "Everywhere I go they tell me about one group who got up like us and the fella tried to play the guitar with his teeth and his teeth fell out all over the stage. That's what you get for not brushing your teeth, I tell 'em. You can't be too careful."

Jimi turned serious when discussing the Experience's upcoming debut album. "First off," he said, "I don't want people to get the idea it's a collection of freak-out material. I've written songs for teeny boppers like 'Can You See Me' and blues things. 'Manic Depression' is so ugly you can feel it and 'May This Be Love' is a kind of 'get your mind together' track. It's a collection of free feeling and imagination. Imagination is very important. There's one lyric line—'let's hold hands and watch the sunrise at the bottom of the sea'—that's just pure imagination!"

In another serious exchange, Hendrix addressed the "deliberate hostility" some members of the press held for him. "There are still a few who have been obviously sent to get me," Jimi observed. "They come back to the dressing room with a kind of 'let's strip him naked and hang him from a tall tree' attitude. They don't bother me too much—there'll always be someone who wants to nail you down." He also offered the view that even though the United States "is still very conservative, Noel and Mitch will go great in the U.S.— they'll love them so much they won't have to wash their own socks." In their final exchange, Altham asked Jimi how he'd changed during his stay in Great Britain. Hendrix quipped, "I've got older and I say more of the things that I want to say."[4]

While Jimi was doing this interview, Mitch was on an office phone, frantically calling authorities. A few weeks earlier he and Noel had pooled their income to rent a split-level flat together near Bayswater. The kitchen was on the top floor and the bedrooms and bathroom below. Not long after moving in, one of them had left the kitchen faucet running and gone out. The overflow had flooded their bedrooms and damaged the ceiling of the flat below theirs. Then, as Jimi spoke with Altham, a friend staying at their flat turned on the bath tap. Altham's tape recorder captured Mitch telling the fire brigade, "The top came off the tap and there's a jet of boiling water about six feet high hitting the ceiling and the water's so deep that we can't open the door because of the pressure and the caretaker doesn't know where the stopcock is."[5] The flow was eventually stopped. Surveying the damage, Mitch and Noel thought it best to immediately evacuate the premises. Mitch moved into Graham Nash's nearby mews house. "I enjoyed sharing his house," Mitch wrote. "Nice house, very pleasant. It was also a place where Hendrix could seek some refuge away from his flat in Upper Berkeley Street with Chas. No offence to Chas, but it was good for Hendrix to get away for an hour or so. Graham and Jimi would often play together at the house, and there was some thought given to them writing together, but I have the feeling it was officially discouraged."[6]

In his country of birth, Jimi got his first important mention in *Jet*. Launched in 1951 as "The Weekly Negro News Magazine," the digest-sized publication was an important voice of the African American community. Issues were commonplace in black beauty parlors, barber shops, waiting rooms, and other gathering places. For an up-and-coming artist, getting a write-up in *Jet* was a *big deal*. Charles L. Sanders wrote in the May 4 issue, "Folks up around Seattle will want to know that their little guitar-playing Jimi Hendrix is now twenty-one [sic], is living in London, and is at the top of the pop-record polls with his tune 'Hey Joe,' and is cleaning up with European tours."[7] In a follow-up article in the June 8 issue, Sanders framed his profile as a rags-to-riches story: "All of the 'great musicians' who used to laugh at little Jimi Hendrix when he was trying to learn guitar, and all of the Greenwich Villagers who used to poke fun at him because of his 'Wild Man of Borneo' get-up (long, long hair and way-out clothes), may not find this a laughing matter. After arriving in London just six months ago with nothing but the clothes on his back, Jimi's at the top of the British record charts (with two hits, 'Purple Haze' and 'Hey Joe'), has just been handed a $150,000 check [sic] to sign with Frank Sinatra's Warner-Reprise record label, and is in line for about a million bucks from a five-year contract. Now he's laughing at himself—all the way to London's Barclays Bank."[8]

On May 4 the Experience met for a session at Olympic Studios. Their first effort, "She's So Fine," spotlighted Noel as lead vocalist. Redding had composed the song on an acoustic guitar during one of the band's day-long waits for an appearance on *Top of the Pops*. The lyrics, he explained, were "about hippies. I had seen some bloke walking about with an alarm clock around his neck, attached by a bit of string. He must have thought that it looked very avant-garde to walk around with an alarm clock hanging off of him."[9] Jimi played bass during their initial run-through. By all accounts the session was lively and entertaining. Chas recalled that every time Noel began to sing, Hendrix burst out laughing. Noel joined Mitch, Chas, and Eddie Kramer in the merriment. By evening's end the band had attempted more than two-dozen takes. Jimi would later lobby hard to have the track included on *Axis: Bold as Love*.

After that, Chandler remembered, the musicians got stoned and wanted to play "a New Orleans walking band type of thing."[10] Jimi began playing a slow blues called "Taking Care of No Business." The song was roughly based on Curtis Knight's somnambulistic "No Business," which Hendrix had played on during a 1965 session. But aside from recycling the line "All I've got to my name is a beat-up guitar with three broken strings," Jimi's version took off in a new direction. Unlike Knight's no-frills performance, the Olympic version captures the feel of a tavern near closing time, complete with clinking glasses and a growled "Get out of here, you bum!" On the initial run-through, an unaccompanied Jimi played the song on electric guitar. He littered his new lyrics with alley imagery and down-and-out lines such as "I'm so broke I can't even pay attention. I'm so poor I couldn't even give you the time." Midway through the take, Jimi said "play the horn" and vocalized a trumpet-like solo. Fun stuff, this track was withheld from release until take two was included in the *The Jimi Hendrix Experience* box set. The Experience finished the session by recording both sections of what would become "If 6 Was 9."

Back at Olympic the following day, the Experience replaced the previous evening's drum and guitar parts for "If 6 Was 9" and layered in Jimi's lead vocal. When Graham Nash and Gary Leeds dropped by, Jimi enlisted them for the foot clomps heard in the song's "I'm the one that's got to die when it's time for me to die" section. As Graham remembered, "Jimi said, 'I need somebody to walk. Come here and listen.' And he put a piece of plywood on the floor and put a microphone down there. He said, 'Okay, I'm going to play the track. Put the 'phones on. When I nod my head, you start walking.' I thought, 'Oh, Jimi!' He put on 'If 6 Was 9' and we started to walk. I mean, I'm known for my high harmony and tinkling western sky music, and here I am walking."[11] Jimi credited Chandler's "big feet" for the fade-out's retreating footsteps. Hendrix played the recorder part at the song's end, using an old wooden instrument he'd purchased from a street vendor. He would later describe "If 6 Was 9" as "a great feeling of blues." The Experience wrapped up the session with "Mr. Bad Luck," a song Jimi had played in Greenwich Village and would subsequently rename "Look Over Yonder" after the song's opening verse: "Look over yonder, here comes the blues." The expression dated back to the Roaring Twenties, when the great Ma Rainey recorded "Yonder Come the Blues" for Paramount Records. In a later version, Jimi would significantly change the lyrics.

On the same day as this session, Track Records officially released the third Jimi Hendrix Experience single, "The Wind Cries Mary" backed with "Highway Chile." Mitch and Noel were unhappy with the jacket's artwork—a solo shot of Jimi—but press reaction was swift and positive. In the next day's issue of *New Musical Express*, Derek Johnson's "Top Singles Reviewed" column proclaimed "The Wind Cries Mary" a "beautiful record, the best showcase yet for Jimi's inherent feeling for the blues. Shades of Ray Charles, Percy Sledge, and the singer's own distinctive quality ... thought provoking ... a subtle flowing accompaniment, with some delicious guitar work, make this a quality blues ballad. Not normally commercial, but with his current popularity, Jimi should notch another hit."[12] In that week's *NME* Top Thirty chart, "Purple Haze" came in at number five, beneath platters by Sandie Shaw, Frank and Nancy Sinatra, the Monkees, and the Mamas and the Papas.

On Saturday, May 6, the Experience journeyed to Nelson, Lancashire, to perform at the Imperial Ballroom. The gig netted them £378—nearly twice as much as they'd earn for their upcoming Saville show. Tony Skinner, on hand to review the concert for *The Leader*, headlined his write-up "An Imperial Victory for Hendrix" and proclaimed Jimi "the most famous exponent of the new psychedelic sound."[13] The Experience's two sold-out Sunday shows at the Saville drew a star-studded audience: Eric Burdon, Spencer Davis, Georgie Fame, Ringo Starr, Brian Jones, Anita Pallenberg, and members of the Moody Blues, the Move, and the Tremeloes were spotted among the crowd. The performance began, in the words of Nick Jones, with a "thick, haunting darkness, suddenly pierced by a single spotlight which fell onto the red-trousered Hendrix, cooly dancing in the pool of white light and then erupting into 'Foxey Lady.'" Swirling shards of multi-colored lights enveloped the band as they played "Can You See Me," "Hey Joe," "Like a Rolling Stone," "Purple Haze," and "The Wind Cries Mary." Jimi had trouble keeping his Stratocaster in tune under the hot stage lights, at one point saying to the audience, "Man, is Eric Clapton in the house? Ask him to come up here and tune this thing." The audience, though, didn't seem to mind a bit. As Hendrix played his "Wild Thing" finale, Jones noted, "Poppers all over London were gesticulating wildly and coming out with the same old sounds: 'Incredible,' 'Fantastic,' 'Ridiculous,' or just plain 'Erotic.'"[14]

Concertgoer Penny Valentine's review for *Disc and Music Echo* contains one of the first accounts of Jimi's fans emulating his look:

> If you could see electricity, it would look like Jimi Hendrix. At London's Saville Theatre on Sunday, Hendrix proved, if proof were needed, that there is no other explosive force on the British pop scene today to match him. He is a resplendent figure. Tall, snakelike in a scarlet velvet suit and frilled shirt. His hair like a black halo round his head, his guitar like another limb to be used with his body. On Sunday he topped the bill for the first time to an audience wholly receptive, filled with Hendrix devotees, many of them looking more like Jimi than Jimi. And they were given what they asked for. The man has changed—he is now confident and entirely at ease. The first time I ever saw him play in London he stood on the stage and played, a quietly dynamic force. He said little to the audience and seemed incredibly humble. On Sunday he showed he is now feeling much more at home with his success. Cracking jokes, talking to the audience, treating the majority like long-lost brothers, knowing they knew what it was all

about, treating the few who he considered didn't with perhaps a slightly mistaken rudeness. To his friends he smiled gently and said: "When I played in my backyard at home, kids used to gather round and heard me and said it was cool. I wanna thank you now for making this my home."[15]

Returning to Olympic on Tuesday, May 9, Jimi discovered a harpsicord tucked away in Studio A. Tape rolling, he began playing a frantic chord progression. After a few measures he halted and said to the engineer, "Wait, let me do it just one more time, okay?" Chording with his left hand and soloing with the right, he played the opening figure and the changes for what would evolve into the first verse of "Burning of the Midnight Lamp." Mitch and Noel began playing along. In less than a minute's time, Hendrix had instrumentally sketched out the song that would become the Experience's fourth single.

The next afternoon Jimi put on his finery—velvet jacket, a lacey Sam Pig in Love shirt, pink scarf—for the Variety Club of Great Britain's Tribute to the Recording Industry. Hendrix, Cat Stevens, and Lulu were feted during the luncheon. After that, it was back to the BBC's Lime Grove Studios for a tea-time rehearsal and an evening performance of "The Wind Cries Mary" for *Top of the Pops*. Reviewing this broadcast for *Disc and Music Echo*, Samantha Just joined the list of journalists obsessed with Jimi's looks:

> Heavens! Did you see Jimi Hendrix on *Top of the Pops*? Didn't he look weird? It just isn't true! Now long hair's O.K.—but his looked quite horrible standing on end like that. It was back-combed to a ridiculous extent. And his drummer, Mitch. Those terrible patterned toweling trousers, that striped shirt and the jacket with a map of America on it. Ugh! If that's supposed to look nice, I give up. I don't get it. If you're that talented, surely you don't need gimmicks? Imagine walking down the street and bumping into those three. The other guitarist [Noel Redding] looked like a girl from St. Trinians! We were making so much fun of him earlier on that he took his funny little glasses off for the show. But wait! Musically there's nothing at all wrong with them. Although I haven't seen them onstage properly. It's not very hard to learn to play an instrument. But it is hard to be a good entertainer.[16]

On Thursday the Experience did a quick jaunt to Paris for an 11:00 P.M. performance seen live by fans at the Theatre d'Issy and broadcast on the *Music Hall de Paris* television program. Jimi had considerable trouble keeping his sunburst Stratocaster in tune, but made the best of it. Near the end, the crowd roared their approval as he stood still behind his microphone, creating waves of feedback while holding his headstock toward the floor and gently rocking his whammy. In just a few seconds he brought his guitar, which had fallen wildly out of tune, back to pitch with a few quick turns of the keys, using the technique of matching notes played on the fifth fret—or in the case of the G string, the fourth fret—to the adjacent higher open string. Hendrix threw many of his patented moves into the "Wild Thing" finale, dropping to his knees between verses and swiping the strings with his jacket sleeve. He quoted Frank Sinatra's "Strangers in the Night" during the solo, then dropped to his knees again and covered his eyes with his picking arm while fretting rapid hammer-ons. He rolled on the floor and played on his back, body jerking spasmodically in time with the music. Ladies screamed as he rose to his knees, finished the solo with his teeth, and returned to microphone to sing the final verse. As the last notes filled the hall, Mitch kicked over his tom-toms and the band exited the scene. The Experience's management charged 5,000 francs for this performance. Noel, though, had to borrow a pound from Kit Lambert to avoid being penniless in Paris.

Upon their return to London on Friday, May 12, the Experience had cause to celebrate: Track Records officially released *Are You Experienced*. Unlike the Reprise version scheduled for summer release in America, Polydor's European pressings contained none of the songs that had been issued as the A or B sides of the three Experience singles. Chris Stamp explained his label's strategy: "We realized that what Jimi was doing was not necessarily going to be accepted as the packaged sort of hits of the day, that it was something that was very different."[17] *Rave* magazine published Jimi's own review: "This is a very personal album, just like all our singles. Luckily, they also seem to be commercial. Nine of the tracks were put together in the studio. I guess you could call it an adlib LP because we did so much on the spot. 'Foxey Lady' we messed about with a couple of times and we were bouncing stuff around in our minds, because if you get a good idea you've got to put it down right away. We just went in and said, 'Let's see what happens.' Maybe some of the stuff is far ahead. I don't know, but I believe the public can still understand it. We don't compromise. I'm very happy with it, but already I can hardly wait for something else!"[18]

According to Noel, 25,000 advanced orders had been placed, but the timing of the release caused a "furor" in the press, since records were typically not released in such close succession. "We never gave it a moment's thought," Chas remembered. "The way Jimi and I looked at the situation was that the singles had paved the way for the album. It wouldn't have said much for him if half of *Are You Experienced* was just those three singles."[19] Chandler's strategy paid off: by month's end, the Jimi Hendrix Experience's debut album had entered the U.K. charts, where it would spend thirty-three weeks and top off at number two, just behind the Beatles' *Sgt. Pepper's Lonely Hearts Club Band*.

Arguably the most revolutionary debut album in rock history, *Are You Experienced* upped the ante for guitarists on both sides of the Atlantic. Jimi modestly described it as "loud and brash and frustrated and rebellious and so forth," but it was far more than that. While others before had experimented with massive volume, feedback, distortion, whammy, octave doubling, and other sonic effects, Hendrix was the first to harness them into music so extraordinarily imaginative and enduring. And then there were the album's innovative songs, imagistic lyrics, multi-layered arrangements, ping-ponging production, and unprecedented approaches to tones, chord voicings, and solos.

In short, *Are You Experienced* surprised *everyone*, even the man whose playing had inspired comparisons to God: "I will never forget returning to London after recording [Cream's] *Disraeli Gears*," Eric Clapton wrote, "with all of us excited by the fact that we had made what we considered to be a groundbreaking album, a magical combination of blues, rock, and jazz. Unfortunately for us, Jimi had just released *Are You Experienced*, and that was all anyone wanted to listen to. He kicked everybody into touch, really, and was the flavor not just of the month but of the year. Everywhere you went it was wall-to-wall Jimi, and I felt really down. I thought we had made our definitive album, only to come home and find that nobody was interested. It was the beginning of a disenchantment with England, where it seemed there wasn't really room for more than one person to be popular at a time."[20]

The Experience had precious little time off to enjoy the album's release. Chandler had scheduled them gigs throughout the weekend, followed by a tour beginning on Monday. On Friday night the Experience played an event at London's Manor House billed as "A Ball in Bluesville '67." Saturday brought them to an 800-seat venue at the Imperial College in Kensington, where 1984, a band featuring future Queen guitarist Brian May, opened the show. On Sunday the Experience journeyed to Manchester for an evening show at the Belle Vue New Elizabethan Theater. An estimated 3,000 people attended the event deejayed by popular TV host Jimmy Savile, who'd later be knighted and, after his death, reviled for his long history of sexually abusing children.

Flying out from Manchester on Monday, May 15, the group embarked on a fifteen-day European tour that would take them to clubs, theaters, and outdoor venues in West Germany, Sweden, Denmark, and Finland. They arrived in Berlin mid-afternoon. A few hours later they played their first of two forty-five-minute shows at the Neue Welt, with Mitch using the drum kit belonging to one of the opening acts, the Beat Cats. While in Berlin, Noel wrote, "We all insisted on seeing the Wall, with gray East Berlin trapped behind it. What a contrast, we thought, to our lives. But touring was a trap too. The only distractions were reading music papers like *Beat Instrumental* (in which I was proud to see myself elected Player of the Month) and the competition for girls we'd use to while away the time otherwise spent fidgeting and getting terminally smashed in interminable terminals while worrying about our two or even three flights per day."[21] While the Experience were in Berlin, Michael Jeffery closed a deal with Barclay Records to release *Are You Experienced* in France. According to Redding, "The 15 May 1967 contract was for ten percent royalties, with no points to the group, and an advance of $35,000."[22]

A flight the next day took the Experience to Munich for two shows at the Big Apple. Backstage between sets, Jimi, Mitch, and Noel were interviewed together for the German-language *Bravo* magazine. The article came out in the June issue, headlined "Ich Bin Nicht Mehr der Dumme!" (I'm Not Dumb Anymore!). Early in the interview, Gerhard Schizel asked the trio how they had become so popular so quickly. "We're raving onstage," Jimi responded. "We put on a show. We are doing exactly what we feel. I believe this is crucial." Jimi took umbrage at the mention of critics: "I couldn't care less what the critics are saying!" But, noted the interviewer, "The critics are now saying you're a genius. Why don't you want to hear about it?" Jimi's answer was remarkably candid: "These are the same people who laughed at first. They sat behind their type-writers and rubbed their bellies. Now they pretend to 'understand.' I don't think they understand my songs. They live in another world. My world—that's hunger, that's the slums, that's burning racial hatred, and the kind of luck that you can hold in one hand, nothing more! It may be that the critics recognize a new sound, but they still don't understand my songs."

Asked what prompted him to join the group, Mitch told Schizel, "Jimi guarantees me freedom. With him my opinion about music is taken into account. He never tells me what to play, like other band-leaders." The interviewer then asked Jimi who he thought was the best guitarist in the world—Chuck Berry? "No," Jimi said. "A 'best guitarist' doesn't exist. There are too many styles of music. It's a matter of taste. Everyone should have his own style. I love Muddy Waters's style, because he plays blues." Their final exchange consisted of a long question, followed by a short, insightful answer: "Jimi, there was a time when you were ejected from every hotel in the world. People were bothered by the color of your skin. Your only possession was your guitar. You had few friends—people such as Solomon Burke, Little Richard, and Jackie Wilson. Today we speak of you as a genius. You could start a company with the people that once went out of their way to avoid you. You have shown them, Jimi. How do you explain this turnaround in people's opinions?" Jimi laughed and answered, "I'm not just that dumb Jimi now, but Mr. Hendrix."[23]

On the 17th, the Experience journeyed to Frankfurt, where Jimi did a radio interview with Hans Carl Schmidt at the Hotel Inter-continental. Asked if he was "putting on an act" or actually feeling the emotions while he performs, Jimi told him, "We mostly feel it. If you see our show, for instance, once every night for about a week, it would probably be very different, because of the different mood you might be in. And the way the music might hit you, it's very emotional like." Asked if it's necessary to have long hair or dress in a "most peculiar way," Jimi said, "Well, I don't consider it actually necessary, because there's a lot of groups around—pop stars like Engelbert Humperdinck, Cat Stevens and all of the beautiful people—they don't necessarily have to have long hair. I believe this goes for the other cats too. I dig it. I think it's very nice, especially in your own style. As far as clothes go, I'll get anything I see that I like, regardless of what it looks like and regardless of what it costs. If it cost only two shillings, I'll get it if I like it, if it would suit me."

Referencing the soul music being produced by Motown Records, Schmidt asked Jimi his opinion of the "Detroit sound." Hendrix responded, "To me it's very commercial, very artificial. Why is that? Synthetic soul sound. It isn't a sound like real Negro artists. It's put together so beautifully that I don't feel anything from it—except the Isley Brothers and maybe the Four Tops. All they do is put a very, very hard beat to it, about a thousand people on tambourines, bells, a thousand horns, a thousand violins, and then a singer who overdubs his voice about a million times or sings in an echo chamber. To me it comes out so artificial. It's very commercial for the younger people." By contrast, Jimi added, he preferred music that's "very primitive . . . a more freeform type of thing. It's what I hope we work up toward: a free style. Quite naturally it has to have a nice beat, where the person can almost feel the music." Schmidt followed up with a question about classical music. "It's very beautiful," Jimi told him, "but I don't listen to it all the time, but I would like to at the most relaxing time. See, different music is supposed to be used different ways. You're supposed to appreciate music. During the bright day, and noise, I don't figure that's the best time to listen to classical. Anytime when it's quiet and your mind is very relaxed and you feel like daydreaming maybe or something, you can turn on the stereo."

In a welcome departure from the typical questions directed to Jimi during this phase of his career, Schmidt said to him, "Kids always think it's easy to grab a guitar and go onstage and make music. Could you tell them that it's not that easy at all?" Jimi responded with a reference to his first band in Seattle, the Rocking Kings. "It was so very hard for me. Like, I joined this band. I knew about three songs, and when it was time for us to play onstage I had to play behind the curtains. I couldn't get up in front. Plus, you get so very discouraged. You hear different bands playing around you, and the guitar player seems like he's always so much better than you are. At first I was so scared I wouldn't dare go onstage. Most people give up at this point because they get very discouraged. But just keep on, keep on—you can make it.... The only way I tried to make it is [by being] very persistent." In another surprising revelation, Jimi responded to Schmidt's question about what's his greatest wish by confiding, "I wish you could send me home so I could see my parents for about three days. [It's been] about five-and-a-half years. They don't know what's happening at all except I called them two times. Once when I came here to England about seven months ago, and once a few days ago when we were in London, and I told them we have three records out. And my father said, 'Yeah?' He didn't know nothing about it."[24]

Al Hendrix, who had just recently married Ayako "June" Fujita, remembered that during this call "Jimi was all excited for me. He said, 'I hear you've moved to another place and you've gotten married again. Sounds like you're getting ready to settle down, dad.' Jimi also told me he felt so good about finally being able to do things for me financially. He said, 'I'm going to buy you a home. I'm gonna buy you this and that. Whatever you need, just let me know.' I said, 'Right now we're in the process of buying a house, so that's taken care of. You just take care of yourself. I'll holler if I need anything. You just keep your nose clean and stay out of trouble and take care of yourself.'"[25]

On May 18, the Experience were filmed at the Stadthalle in Offenbach am Main, performing three songs for *Beat Beat Beat*. The surviving black-and-white footage begins with a serious-looking Jimi playing "Stone Free" on a solid-color Stratocaster with a rosewood fingerboard. In the broadcast version, the song was cut short at the end of his solo. Jimi perked up during "Purple Haze," breaking into a grin as he sang "'scuse me while I kiss this guy" and pointed toward Noel. He played the middle solo with his teeth. Apparently, his ending solo was deemed too wild for home consumption, since the cameras stayed focused on Mitch, Noel, and teenaged dancers during the sonic assault. The Experience concluded with a heartfelt arrangement of "Hey Joe," the camera swooping in for a close-up of Jimi soloing with his teeth. Jimi played the ending solo with the guitar held behind his head. Following the performance, the Experience joined in an after-hours jam session with Dave Dee and Beaky at the K-52 Club, Jimi playing bass while Noel played lead guitar.

That night, Noel told Hugh Nolan during a phoner for *Disc and Music Echo*, the Experience were thrown out of their hotel. "Not for any particular reason," Noel claimed, "just because they didn't like the look of us. I think! And everyone stares at us all the time—in hotels, in the street. But the kids are great. They love us. The whole scene is so funny—but we're going down a bomb and that's all that matters." Noel also reported that they already had five numbers down for the second Experience album, including "She's So Fine" and a Mitch Mitchell composition called "Mind Octopus." Asked about the next leg of the tour—to the lands of the "staid Swedes and disapproving Danes," as Nolan put it—Redding responded, "It should be a bit of a laugh!"[26]

The final leg of this tour would bring the Experience to Sweden, Denmark, and Finland. In advance of these dates, Jimi had given a brief interview to Keith Keller of *Expressen* magazine, which was decidedly unkind in its introductory description: "Jimi Hendrix looks like a cross between a floor mop and an Australian bush Negro." Jimi told Keller, "I look the way I do to fulfill my dreams." His dream, Jimi demurred, was that "I was sent by Fidel Castro to infiltrate the Confederate lines in 1864. I'm a believer and a rebel." Keller noted that Jimi's style was "adapted soul—not black, more white, as the audience in Europe prefers: Black inspiration, white stars onstage." Asked whether he considered himself white or black, Hendrix quipped, "I'm Cuban, man. I'm from Mars."[27] Finland's *Helsingin Sanomat* likewise sought to diminish Jimi's stature: "Why is this American 'Powder Man' coming to Finland is a question only few can answer.... He hasn't the strength to become a myth like Dylan or Donovan. Even so, Mitchell's drums give the music enough charm to make it fairly bearable. It seems that Hendrix wants to say something with his songs, though the time of the message is considered to have passed."[28]

On Friday, May 19, Jimi and his entourage flew to Copenhagen and then on to Göteborg, Sweden. Backstage at the concert hall at Liseberg Nojespark, they discovered they were co-billed with Cat Stevens. Hendrix and Stevens got into a disagreement over who'd perform first. "Both considered themselves to be the top attraction of the evening," reported journalist Gösta Hanson. "Well, it solved itself with Cat Stevens starting off while Jimi Hendrix kept everybody waiting. A broken amplifier had to be mended.... When Jimi Hendrix finally had fixed his equipment, we all experienced a quite pleasant form of pop music—not so fierce as the rumors had told us. Instead, the trio turned out to be a relaxed and amusing combination, which occasionally hovered out in howling sounds from Mr. Hendrix's guitar. Nowadays there must be a show in the pop music too. Therefore he performed his famous tricks: played the strings with his teeth or his elbow and stroked the guitar all over his body, but an obviously true feeling for soul music allowed the audience to forgive quite a lot of his circus tricks."[29] Brief, grainy film footage from the event shows Jimi playing "Hey Joe" on a red Stratocaster.

On Saturday the Experience were booked to play at the Mariebergsskogen, a city park in Karlstad. They were mystified at finding buckets of fish in the shared dressing room, and then learned that their opening act was a team of trained seals. The receptive crowd of 3,500 gave the Experience a standing ovation during their "Wild Thing" encore. On Sunday morning, May 21, the band flew to Copenhagen a day ahead of their sold-out concert at the Falkoner Centret. The Danish publication *Berlingske Tidende* predicted that Hendrix would get "sharp competition" from the warm-up bands: the Danish-American group Harlem Kiddies featuring soul singer King George; "our best Danish soul group," the Beefeaters; and the "immortal and invincible" Defenders.[30] The Experience opened with "Foxey Lady," followed by "Hey Joe," "Rock Me Baby," "Purple Haze," and "The Wind Cries Mary." Before going into the "Wild Thing" finale, Jimi told the audience, "It's been a beautiful pleasure playing for you."

The following day, no fewer than a half dozen Danish publications covered the concert. *Aktuelt* proclaimed "Hendrix is a Master" and called the concert "the most provocative performance ever seen on a Danish stage. Jimi Hendrix drew in a capacity crowd with his electrified sex last night at the Falkoner. There was such a violent reaction that his rape attempts on the amplifier and the guitar seemed to have worked organically on each individual present. Hendrix plays with his teeth; he simply puts the guitar strings to his mouth and bites them. He uses his elbows to rub the strings. In every case it is a master who is playing. Jimi Hendrix must be seen and experienced. It is true that his music is in a special class, but it is just as much his overall performance, behavior, and appearance, which makes him a phenomenon."[31] In *Ekstra Bladet*, Nils Gudme covered all three musicians: "It is fascinating to watch the group in action onstage. Apart from his instrumental skills, Hendrix himself is a wonder of ingenuity.... The bass player Noel Redding and the drummer Mitch Mitchell also play and look like they are both wild and mad. The drummer almost looks like Harpo Marx dressed up like a frantic rococo clown. He is, by the way, one of the most wild and hard-playing drummers I have ever heard.... The group seems decorative, fresh, strong and stunning."[32]

Arriving in Helsinki, Finland, on May 22, Jimi gave a press conference at the Hotel Vaakuna and the band mimed "Hey Joe" and "The Wind Cries Mary" at a television studio. They wrapped up their busy day with a concert at the Kulttuuritalo. Ilpo Saunio, writing for the Finnish monthly jazz magazine *Rythmi*, likened Jimi's guitar technique to that of violist Johannes Fritsch, who'd recently performed with Karlheinz Stockhausen's ensemble: "Here comes Jimi Hendrix playing pop music with a clear resemblance to the music played at Stockhausen's concert. Hendrix uses electric guitar just like Stockhausen's Johannes Fritsch uses viola: knocking it, scratching it, tearing it with his teeth, and finally raping it."[33]

Finland's *Hufvudstadsbladet* likened the Kulttuuritalo performance to

> wave after wave crashing over the exalted, shaken, trampled, and enthralled audience. Jimi Hendrix is a fantastic guitarist. To compare him with Segovia fails because the Spanish maestro dates back to the previous century's upper-class salons, while this Seattle youth is more a voice from the reality of today's worldwide information network that effectively spreads both terror and delights. The instrument Hendrix worked on is no ordinary solid-body guitar that bluntly amplifies undistorted mellifluous tones. What he played with was a veritable sound laboratory. He stunned the audience with powerful glissandi and eruptive chunks of sound, produced in the most variable tonal combinations. He would get the whole instrument to sustain so that he need do nothing

other than play on the neck of the guitar as one plays the keys of an organ.

Hendrix is clearly the group's dominant personality.... In fact, Hendrix's performance was one of the most erotic musical acts I have ever seen. His lustful, audience-aware handling of his instrument with caresses of the guitar neck, sudden pointing to the crowd, etc., is filled with emotion both in reference to the instrument and the audience. A love-hate relationship. At the same time this greatly solidifies Hendrix's presence. He never becomes a mystical performer, rather he is very much in the here and now. Visually, Hendrix could seem ridiculous if one were to experience him without sound. But the strong music, from which the audience cannot escape unless they stuff their ears or go outside, makes him convincing and merciless. Hendrix's music combines the sound of fear, the machine gun's rattle, bomb bursts, and orgiastic pleasure.[34]

Audience expectations were high for Experience's May 23 concerts at Klubb Bongo in Malmö, Sweden. This time, though, the shows fell flat. "Mediocre Hendrix gala," described the *Sydsvenska Dagbladet*. "Jimi Hendrix's visit to Malmö had been preceded by joyful reports from earlier performances in Sweden, but for the large, expectant audience at Klubb Bongo, the left-handed, curly-haired Negro became a disappointment.... Despite Jimi's superb treatment of the guitar, the overall impact of the concert is that Jimi Hendrix and his Experience are three overrated gentlemen."[35] Journalist Karre Erichs affixed the blame on the club rather than the Experience: "The electrical system in the building was too weak for Jimi Hendrix to play at 'full steam.' Because of that the audience—at least during the first show—missed a lot of the show, as the vocal equipment broke down all the time and caused trouble. It was as hot as a sauna in the relatively small hall, where about 500 people were packed like sardines in a can. A bigger hall would have been better. I'm sure Jimi Hendrix would have wanted that, as he hardly had room for all his equipment on the small stage."[36]

The Experience fared better on the 24th, when they played a subdued "The Wind Cries Mary" and a toothy, rip-roaring, out-of-tune "Purple Haze" for the *Popside* television program. That evening they performed two concerts in Stockholm. In advance of the shows, the influential newspaper *Aftonbladet* ran a brief article focusing on Jimi's popularity and sexuality. "Jimi Hendrix, wild man with guitar, plays in Stockholm tonight," wrote Sven-Oskar Ruhmén. "His guest appearance is much longed for. Jimi is considered to be the best on the music scene today. The Beatles and Rolling Stones think that Jimi is 'the greatest.'"[37]

An estimated 13,000 people attended the Experience's two concerts at Gröna Lund, Sweden's oldest amusement park, the vast majority showing up for the second show. When introduced for the first set, the band received little applause. They then spent two minutes tuning up, testing levels, and trying to control extraneous noise. The buzzes and microphonic squeals would continue as they played. "The PA system was very bad," Jimi said of the first show, "and the audience didn't really help too much." Before going into "Hey Joe," Jimi told the audience, "Now we'd like to do the song that got us here in the first place. We'd like to dedicate it to everybody, all thirteen of you."[38] By contrast, the second show, performed on the larger Stora Scenen stage, was, in Jimi's words, "very, very good. The kids are great. They sit still and listen to my music, and I believe they understand it."[39] Jimi led his band through "Foxey Lady," "Rock Me Baby," "Hey Joe," "Can You See Me," "Purple Haze," and "Wild Thing." After the event, Noel happily jotted in his diary, "We broke the Beach Boys' attendance record!"

The Swedish daily newspaper *Dagens Nyheter* declared the performance "a true knock-out experience." Lars Weck described, "With only three men (with bushy perms), Hendrix produces more sound than most pop groups and leaves the Who far behind when it comes to musical control. A more excellent, sexy show by a small format pop band is unimaginable. . . . The introduction to 'Wild Thing' (which completely destroyed the original) was a masterpiece of electronic music, a furious sound painting of jet-plane-like effects, shots, and other harder-to-describe sounds. . . . Jimi Hendrix is one of the trendsetters in today's pop music and one of its most valid representatives."[40] The *Expressen* deemed Noel and Mitch "the perfect rhythm section," while the Swedish daily *Svenska Dagbladet* declared that Jimi was "probably the most advanced guitarist in the world just now, not just in pop music, but in the whole area—jazz, serious folk or whatever you like. He extends the possibilities of the guitar to the maximum, especially show-wise. He plays it behind his back, between his legs, pulls the strings over the microphone stand, and plays it with his teeth. And it's not only to get everyone's attention—which he naturally gets. The fact is that this unconventional technique also creates new and fantastic sounds—and this is, of course, the most striking.... The trio's exit was as fantastic as their performance. Without having finished 'Wild Thing,' Hendrix said 'Thank you' into the microphone, threw his guitar nonchalantly onto the floor, and walked unaffectedly out while the loudspeakers kept going. The near-record audience applauded enthusiastically."[41]

After the concerts, Jimi, Mitch, and Noel sat in on a jazz jam at En Till, a private club in Stockholm. A reporter for *Dagens Nyheter* noted that "they surprised everyone by playing a rather conventional form of jazz music. When Hendrix joined in and completed the trio, the character of the music changed, but it was naturally very different compared to the group's stage act. Hendrix and Redding effortlessly swapped instruments (despite Hendrix being left-handed and therefore having to play the wrong way round). Those not surprised by Hendrix being an excellent bass player were probably more surprised by Redding, the bassist, being a brilliant lead guitarist, almost as good as Hendrix."[42] Returning to their hotel afterward, Jimi, Mitch, and Noel were refused admittance. Unable to find another hotel that would accommodate them, they flew out of Copenhagen earlier than scheduled. "It seems that people in Scandinavia just aren't ready for the way we look," Jimi told a reporter.[43]

The final two bookings of the tour brought the Experience to the Star Palace in Kiel on Saturday and to the Jaguar Club in Herford, Germany, on Sunday. At both concerts Jimi was photographed playing his red Stratocaster. During one of the concerts, most likely the Star Palace, Jimi was too incapacitated to play. "Hendrix had taken something or someone had given him something," Noel told an interviewer. "We sort of wandered onstage, and I noticed that he was just standing there laughing. He couldn't tune the guitar, so I had to put the bass down, go across there, get the guitar, tune it backwards for him, hand it to him, and he just sort of sat on the chair, laughing because he was tripping. And he couldn't sing or nothing. And in those days I couldn't sing—I just did backing vocals or whatever. Luckily, I could speak a bit of German. So we fumbled through a few songs without vocals, and in the end I said in German that he's a bit ill, and we split quick."[44]

In his autobiography, Redding described how this event triggered a heart-to-heart conversation with his bandmates: "It angered me to think he'd do that and risk everything we'd worked for. I considered it highly selfish. He could just as easily have taken it after the gig. It brought on a serious discussion about the group, and we discovered we were making over £300 a night—a fortune then, when flights were as cheap as our shared hotel rooms. And yet I was living on the same income as in my Burnettes days. This was a sobering thought. We'd had no account to date, though we were due one. I was assigned the task of writing to Chas. We all signed the letter (no copy, of course), the gist of which was: 'We know what we're making. We have nothing. We want to part company.'"[45]

On Monday, May 29, a bank holiday, the Experience returned to England to perform at Barbecue 67, one of the first major rock festivals. The event took place in the Tulip Bulb Auction Hall in the market town of Spalding, Lincolnshire. In addition to the performing bands—the Jimi Hendrix Experience, Cream, Geno Washington and the Ram Jam Band, Pink Floyd, the Move, and Zoot Money and His Big Roll Band—the Barbecue 67 promo poster listed nonstop dancing, "soft ultraviolet lighting," and "knockout atmosphere." Despite the event's title, no barbecue was served; instead, bottles of Coke and hot dogs were available for purchase. The "knockout atmosphere" tag belied the fact that the event was held in a large, sweltering, odorous shed used for cattle auctions.

The bookings for the Experience, Cream, and Pink Floyd had been confirmed the year before, before they'd achieved headliner status. Having priced their tickets at £1, the promoters were woefully unprepared for the crowd attracted to the event—various accounts at the time claimed that from 4,000 to 10,000 people, most of them ticketless, showed up. As fans stood in the slow-moving line, a local band, Sounds Force Five, performed on a side stage. Pink Floyd came on next, an overhead projector creating a primitive oil-bubble lightshow on a sheet hung behind them. Tight sets by Zoot Money and especially Geno Washington's band were very well received. When Cream came onstage, Clapton-watchers were surprised to see Eric, his hair permed to resemble Jimi's, playing a Gibson SG painted in bright psychedelic colors.

The long delay before the Experience stepped onstage set the tone for their performance. As they began to play, Jimi, clearly in a bad mood, had problems keeping his guitar in tune. When his ongoing attempts to retune the guitar caused additional delays, some attendees began to jeer. "Fuck you," Jimi told them. "I'm gonna get my guitar in tune if it takes all fucking night." Germaine Greer, still a few years away from the *Life* magazine cover that would declare her the "Saucy Feminist That Even Men Like," wrote that the audience "didn't even care whether 'Hey Joe' was in tune or not. They just wanted to hear something and adulate. They wanted him to give head to his guitar and rub his cock over it. They didn't want to hear him play. But Jimi wanted, like he always wanted, to play it sweet and high. So he did it, and he fucked with the guitar, and they moaned and swayed about, and he looked at them heavily and knew they couldn't hear what he was trying to do and never would."[46] Jimi ended the set early, shoving his red Stratocaster's headstock through the grille of his Marshall stack, toppling over an amp or two, and walking offstage. The general consensus among concertgoers was that Clapton had easily outplayed Hendrix. On Tuesday morning the band was driven home to London.

At month's end, having received the letter of complaint signed by all three musicians, Jeffery called a meeting. According to Noel, he agreed to a "50/25/25 split (Jimi/Mitch/me), with the management percentage coming off the top. There was never any mention of us being employed, and foolishly we never discussed what we were splitting. It was agreed orally, and confirmed to the office lawyers and accountants, but never documented. £500 was deposited into each of the accounts for expenses on our U.S. tour, and our weekly wage was raised to £45. We were happy—it didn't take much. This pattern continued. We'd get upset and instantly some cash would appear. I tried to think about business, but I was all questions and no answers."[47]

11:June 1967

Setting the World on Fire

Jimi Hendrix, baby, believe me, set the world on fire.
—Eric Burdon[1]

The Jimi Hendrix Experience began the month of June with only one night of performances scheduled before their departure for the United States on the 13th. On the first day of the month, Jimi did an at-home interview with Dawn James for *Rave*. The conversation began with a moment of levity when Jimi told her, "There's one thing I never do—clean my teeth with hair spray!" But it quickly turned revelatory when Jimi, who admitted to feeling "quite melancholy" that day, was asked if he needs people around him. "I guess I could do without them," he confided. "In fact, sometimes I'd rather be alone. I like to think. Yes, gee, man, I'm a thinker. I can really get lost thinking about my music. But then I think so much I have to get out among people again. I hear music in my head all the time. Sometimes it makes my brain throb and the room starts to turn. I feel I'm going mad. So I go to the clubs and get plastered. Man, I get real paralytic. But it saves me."

Asked whether his "hopes are married to music," Jimi revealed, "It's all I really care for. My ambitions are tied up with it. Even my girlfriends are part of it because I meet them where there is music, and they are part of the scene I associate with music." Jimi rolled his eyes, shrugged, and continued. "I don't meet any girls I could be serious about. Sure, I'd like to meet a real nice girl, one I could talk to like she was a fellow. But I've had so many girls and they're all the same. The ones I meet look good and make you feel like a man, but you can't talk to them. I get cross with them because they just talk gossip. I get sad about all the girls I see walking on the street when I'm in a taxicab, because I'll never meet them, and perhaps one of them is the right girl for me." Midway through this quote, Dawn James added a parenthetical aside: "He doesn't have a steady girl."[2] While Jimi's words here might suggest that he was being insensitive—cruel, even—to the woman he'd been living with since his arrival in London, Kathy Etchingham was in on this charade. During Jimi's at-home interviews, she explained, "I had to be kept hidden, since a steady girlfriend would have damaged the sexy image. Jimi was briefed never to mention me and I would stay downstairs, usually in the bath, while he entertained the journalists above. It didn't bother me. I knew it was the way things were done."[3]

When Dawn James mentioned that Jimi's mother had died when he was young and that he'd been sent to live with relatives, Hendrix replied, "So? Lots of kids have it tough. I ran away from home a couple of times because I was so miserable. When my dad found out I'd gone, he went pretty mad with worry. But then I don't really care about other people's feelings." Hendrix added that he returned home "when I realized my dad was upset. Not that I cared, but well, he is my dad."

In another telling exchange, Jimi shared his thoughts on negative critics and how he psyches himself to go onstage: "I must say that people being rude about me doesn't ever bother me now. The only time I get uneasy is when I know that pop critics and writers are waiting for me to fail so they can jump all over me. This is how pop is. You have a hit record and, gee, they love you! But you have one failure and they kill you. It's like a tightrope. I get kind of tense before a show. I like to be left alone to think. My road manager tries to keep the dressing room free from people then. If people come in, I find a corner somewhere else. I have to think myself into my act. I can't just turn on." James wondered if other people's music affected Jimi. "I can't define it," he told her. "A blues or a sad melody can make me real happy. I am affected by sounds, though. They can change my mood."

Near the interview's end Jimi revealed that he did not follow any organized religion, explaining that "religion is all the same—Catholic, Protestant, Jewish. It's just a lot of reasonable commercial quotes that sell because they're somewhere between very good and very bad, and people can easily hang on to that. It gives them something to believe in."[4] In other interviews, Jimi expressed a belief that his spirituality was entwined with his music: "We call our music 'Electric Church' music. Yeah, because it's like a religion to us. What we're saying is not protesting, but saying the answers, some kind of solution."[5]

Like others before her, Dawn James noted that Jimi projected an entirely different persona at home than he did onstage. "Jimi has super manners," she wrote. "When he asks you out, he says, 'Would you do me the honor of dating me tonight?' When he leaves a room you are in, he says, 'Excuse me for a moment, please.' When he meets you, he shakes hands and says, 'Nice seeing you.' Somewhere deep down beneath the raving recording star there is a lot of old-world charm."[6]

In a newsletter sent out that week by his official U.K. fan club, Jimi offered this view of *Are You Experienced*: "I don't want anyone to stick a psychedelic label around my neck. Imagination is the key to my lyric and the rest is painted with a little science fiction. I could never keep to one particular musical style. 'May This Be Love' is 'getyourmindtogether' music, 'Manic Depression' is 'ugly times' music, and 'Red House' is a kind of R&B number which could possibly make the Top 500."[7] Mitch later noted that while most of the album's tracks became staples of Experience concerts, the band did not add "May This Be Love" or "Remember" to their stage repertoire, "because, in all honesty, they were album fillers, not because we couldn't re-create them onstage."[8]

The album rapidly ascended the charts. A June 3 issue of *New Musical Express* ranked *Are You Experienced* number three in Britain's Top-Fifteen LPs, with the *The Sound of Music* soundtrack coming in second and the Beatles' *Sgt. Pepper's Lonely Hearts Club Band* on top. As Chas noted, "*Sgt. Pepper* became a watershed album. And so there we were with *Are You Experienced* coming out, right on the coattails of a very innovative album by the Beatles, which really did make a significant change. Albums became a much more serious piece of work at that time."[9]

Back home in America, the Monterey International Pop Festival, the first of its kind, was gaining attention. *Billboard*'s front page announced that the "multi million-dollar" lineup had agreed to play for free, with all income going to charities. "We are running this festival as a non-profit foundation set up by artists in the name of pop music," explained cofounder Lou Adler. "People don't think of pop music as an art form. They think of it as single records. It needs an artistic image. It's more than just a business." A film was in the works. The Mamas and the Papas, Lou Rawls, the Beach Boys, the Byrds, Simon and Garfunkel, Dionne Warwick, Johnny Rivers, the Association, Otis Redding, and the Jefferson Airplane made it into the top paragraphs. Among the names at the article's end, bookended by the Who and Mike Bloomfield on page ten, was "Jimmy Hendrix."[10]

Paul McCartney, it turned out, was responsible for the Jimi Hendrix Experience being invited to make their first North American appearance at the Monterey festival. "You gotta remember how *huge* the Beatles were in them days," Chas explained.

> They were just a colossus. And when the Mamas and Papas and John Phillips and them come up with the Monterey thing, they asked Paul to be part of the board that was set up in front and would guarantee the Monterey festival. Paul just basically said, "I'll join the board at Monterey *if* the Jimi Hendrix Experience are on the show." That was his condition on joining it. Brian Jones was a good pal of Jimi's and mine—he used to be at our house all the time. It was Brian that answered the phone from California when John came on the phone asking us to go to Monterey. Because Brian answered the phone, we turned around and said, "Yeah—if Brian will come out and do the announcing for Jimi." So Brian went out with us and announced Jimi onstage.[11]

At the moment, though, Jimi had more immediate concerns. Well aware that the June 4 Saville shows would draw intense scrutiny, the Experience spent two afternoons in rehearsals there. Tickets were selling fast. Four bands were slated to open: the Stormsville Shakers, Procol Harum, the Chiffons, and Denny Laine and his Electric String Band. "The 'farewell' show at the Saville Theatre is bound to be a biggie," Noel predicted.[12] In preparation, Jimi painted flowers and words onto the back of the 1965 Stratocaster he planned to use for the finale. His painted message, all in caps, read, "May this be love or just confusion born out of frustration-wracked feelings of not being able to make true physical love to the universal gypsie queen of true, free expressed music. My darling guitar ... Please rest in peace, Amen." Off to the side he added "London."[13]

On the day of the Experience's sold-out Saville shows, hundreds of fans were turned away at the door. Inside, Paul McCartney and Jane Asher, George and Pattie Boyd Harrison, Charlie and Shirley Watts, Graham and Rose Nash, Spencer Davis, and Terence Stamp mingled among the crowd. According to Charles Cross, thirty minutes before the Experience were scheduled to go onstage, Jimi toted a portable record player and a copy of the new Beatles album into the dressing room. He dropped the needle onto the LP's title track, "Sgt. Pepper's Lonely Hearts Club Band," and told Mitch and Noel, "We'll open with this."[14] Hendrix quickly showed them an arrangement on his guitar. "We thought he'd gone daft," Noel recalled, but they learned their parts.

At the start of the second set, Jimi stepped onstage in a flame-orange velvet suit. As Paul McCartney and George Harrison watched from Brian Epstein's box, Jimi, Mitch, and Noel launched into the song they'd just learned. Unlike the multi-textured original, with its overdubbed horns and music hall vibe, Jimi set the song to a hard-driving guitar riff and went full-feedback on the solo. "Jimi was just a fantastic guy, a very humble guy," McCartney remembered,

and I think one of the greatest tributes he could have ever paid me was we had released *Sgt. Pepper's Lonely Hearts Club Band* on Friday, and by that Sunday, a couple of days later, he'd learned it, and he opened with it with his band. Now that's cool! He played this really long solo in it, and he had his whammy bar and he was doing all this stuff. He was going crazy in those days with that whammy bar. The trouble was that it would put your guitar *very* out of tune. So at the end of that song, at the end of that solo, he was looking down and didn't know what to do. So he looks at the audience and says, "Is Eric out there, man?" He's looking out for Eric Clapton, who was there. So he looks at him and says, "Could you come up here and tune this for me, mate?"[15]

Then came the first delay, caused by a microphone malfunction. Roadies darted about the stage and made repairs. The Experience resumed with "Foxey Lady" and "Like a Rolling Stone." Then an amp blew. Noel filled in some of the time by chatting with the audience. Mitch gave an impromptu drum solo. Jimi, who stayed calm and upbeat, told the audience, "This is our last gig here for a long time, so we're gonna make it nice!" When the amplifier was finally restored, Jimi told the audience, "I feel like getting nasty." They then played "Manic Depression," "Hey Joe," "Purple Haze," and "The Wind Cries Mary." "It was a really good, loose show," Noel remembered. "Jimi liked rolling around on the stage and kept nudging me and shouting at me to do the same. I'm not athletic, and in my shyness I hesitated. But he went on bumping me until I gave in. We wrestled together, then fell over and tumbled round the stage. Once down, I felt freer than I had since my carefree days in Germany."[16] The group began their final number. As "Are You Experienced?" built to a freak-out climax, Jimi was handed the guitar he'd painted in swirling colors. Strobe lights flashing, he smashed the guitar against the stage and tossed pieces to the clamoring crowd.

Hugh Nolan reported in *Disc and Music Echo* that the Saville show "was the highpoint of Jimi's meteoric rise to fame in this country—and of a superb night's exciting sounds at the Saville, with a bill which included current chart-toppers, Procol Harum, and a mind-blowing set from ex–Moody Blue Denny Laine and his Electric String Band. But it was Jimi's audience and Jimi's night. In all the scenes of wild acclaim with which Jimi Hendrix and his Experience have been greeted since they first exploded onto our rather tired ears, none equaled Sunday's, when after a raving and tumultuous set the whole audience rose to its feet. . . . If he ever returns to Britain or not, Jimi Hendrix can be sure that things will never be the same again here since his Experience hit town with all the impact of a 50-megaton H-Bomb."[17] Arriving at an after-gig party at Brian Epstein's home, Jimi, Mitch, and Noel were shocked when Paul McCartney, smoking a large joint, opened the door to let them in. Noel wrote that he spent most of the night "just watching people and marveling that I was there. . . . The show at the Saville really capped things off. We'd got the music together, got the recording together, got the audience together, and now it was time to get America together."[18]

The morning after the Saville show, Jimi was visited by Norrie Drummond, on assignment from *New Musical Express*. Inviting

Drummond into the flat, Jimi woke up Chas, who put on a copy of the *Sgt. Pepper's* album. Drummond wrote,

> Jimi really wasn't in the best of spirits when I met him. The previous evening his concert at London's Saville Theatre had been plagued with amplifier problems and it was still worrying him. "Man, it really brings me down when these amps don't work," he said, lighting his first cigarette of the day, "and they were new ones too." ... Many people have the impression that Jimi Hendrix is moody and introverted, but he is not. Certainly, compared to many other pop artistes he is quiet, but once he starts talking about something which interests him—mainly music, obviously—he rambles on at great length. "I know people think I'm moody," he admitted, "but that's only because I'm thinking of music most of the time. If I suddenly clam up it's because I've just hit on an idea."

Hendrix spoke with Drummond about his imminent return to the United States. "I don't really think we'll achieve as much success there as we have done here. We have been told that we'll do well, but I'm not sure that we will be accepted as readily there. In America people are much more narrow-minded than they are in Britain. If they do like us—great! If not—too bad! In the States the disc jockeys stopped playing 'Hey Joe' because people complained about the lyrics." At the interview's conclusion, Drummond asked Jimi about his main ambition in life. "Oh, that changes a hundred times a day," Hendrix answered. "I really just want to continue playing and recording what gives me pleasure. What we play is straight from us. I don't ever want to have to bow to commercialism."[19]

Later that day the Experience met at Olympic Studios to record another original, "Cat Talkin' to Me." After plowing through seventeen takes, they chose the second one and Jimi and Mitch overdubbed additional parts. The unfinished recording was shelved until 1987, when Chas, Mitch, and Noel reworked it with new lyrics written and sung by Mitchell. This, too, was deemed unworthy of release.

Jimi's next several days were devoted to photo shoots. The most important of these were with Karl Ferris, whose cover shot of the Hollies' *Evolution* album had caught Jimi's eye. Before the shoot, Ferris dressed Noel in a long, Victorian-style yellow coat with black buttons, and Mitch in striped pants, wide belt, flowery shirt, and scarf. He made a pilgrimage to Jimi's flat to rifle through his wardrobe, selecting what Jimi called his "Gypsy Eyes jacket." To match the inventive nature of the trio's music, Ferris decided to use infrared film and a fisheye lens. Their photoshoot at London's Royal Botanical Gardens on Kew Road produced the iconic psychedelic image on the front cover of the American release of *Are You Experienced*. Per Chas's instructions, none of the musicians are smiling in the photo. Ferris's artwork would also be featured on the back cover of the American release of *Are You Experienced*, as well as on the *Axis: Bold as Love* and *Electric Ladyland* albums.

Are You Experienced climbed to number two on the British charts on June 10. In an interview with *Disc and Music Echo*, Jimi expressed gratitude to his British fans: "I always think how lucky I am that people like what I'm doing enough to buy my records, because I haven't set out to produce a commercial sound. I don't even know what a hit record sounds like. Those records just came to us—I'm convinced it was luck." He also mentioned his love for London, tourist spots and all, adding, "I'm not just saying that.... It's the little streets and all those little shops, the little things that I love."[20]

On Tuesday, June 13, Mike Jeffery and Keith Altham picked up Chas and Jimi at their London flat and drove them to Heathrow in Jeffery's Rolls Royce. Before taking his seat in the TWA flight's first-class section, Jimi scoured the airport bookstalls for a science fiction novel. A stewardess, delighted to have such an unusual passenger in her section, sat alongside Jimi for part of the flight, chatting with him about beat groups. "I sat next to him on the plane going over," Keith Altham remembered, "and he said that he was a bit frightened because he didn't really know if he'd be able to get across what he was trying to do."[21] During the flight Jimi amused himself by scrolling through the taped music channels: "Every so often Jimi would throw up an assortment of fingers indicating a new delight on a particular channel," Altham wrote. "He seemed to get a perverse enjoyment from Bing Crosby, Al Jolson and [Jimmy] Durante. But more genuine was his interest in the Bach tapes."[22]

After their arrival at Kennedy International Airport, Jimi directed their limousine driver to go straight to Colony Records in Times Square, where he bought albums by the Doors and the

Mothers of Invention. The entourage attempted to check in at the Chelsea on West Twenty-Third—a "dreadful, notorious hotel," in Altham's words. In the lobby, an overdressed woman mistook Jimi for a bellman and ordered him to carry her luggage. The entourage relocated to the Buckingham Hotel on West Fifty-Seventh. That evening Jimi showed his traveling companions around the Village. He pointed out Cafe Wha?, took them to dine at the Tin Angel, and stopped in at Cafe au Go Go for a Richie Havens performance. "He's worth listening to hard," said Hendrix.

The following day Mitch, Noel, Brian Jones, and Eric Burdon took their first-class seats on a TWA flight from London to New York City. En route, Noel ingested what he described as "purple Owsley" LSD: "I was sitting beside Brian Jones and he gave me this little tablet and he said, 'Take it.' So I took it because, like, he was Brian Jones. The next thing I remember was that I was on some boat in New York and I said, 'Well, this doesn't affect me.'"[23] Mitch, who didn't drop acid en route, wrote that after landing, he and Noel were chauffeured to their hotel, where they were to share a room. Noel decided to take a bath and began running the water. "I'm unpacking the case and I hear this screech," Mitch wrote, "and Noel's standing on the side of the bath and I'm going, 'What's wrong, what's wrong?' It was our first experience with cockroaches.... So I open a drawer in the kitchen cabinet and it's the wrong move. The rest of the family is in there—thousands of them. Quick phone call to Chas, 'Get us out of here *now*.' We managed to transfer to another hotel, which was okay."[24] That evening Mitch and Noel were invited by Chas's friend Deering Howe, an heir to the International Harvester fortune, to take a cruise on his yacht. "We were treated very regally," Mitch wrote. "It was an amazing situation—first night in New York and we're sailing around the Hudson and the East River in this yacht—very decadent." Noel dropped more LSD during the cruise.

Jimi began his first full day back in New York City by donning white pants, a bright floral jacket, an emerald green scarf, and a gold medallion inscribed "Champion Bird Watcher." The downside of such striking garb, Keith Altham reported, quickly became apparent: "Getting cabs was a lot of fun at that time with Jimi, because you had three chances of not getting a cab in the Village: 1. If you were sort of a weird-looking hippie; 2. if you had long hair; and

3. if you were black. And he made it on all three accounts! So not only would the cabs not stop for him, they would try and run him over. So we would have to hide him in doorways and go and stop a cab, then we would get in the cab and even then the cabbies would tell him to get out. We had to get out of a couple of cabs and I'd get a bit humpty about it.... But, of course, a year or two later when Jimi went back as a superstar, they couldn't do enough for him."[25] Eventually they were able to get Hendrix and Jeffery to their meetings with the Experience's American booking agent, Premier Talent, and with the organizers of Teen Mail Ltd., who would create a Jimi Hendrix fan club and handle his licensing and merchandising. That evening Chas and Jimi went to the Scene to watch the Doors perform selections from their debut album, as well as their epic, as-yet-unreleased "When the Music's Over."

On Thursday Jimi and company flew to San Francisco International Airport. Keith Altham remembered that Hendrix had "a little sulk when he discovered I had left his *Mad* magazine in my room at the hotel, but he got over it."[26] Barry Jenkins, who'd drummed for the Nashville Teens before joining the Animals, sat near Jimi on the flight. "I'll never forget seeing Hendrix sitting in his seat with his ear pushed up against the side wall of the plane," Jenkins remembered. "I asked him what he was doing, and he said, 'I'm getting inspiration for the next album, man.' He was listening to the sounds of the engine vibrating inside the walls."[27]

After an overnight stay in San Francisco, Altham reported, they began their day by trying to "find an 'indestructible' guitar for Jimi. 'I need a Fender,' explained Jimi. 'It gets used pretty hard in the act and they are the only make which will stand up to it.' We failed to get the model Jimi wanted but somehow he later acquired one in Monterey. It was the wrong color but he remedied that by spraying it white and drawing swirling designs all over it with a felt pen."[28] Mitch and Noel, meanwhile, enjoyed frolicking in the hotel pool with several young women. On Friday morning Eric Burdon, Tiny Tim, and Jefferson Airplane singer Grace Slick joined Jimi, Mitch, Noel, and Chas on the Pacific Airlines flight to Monterey's Peninsular Airport. Jimi touched ground just fifteen miles from Fort Ord, where a half-dozen years earlier he'd done his military basic training.

Held at the beginning of the "Summer of Love," the first and only Monterey International Pop Festival would turn out to be an historic event. From the vantage point of a quarter-century later, San Francisco–based music critic Joel Selvin offered this telling perspective:

> The Monterey International Pop Festival was not only an unprecedented and unmatched collection of talent, the three-day event was also an axis on which the world of rock music turned. Music would never be the same again. Over that weekend, the Monterey Pop Festival managed to simultaneously sum up and accelerate the dramatic changes sweeping through pop music. It was a festival taking place on the cusp of innocence. Never again would rock music be the charmingly uncorrupted force it was at Monterey. But, for one weekend at least, rock music was everything it was supposed to be: music, love, and flowers.[29]

And drugs, as Mitch Mitchell would discover during his first stroll around the fairgrounds. As Mitch snacked on some strawberries, a stranger asked him for one. Mitch obliged, and the stranger asked him to put down the strawberries and hold out his hands. "I'm not sure what's going on," Mitch wrote, "but I put them down and he puts this gigantic quantity of these purple pills into my hands. Of course, it's Owsley, the legendary acid chemist. I had heard of him and knew of his reputation, but I wasn't sure what to do with these things, so I just stuffed them in my pocket, said 'Thank you,' and walked off."[30] The sheer size of the event shocked Noel: "It was freaky, you know. The first gig in America, doing this *huge* festival. All these people leaping about, taking various things and hair everywhere, and women—of course."[31]

The festival officially opened on Friday night. "Everyone," wrote Noel, "was convinced that the three-day Monterey Pop Festival marked the beginning of a new era.... The exotic crowd ranged from madras to velvet. You only had to breathe the air filled with incense and marijuana to be high. Everyone believed something awesome was happening, that some amazing vibration was breaking out. The whole concept of this stupendous concert made everything previous pale into insignificance."[32] By 9:00 P.M., an estimated 10,000 people had congregated on the fairgrounds, with far more milling outside the fences. The evening's lineup featured the

Association, Lou Rawls, Eric Burdon and the Animals, Simon and Garfunkel, and Johnny Rivers.

Dew glistened on the fairground grass on Saturday morning. Canned Heat opened, followed by Janis Joplin with Big Brother and the Holding Company, and then Country Joe and the Fish. Over at a booth set up by the Guild guitar company, Paul Simon watched as Jimi and the Grateful Dead's Bob Weir had a jam session, both playing through the same amp. The Paul Butterfield Blues Band took the main stage, with Elvin Bishop taking over on guitar for Michael Bloomfield, who'd recently quit the band. The as-yet-unsigned Quicksilver Messenger Service, with their three lead guitarists, came on next, followed by the Steve Miller Blues Band. Described in the advance press as the Michael Bloomfield Thing, the newly formed, newly named Electric Flag climaxed the afternoon performances with their first public concert. Jimi watched from the audience as Bloomfield and drummer Buddy Miles played brilliantly. (Miles would later join Hendrix and Billy Cox in Band of Gypsys.)

The Saturday evening show brought onstage Booker T. and the MG's, the Byrds, Jefferson Airplane, and Otis Redding, who drew thunderous applause. Mitch recalled that "Otis Redding with most of Booker T. and The MG's was amazing. Some of it wasn't so good, but after Otis maybe we were expecting too much. Other bands like the Byrds—great records, one of our favorite bands, but we thought they were having a bad night. Some of the bands, like the Jefferson Airplane, we'd heard of, but this was our first exposure to them. We were well aware of the West Coast movement, but hadn't paid much attention to it until then. Some of them turned out to be very good, but we still thought, 'Well, if this is the best they can do . . . can't wait to play. Let me up onstage—we'll show these mothers."[33] After the concert Jimi jammed on a side stage with members of the Grateful Dead and Jefferson Airplane.

On Sunday morning the Experience and the Who went together to a late-morning rehearsal, where Jimi was brilliantly photographed by Jim Marshall. Jimi attended the first performance of the day, Ravi Shankar's three-hour afternoon set. Incense wafted through the air as Shankar explained the working of his sitar and serenely played ragas accompanied by Alla Rakha on tabla. Afterward, Jimi and Brian Jones strolled together backstage. Jim Marshall's iconic photo of the pair depicts Jones, resplendent in a gold lame coat, lace, scarves, and necklaces, holding a can of Budweiser, while Jimi wears his military coat, ornate vest, jewelry, and a lapel button that reads "I'm a Virgin."

With the Who and Jimi Hendrix Experience both scheduled to perform Sunday evening, the big question was which act would go on first. Mitchell wrote, "Of course, it got down to who was going to follow whom, or Who, as the case may be. . . . Let's face it: the Who were a bloody hard act to follow at any time."[34] Neither act wanted to follow the other. Finally, John Phillips declared that he'd flip a coin into the air, with the loser having to go on after the winner. Pete Townshend remembered Jimi's reaction when the Who won the toss: "There was a certain look up in his eye and he got on a chair and he played some amazing guitar, just standing on the chair in the dressing room. Janis Joplin was there, Brian Jones, Eric [Burdon]. And then he got down off the chair, turned round to me, and said, 'If I follow you, I'm gonna pull *all* the stops.'"[35] The organizers asked the Grateful Dead to perform between the sets by the Who and the Experience.

Tommy Smothers emceed the Sunday evening show, delivering zingers with his patented deadpan humor. The Blues Project played first, bridging jazz and rock. Peter Tork of the Monkees came out to introduce Buffalo Springfield, with David Crosby sitting in on guitar. Eric Burdon introduced the Who, telling the audience, "This is a group that will destroy you completely in more ways than one." Dressed in foppish finery, the Who opened with "Substitute." Then came a devastating cover of Eddie Cochran's "Summertime Blues," with Keith Moon playing fantastic figures on his double drum set as Pete Townshend, looking like a "berserk British aristocrat" as Keith Altham described, engaged in guitar gymnastics. Next up were "Pictures of Lily," "A Quick One (While He's Away)," and their then-current single, "Happy Jack." The Who concluded with an impassioned "My Generation," Roger Daltrey stammering his words, Keith Moon pounding hard, John Entwistle thundering on bass, and Pete Townshend windmilling his guitar. At the end, Townshend set off smoke bombs and savagely destroyed his guitar. The stunned audience, most of whom had never seen anything like this before, erupted into applause.

Noel, for one, was filled with apprehension: "Nobody knew

how we'd come off. The Who's 'smashing' act had taken America by storm, but we were coming to the audience as total unknowns. Whereas in England Jimi's being an American had helped us get noticed, it was the Englishness of the group that was being stressed in America. The press played up to our 'black English guitarist who could play with his teeth.' Suddenly it didn't seem like much."[36] Mitch, watching on backstage monitors, thought that the Who "were incredibly good, as usual, but we were too on-edge to enjoy it. When Pete Townshend broke up his guitar, which I seem to remember took quite a while—unusual for him—we thought, 'How do you top this?'"[37] Jimi seemed to have taken the Who's finale in stride. As he stood alongside Jim Marshall, watching the destruction, Marshall asked him, "Well, Jimi, how are you gonna top that?" Jimi just looked at him and said, "Make sure you've got plenty of film in your camera."[38]

The Grateful Dead, placed in the unenviable position of buttressing the Who and the Experience, took a laid-back approach, delighting listeners with their exploratory jams. Huddling backstage, the Experience decided it was time, in Mitch's words, to "roast the Fender" again. As agreed, Brian Jones came onstage to introduce the trio: "I'd like to introduce a very good friend, a fellow countryman of yours, the greatest performer, the most exciting guitarist I have ever heard: the Jimi Hendrix Experience." For Jimi, watching from the wings, this was the moment he'd long dreamed of. "It's amazing that he had to come to England to make it back in the U.S.," Mitch remembered. "The guy wanted to get in there and hit hard."[39]

A far cry from the neatly coiffed, suit-wearing soul musicians who'd performed earlier in the festival, a gum-chewing Jimi came onstage in full hippie regalia—red velvet pants, brightly colored shirt, headband, pink feather boa slung around his neck. Most of the audience had never seen anything like him. "Thanks to the Who," Noel noted, "the audience was already in a frenzy."[40] Jimi began with a flurry of strummed chords, leading Mitch and Noel into a sped-up rendition of "Killing Floor." He played a quick solo, picking hand upraised as he fretted, and then sang the opening verses. He threw his whole body into the next solo, swaying like a snake charmer, playing one-handed, grazing the strings with his sleeve, and rapidly flicking his tongue as he trilled a note. He repeated this move after the final verse, lowering and letting up on his whammy mid-trill for added effect. Jimi concluded the song with a flash of feedback.

"Yeah, what's happening, brother," Hendrix spoke into the microphone. "Here's something else. We got a little thing called 'Foxey Lady.' My fingers will move, as you see. Dig this." With that he went into the song's distinctive opening. Perpetual motion incarnate, Hendrix began his solo with a dance step, played with the guitar's headstock between his legs and furiously stroked its neck—all in perfect time. He ended with a passage that was as much soundscape as notes.

Jimi stepped up to the microphone and said, "Dig. Let's get down to business. Just give me one second to get down." The film crew panned through the crowd, showing everyone on their feet. Jimi slipped off his boa, revealing a golden-yellow shirt and brocaded vest. Perfectly at ease, he continued his relaxed, friendly patter. "Yeah, it's really outta sight. It didn't even rain. No buttons to push. Right now I'd like to dedicate this song to everybody here with any kind of heart and ears. It goes something like this here." Jimi strummed the opening chords of "Like a Rolling Stone" and fired off a quick solo inspired by Bloomfield's leads on Dylan's original version. Instead of going into the first verse, he kept playing and said, "Yes, as I said before, it's really groovy. I'd like to bore you for about six or seven minutes and do a little thing, yeah . . ." Flashing a charismatic smile, he then quipped, "Yeah, you have to excuse me for a minute and just let me play my guitar, alright?" Another flourish à la Bloomfield. "Right now we're gonna do a thing by Bob Dylan—that's his grandmother over there," he said, pointing to Mitch. "It's a little thing called 'Like a Rolling Stone.'" A case study in cool, Jimi toned down the theatrics and turned on the charm. He wrapped his half-spoken, half-sung lyrics in superlative rhythm-guitar playing.

The Experience next went into a frantic version of "Rock Me Baby," pushing the song far beyond its blues roots. In another display of stunning guitar playing, Jimi punctuated his vocals with matching multi-string bends. The band segued into "Hey Joe." Jimi played the first solo with his teeth, the second behind his head, both note-perfect. At song's end, the film crew had to reload their cameras, so the next song, "Can You See Me," did not make it into the *Jimi Plays Monterey* film. The Experience followed their tender, no-frills, poetic reading of "The Wind Cries Mary" with a majestic version of "Purple Haze."

Jimi changed guitars, strapping on the one he'd just repainted and decorated, and stepped up to the microphone. He asked the audience if they'd heard "about the story that we couldn't make it here, so we go to England and America doesn't like us because, you know, our feet's too big, we got fat mattresses, and we wear golden underwear. Ain't no scene like that, brother. Dig, man, I was layin' around and went to England and picked up these two cats, and now here we are, man. It was so, you know, groovy to come back here this way and really get a chance to really play, you know." The audience erupted in applause. "I could sit up here all night and say 'thank you, thank you, thank you.' I wish I could just grab you, man, and just, ooh [*kissing sounds*]. One of those things, man, one of those things. But, dig, I just can't do that. So what I wanna do, I'm gonna sacrifice something right here I really love.... Don't think I'm silly doing this, you know, because I don't think I'm losing my mind. Last night, man, ooh God.... But today I think it's the right thing, so I'm not losing my mind. This is for everybody here, man. It's the only way I can do it. So we're gonna do the English and American combined anthem together, okay? Don't get mad—noooo. Don't get mad. I want everybody to join in, too, alright? And don't get mad. This is it. There's nothing more I can do ..."

Feedback building, Jimi raised his guitar in front of him, headstock toward his feet, and pressed on his whammy arm, conjuring otherworldly sounds. He lowered his instrument, thrust his groin against its back, slipped his pick between his lips, and slapped a veritable symphony in feedback as his picking hand worked the whammy. Suddenly, with a little leap into the air, he retrieved his pick and slammed into the opening chords of "Wild Thing." "C'mon, man," he exhorted the audience, "sing with me!" Noel joined in with harmony vocals. Left arm pointed skyward, Jimi began his solo with a legato, one-handed quote from Frank Sinatra's "Strangers in the Night" and then made good on his backstage promise to Townshend, unleashing an astonishing barrage of sound. He somersaulted across the stage, dropped to his knees and returned to his feet, without missing a note. For a moment the band fell silent as Jimi put his own stamp on the chorus: "C'mon and sock it to me one more time again. Aw, shucks, I love ya."

He performed the final verse with his guitar behind his back. With Mitch frantically pounding drums and Noel anchoring on bass, Jimi climaxed the set with several of the techniques and moves he'd perfected in England. Feedback squealing, he spasmodically humped his guitar against an amp. He turned toward the crowd, fell to his knees, and jerked his whammy between his legs. He wiggled his fingers skyward above his guitar, as if magically summoning its roar. He jerked the whammy as if he were frantically masturbating. Then he stood and retrieved a can of lighter fluid from behind his amplifier. He doused the guitar, knelt down and kissed it, and struck a match. Like a scene from the Old Testament, the Stratocaster burst into flames. Amid thunderous feedback, Hendrix swung the burning guitar overhead and crashed it into the stage, again and again, and then gently tossed the pieces to the audience. The Experience left the stage to stunned looks and rapturous applause.

Drenched in sweat, they worked their way through the ecstatic crowd of musicians offering congratulations. "That meant so much to us," Mitch remembered, "not only the audience approval, but our peers as well. We'd done incredibly well in Europe in a very short time, we'd got to America, gone down really well. We thought we'd arrived."[41] As Joel Selvin sagely noted, "No single performance has been more deeply embedded into the firmament of rock than Hendrix at Monterey. He walked onstage a nobody and walked off a major star, ready to rewrite the language of the guitar."[42]

Looking back, Jimi offered this view of the Monterey performance:

That was our start in America. When I was in Britain I used to think about America every day. I'm American. I wanted people here to see me. I also wanted to see whether we could make it back here. And we made it, man, because we did our own thing—and it really was our own thing and nobody else's. We had our beautiful rock-blues-country-funky-freaky sound, and it was really turning people on. I felt like we were turning the whole world on to this new thing, the best, most lovely thing.

So I decided to destroy my guitar at the end of the song as a sacrifice. You sacrifice things you love. I love my guitar.[43]

Thus, in nine months' time, Jimi Hendrix overcame the poverty he'd endured in the land of his birth. Reinventing himself in another country, he created mind-expanding songs and became the ultimate embodiment of the rock guitarist. His music, ever fresh and inspirational, endures as a celebration of creativity, individuality, and the human spirit.

ACKNOWLEDGMENTS

First and foremost, kudos to those who knew Jimi Hendrix and recorded their memories for future generations: Keith Altham, Brian Auger, Jeff Beck, Michael Bloomfield, Jack Bruce, Paul Caruso, Chas Chandler, Eric Clapton, Billy Cox, Bruce Fleming, James Gurley, John Hammond, James "Al" Hendrix, Leon Hendrix, Mick Jagger, Andy Johns, Linda Keith, Curtis Knight, Eddie Kramer, Bob Kulick, Dave Mason, Paul McCartney, John McLaughlin, Mitch Mitchell, Noel Redding, Keith Richards, Carlos Santana, Chris Stamp, Sting, and Randy "California" Wolfe.

I am especially indebted to Kathy Etchingham for reading the manuscript and allowing me to quote liberally from her memoir, *Through Gypsy Eyes: My Life, The Sixties, and Jimi Hendrix*, a must-read for Hendrix fans and scholars.

I owe gratitude to many other authors as well, notably the late Carol Appleby (Noel Redding's coauthor), Tony Brown, Andrew Crofts (Kathy Etchingham's coauthor), Charles R. Cross, Caesar Glebeek, Sharon Lawrence, John McDermott, Charles Shaar Murray, John Platt (Mitch Mitchell's coauthor), Harry Shapiro, and Brian Southall. Your inspiring books served as my companions and guides during parts of this journey.

With its postings of hundreds of Hendrix articles culled from old newspapers and magazines, the amazing *Crosstown Torrents* website (crosstowntorrents.org) proved to be a Hendrix researcher's dream come true—a stirring round of applause for its staff and contributors. The *Jimi Hendrix Lifelines* website (jimihendrix-lifelines.net) also provided valuable insight into Jimi's day-to-day activities, as well as scans of posters and ticket stubs, photos, and other relevant images. My thanks to its staff, especially Ben Valkhoff. I also send my appreciation to those who helped secure images of the Experience's original 45 and album artwork: Matt Bradish, Sean Westergaard, and especially Jim Hawthorn at the Jimi Hendrix Record Guide (hendrix.guide.pagesperso-orange.fr), a wonderful asset for Hendrix scholars and fans.

The writings of many other music historians and journalists informed these pages: Stuart Arnold, Steve Barker, Josephine Bayne, James Belsey, Bruce Bergman, Donal Bruce, Klas Burling, Norrie Drummond, Karre Erichs, Jym Fahey, Michael Fairchild, Alan Freeman, Tony Gale, Bob Garcia, Richard Green, Germaine Greer, Jesse Gress, Nils Gudme, Gösta Hanson, Dawn James, Barry Jenkins, Derek Johnson, Nick Jones, Peter

Jones, Keith Keller, John King, Mike Ledgerwood, Chris Lloyd, Ann Nightingale, Hugh Nolan, Barbro Nordström, Graham Oliver, Steven C. Pesant, Steven Roby, Sven-Oskar Ruhmén, Charles L. Sanders, Ilpo Saunio, Gerhard Schizel, Hans Carl Schmidt, Joel Selvin, Keith Shadwick, Harry Shapiro, Tony Skinner, June Southworth, Mike Stafford, Kevin Swift, Eliot Tiegel, Penny Valentine, Jan Waldrop, Lorraine Walsh, Lars Weck, Chris Welch, Jann Wenner, and Nicholas Williams. Thank you all.

One of the great pleasures of writing this book was the time spent in the Ann Arbor home studio of Brian Delaney, a gifted jazz and rock guitarist. As we listened carefully to each of Jimi's released recordings, Brian continually astounded me with his uncanny ability to reproduce every unusual Hendrixian guitar sound coming through the speakers. I also thank Jim Dapongy for his musical clarifications. I am likewise grateful to Randy Hansen, Eric Johnson, and Stevie Ray Vaughan for sharing their thoughts on Jimi's playing techniques. I am indebted to Nicola Matthews for deciphering the meanings of British slang and musician-speak, and to Sylvestre "Steve" Novak for his French-to-English translations.

Special shout-outs go to Lawrence Townsend and Bob Gordon for generously sharing their insights into contractual and other legal issues faced by Jimi Hendrix. I am likewise grateful to David Abbott, Head of Brand Partnerships for Time Inc. (UK) Ltd., for permission to quote extensively from 1960s issues of *New Musical Express* and *Melody Maker*. I extend my gratitude to all other publications quoted in the manuscript.

My background as an Editor for *Guitar Player* magazine all those years ago deeply informed my knowledge of Jimi Hendrix and the arts of research, writing, and editing. Here's to my colleagues during those fine, fine days, especially Janine Cooper Ayers, Jim Crockett, Andy Ellis, Judie Eremo, Dan Forte, Dennis and Cheryl Fullerton, Lonni Elrod Gauss, Joe Gore, Saroyan Humphrey, Richard Johnston, John Lescroart, Don Menn, Michael Molenda, Tom Mulhern, Matt Resnicoff, James Rotondi, Jim Schwartz, Peggy Shea, Jon Sievert, Sherry Thomas-Zon, Art Thompson, and especially Tom Wheeler—RIP, pal.

I send heartfelt thanks to my friends and colleagues who looked out for me and encouraged me as I worked on the manuscript: Bill Abernethy, Sotiri Adamopoulos, Kim Aikin, David Ammer, Helen Costa, Rosalie Denenfeld, Ira Fried, Mike and Abbie Gentry, Kris Good, Margaret Green, Amy Rust Higgins, Steve "Hideaway" Hilla, Dave Horowitz, Theresa Hunt, Mike Kappus, Karen Karatzas, Ala Kaymaram, Julie Skiendziel Kissel, Carrie Krantz, Diane Laboda, Teresa DeRuntz Leonard, Susan Mann, Lynda Mills, Chris Moriarty, Michael Moriarty, Nancy Nelson, Thornton Perkins, John Pitcher, Michael Pitcher, Helena Solano Reed, Dave and Nancy Solo, George and Marie Staley, Mason Williams, Tom Wilson,

Jessica Winn, Scott Wood, David Noam Zacks, and Tom Zimmerman.
I send my appreciation to my colleagues at the University of North
Carolina at Chapel Hill: my friend and inspiration, William Ferris; my
astute and supportive editors at UNC Press, Mark Simpson-Vos, Jay
Mazzocchi, and Jessica Newman; Cate Hodorowicz, who helped with
photos; and Steve Weiss, curator of the Southern Folklife Collection.
And a tip of the hat to Matthew Somoroff for the expert copyedit; to
Jennifer Schaper for arranging the U.K. and foreign-language versions
of *Stone Free*; and to Rich Hendel, book designer extraordinaire, for his
beautiful work on *Stone Free* and *Talking Guitar*.

Most of all, I express my love and appreciation for my family: my
brothers, Tom and John; my sisters-in-law Kathy and Mary Ellen; my
nieces and nephews, Greg, Annie, Liz, Sean, Kevin, and Paul Obrecht;
my sisters-in-law Viana and Maria La Place; and Sheridan, Betsey,
Rebecca, Dan, and Doug Warrick. Blessings upon you all. And a lifetime
of thanks goes to my beloved wife, Michelle La Place Obrecht, and our
daughter Ava, who brightens every day. Fly on, my sweet angels ...

NOTES

PREFACE

1   Pete Townshend interview, *A Film about Jimi Hendrix*, directed by Joe Boyd, John Head, and Gary Weis (Warner Bros., 1973).

2   Carlos Santana interview with Jas Obrecht, Summer 1994.

3   Eric Johnson interview with Jas Obrecht, October 4, 2010.

4   Eric Johnson interview with Jas Obrecht, October 12, 2012.

CHAPTER 1

1   Bob Garcia, "Our Experience with Jimi," *Open City*, August 24–30, 1967; reprinted in *Hendrix on Hendrix: Interviews and Encounters with Jimi Hendrix*, ed. Steven Roby (Chicago: Chicago Review Press, 2012), 53.

2   Sharon Lawrence, *Jimi Hendrix: The Man, the Magic, the Truth* (New York: Harper Entertainment, 2005), 38.

3   Garcia, "Our Experience with Jimi."

4   Jas Obrecht, "Ernie Isley: Psychedelic Soul of the Isley Brothers," *Guitar Player*, September 1981, 58.

5   Henry "Juggy" Murray interview, *A Film about Jimi Hendrix*, directed by Joe Boyd, John Head, and Gary Weis (Warner Bros., 1973).

6   James A. Hendrix with Jas Obrecht, *My Son Jimi* (Seattle: AlJas Enterprises, 1999), 139–40.

7   Ace Hall interview, "Ace Hall Talks about Jimi Hendrix," transcribed from the YouTube video, https://www.youtube.com/watch?v=Vpa HTX-hwLA.

8   Transcribed by author from a scan of the original document.

9   Fayne Pridgeon interview, *A Film about Jimi Hendrix*.

10   Lawrence Townsend, email correspondence with the author, January 28, 2018.

11   Hendrix, *My Son Jimi*, 140.

12   Curtis Knight, *Jimi* (New York: Praeger, 1974), 35.

13   BBC interview: Sam Chatmon, Hollandale, Mississippi, 1976; reprinted in Giles Oakley's *The Devil's Music: A History of the Blues* (New York: Harcourt Brace Jovanovich, 1976), 54.

14   Randy Hansen interview with Jas Obrecht, April 1979; for the complete interview, see "Randy Hansen: Pro's Reply," *Guitar Player*, July 1979, 120.

15   Knight, *Jimi*, 36.

16 Linda Keith interview, *A Film about Jimi Hendrix*.

17 Charles R. Cross, *Room Full of Mirrors: A Biography of Jimi Hendrix* (New York: Hyperion, 2005), 132.

18 Linda Keith interview, *A Film about Jimi Hendrix*.

19 Linda Keith interview, *Jimi Hendrix: Hear My Train A Comin'*, PBS *American Masters* television series, aired November 5, 2013.

20 Ace Hall interview.

21 Paul Caruso interview, *Jimi Hendrix: Hear My Train A Comin'*.

22 Randy Wolfe quoted in Steven C. Pesant and John McDermott, "30 Years of Experiences: The Making of *Are You Experienced*," *Experience Hendrix* 3 (July/August 1997): 35.

23 Steve Barker, "Jimi Hendrix: The Complete January 1967 Interview with Steve Barker," Jas Obrecht Music Archive; http://jasobrecht .com/jimi-hendrix-london-complete-january-1967-interview-steve -barker/.

24 Linda Keith interview, *A Film about Jimi Hendrix*.

25 Keith Richards with James Fox, *Life* (New York: Little, Brown, 2010), 186.

26 Chris Welch, "Who Says Jimi Hendrix Can't Sing? (He Does!)," *Melody Maker*, April 15, 1967; reprinted in *The Jimi Hendrix Companion: Three Decades of Commentary*, ed. Chris Potash (New York: Schirmer, 1996), 9–10.

27 Chas Chandler interview, "Jimi Hendrix," *The South Bank Show*, ITV, October 1, 1989; retrieved from "Jimi Hendrix Documentary," https:// www.youtube.com/watch?v=pRg9h-XCHKs).

28 John McDermott with Billy Cox and Eddie Kramer, *Jimi Hendrix Sessions: The Complete Studio Recording Sessions, 1963–1970* (New York: Little, Brown, 1995), 12.

29 Lawrence, *Jimi Hendrix: The Man, the Magic, the Truth*, 41.

30 Don Menn, "John Paul Hammond Reminisces," *Guitar Player*, September 1975, 20.

31 Menn, "John Paul Hammond Reminisces," 20.

32 Don Menn, "Michael Bloomfield Reminisces," *Guitar Player*, September 1975, 22.

33 Menn, "Michael Bloomfield Reminisces," 22.

34 Menn, "Michael Bloomfield Reminisces," 22. Here Bloomfield is likely referring to the 15:01 version of "Voodoo Chile" on the Jimi Hendrix Experience's 1968 album *Electric Ladyland*.

35 Hendrix, *My Son Jimi*, 126.

36 Menn, "Michael Bloomfield Reminisces," 22.

37 Bob Kulick, "Spirit of '66: When Jimi Was Jimmy James," *Guitar Player*, September 1995, 71.

38 Chas Chandler interview, *Jimi Hendrix: Hear My Train A Comin'*.

39 Jimi Hendrix interview, *Jimi Hendrix: Hear My Train A Comin'*.

40 Lawrence, *Jimi Hendrix: The Man, the Magic, the Truth*, 42.

41 Lawrence, *Jimi Hendrix: The Man, the Magic, the Truth*, 43.

42 John McDermott with Eddie Kramer and Billy Cox, *Ultimate Hendrix: An Illustrated Encyclopedia of Live Concerts and Sessions* (New York: Backbeat Books, 2009), 21.

43 Unbylined essay, *The Jimi Hendrix Exhibition* catalog, The Jimi Hendrix Scholarship Foundation, London, 1992, 6.

44 Menn, "John Paul Hammond Reminisces," 20.

45 Lawrence, *Jimi Hendrix: The Man, the Magic, the Truth*, 42.

CHAPTER 2

1 "Great Britain: You Can Walk Across It on the Grass," *Time* magazine, April 15, 1966; retrieved from http://content.time.com/time/magazine/article/0,9171,835349,00.html.

2 Alan Freeman, "Quite an Experience," *Rave*, June 1967; reprinted in *Hendrix on Hendrix: Interviews and Encounters with Jimi Hendrix*, ed. Steven Roby (Chicago: Chicago Review Press, 2012), 27.

3 Keith Altham interview, *Jimi Hendrix: The Uncut Story*, directed by Steven Vosburgh (Passport International, 2004).

4 Kathy Etchingham and Andrew Crofts, *Through Gypsy Eyes: My Life, the 60s, and Jimi Hendrix* (London: Orion, 1999).

5 Kathy Etchingham, "At the Scotch of St. James," posted February 13, 2013; retrieved from http://www.kathyetchingham.com.

6 Etchingham and Crofts, *Through Gypsy Eyes*.

7 Dave Mason interview, *Jimi Hendrix: Hear My Train A Comin'*, PBS *American Masters* television series, aired November 5, 2013.

8 Paul McCartney interview, *Jimi Hendrix: Hear My Train A Comin'*.

9 Andy Johns interview, *Jimi Hendrix: The Uncut Story*.

10 Keith Richards with James Fox, *Life* (New York: Little, Brown, 2010), 186.

11 McCartney interview, *Jimi Hendrix: Hear My Train A Comin'*.

12 Kathy Etchingham interview, *Jimi Hendrix: Hear My Train' A Comin'*.

13 Kathy Etchingham interview, *Jimi Hendrix: The Uncut Story*.

14 "Black British," Wikipedia; https://en.wikipedia.org/wiki/Black_British.

15 James A. Hendrix with Jas Obrecht, *My Son Jimi* (Seattle: AlJas Enterprises, 1999), 10.

16 Sharon Lawrence, *Jimi Hendrix: The Man, the Magic, the Truth* (New York: Harper Entertainment, 2005), 71.

17 Lawrence, *Jimi Hendrix: The Man, the Magic, the Truth*, 71.

18 Etchingham and Crofts, *Through Gypsy Eyes*.

19 Etchingham and Crofts, *Through Gypsy Eyes*.

20 Hendrix, *My Son Jimi*, 20.

21 Etchingham interview, *Jimi Hendrix: The Uncut Story*.

22 Hendrix, *My Son Jimi*, 142, 144.

23 Kathy Etchingham interview, *Jimi Hendrix: My Story*, A&E *Biography* series, 2004.

24 Jan Waldrop, "Jimi Hendrix Shows His Teeth," *Humo*, March 1967; reprinted in Roby, *Hendrix on Hendrix*, 20.

25 Several sources list October 5 as the date of Jimi's Les Cousins appearance, but the article "U.S. Folk Blues Fest Takes to the European Road" in the October 1, 1966, issue of *Billboard*, p. 27, confirms that the American Folk Blues Festival was scheduled to perform in London on September 28. On October 5, the musicians were in Mainz, Germany.

26 Chris Welch interview, *Jimi Hendrix: Hear My Train A Comin'*.

27 John Lee Hooker interview with Jas Obrecht, July 19, 1989.

28 Willie Dixon with Don Snowden, *I Am the Blues: The Willie Dixon Story* (New York: Da Capo Press, 1989), 130.

29 Tony Brown, *Jimi Hendrix: A Visual Documentary* (London: Omnibus Press, 1992), 43.

30 Billy Cox interview with Jas Obrecht, June 22, 1987.

31 John McLaughlin interview, *Jimi Hendrix: The Uncut Story*.

32 "Brian Auger Talks about Jimi Hendrix's First Gig in London," YouTube, https://www.youtube.com/watch?v=6GMjtYpTlIY.

33 *The Jimi Hendrix Exhibition* catalog, The Jimi Hendrix Scholarship Foundation, London, 1992, 10.

34 Noel Redding and Carol Appleby, *Are You Experienced: The Inside Story of the Jimi Hendrix Experience* (London: Fourth Estate, 1990; repr., Da Capo Press, 1996), 18.

35 Redding and Appleby, *Are You Experienced*, 18–19.

36 "Brian Auger Talks about Jimi Hendrix's First Gig in London."

37 "Brian Auger Talks about Jimi Hendrix's First Gig in London."

38 "Brian Auger Talks about Jimi Hendrix's First Gig in London."

39 John McDermott with Eddie Kramer and Billy Cox, *Ultimate Hendrix: An Illustrated Encyclopedia of Live Concerts and Sessions* (New York: Backbeat Books, 2009), 22.

40 "Jeff Beck Talks about Meeting Jimi Hendrix," YouTube, https://www.youtube.com/watch?v=EVBf-N4smZ4; and *Jimi Hendrix: The Uncut Story*.

41 Redding and Appleby, *Are You Experienced*, 21.

42 Redding and Appleby, *Are You Experienced*, 1.

43 Redding and Appleby, *Are You Experienced*, 2.

44 Redding and Appleby, *Are You Experienced*, 2–3.

45 Redding and Appleby, *Are You Experienced*, 11. Captagon is a brand name for the synthetic stimulant fenethylline.

46 Redding and Appleby, *Are You Experienced*, 17.

47 Etchingham and Crofts, *Through Gypsy Eyes*.

CHAPTER 3

1 Captions, *The Jimi Hendrix Exhibition* catalog, The Jimi Hendrix Scholarship Foundation, London, 1992, 10.

2 Johnny Shines interview with Jas Obrecht, January 23, 1989.

3 Jas Obrecht, "Muddy Waters," *Rollin' and Tumblin': The Postwar Blues Guitarists* (San Francisco: Miller Freeman Books, 2000), 104; this quote originally appeared in *Down Beat*.

4 "Eric Clapton," *Record Mirror*, August 10, 1966; retrieved from http://crosstowntorrents.org/archive/index.php/t-27265.html.

5 Chas Chandler interview, "Jimi Hendrix," *The South Bank Show*, ITV, October 1, 1989; retrieved from "Jimi Hendrix Documentary," https://www.youtube.com/watch?v=pRg9h-XCHKs.

6 Eric Clapton interview, *South Bank Show*.

7 Eric Clapton, *Clapton: The Autobiography* (New York: Broadway Books, 2007), 80.

8 Steve Barker email correspondence with the author, August 2010.

9 Chas Chandler interview, *The Birth of Rock*, BBC television; retrieved from https://www.youtube.com/watch?v=6t4qXH_YaBs.

10 Kathy Etchingham and Andrew Crofts, *Through Gypsy Eyes: My Life, the 60s, and Jimi Hendrix*, (London: Orion, 1999).

11 Clapton, *Clapton*, 80.

12 Jack Bruce interview, *Birth of Rock*.

13 Ginger Baker interview, *Birth of Rock*.

14 Sharon Lawrence, *Jimi Hendrix: The Man, the Magic, the Truth* (New York: Harper Entertainment, 2005), 53–54.

15 Clapton interview, *South Bank Show*.

16 Clapton interview, *South Bank Show*.

17 Noel Redding and Carol Appleby, *Are You Experienced: The Inside Story of the Jimi Hendrix Experience* (London: Fourth Estate, 1990; repr., Da Capo Press, 1996), 25–26.

18 Redding and Appleby, *Are You Experienced*, 26.

19 Stevie Ray Vaughan interview with the author, February 9, 1989. The entire interview appears in Jas Obrecht, *Talking Guitar: Conversations with Musicians Who Shaped Twentieth-Century American Music* (Chapel Hill: University of North Carolina Press, 2017), 109–16.

20 Mitch Mitchell with John Platt, *Jimi Hendrix: Inside the Experience* (New York: Harmony Books, 1990), 15.

21 Mitchell with Platt, *Jimi Hendrix: Inside the Experience*, 13.

22 Captions, *Jimi Hendrix Exhibition*, 13.

23 Mitchell with Platt, *Jimi Hendrix: Inside the Experience*, 16–17.

24 Chandler interview, *South Bank Show*.

25 Redding and Appleby, *Are You Experienced*, 26.

26 Redding and Appleby, *Are You Experienced*, 26.

27 Redding and Appleby, *Are You Experienced*, 26.

28 Mitchell with Platt, *Jimi Hendrix: Inside the Experience*, 17–18.

29 Etchingham and Crofts, *Through Gypsy Eyes*.

30 Mitchell with Platt, *Jimi Hendrix: Inside the Experience*, 18.

31 Tony Brown, *Jimi Hendrix: A Visual Documentary* (London: Omnibus Press, 1992), 43.

32 Redding and Appleby, *Are You Experienced*, 28.

33 Lawrence Townsend email correspondence with the author, January 28, 2018.

34 Redding and Appleby, *Are You Experienced*, 23.

35 Redding and Appleby, *Are You Experienced*, 30.

36 Mitchell with Platt, *Jimi Hendrix: Inside the Experience*, 21–22.

37 Kathy Etchingham, "Jimi Hendrix Experience Evreux Anniversary Plaque 1996," posted October 12, 2012; retrieved online at http://www.kathyetchingham.com/evreux-anniversary-plaque-1996/.

38 Translation courtesy Sylvestre Novak.

39 Redding and Appleby, *Are You Experienced*, 31.

40 *L'Est Républicain*, October 15, 1966; translation retrieved from http://crosstowntorrents.org/showthread.php?1403-Newspaper-amp-Magazine-Articles-(Text-Only)-1960-s-1970-s.

41 Lawrence, *Jimi Hendrix: The Man, the Magic, the Truth*, 58.

42 *L'Est Républicain*, October 17, 1966; translation retrieved from http://crosstowntorrents.org/showthread.php?1401-Newspaper-amp-Magazine-Article-Scans-1960-s-1970-s/page3.

43 Sylvestre Novak clarifies the "Papuan" reference: "Nowadays, of course, you could not write something like this, but the reference is directly aimed at his hair style. In the mind of the French at that time, Papuans had very wild bushy hair styles. We saw them sometimes when they came to play rugby in France during the 1960s. So at that time it would have been registered by the reading public as a wild style—a hair style in particular." Email correspondence with the author, April 4, 2017.

44 Redding and Appleby, *Are You Experienced*, 31.

45 Lawrence, *Jimi Hendrix: The Man, the Magic, the Truth*, 58–59.
46 "Brian Auger Talks about Jimi Hendrix's First Gig in London," video retrieved from YouTube, https://www.youtube.com/watch?v=6GMjt YpTlIY.
47 Redding and Appleby, *Are You Experienced*, 31.
48 John McDermott with Billy Cox and Eddie Kramer, *Jimi Hendrix Sessions: The Complete Studio Recording Sessions, 1963–1970* (New York: Little, Brown, 1995), 16.
49 Steven C. Pesant and John McDermott, "30 Years of Experiences: The Making of *Are You Experienced*," *Experience Hendrix* 3 (July/August 1997): 37.
50 McDermott, *Jimi Hendrix Sessions*, 16.
51 *Jimi Hendrix Exhibition*, 12.
52 *Jimi Hendrix Exhibition*, 12.
53 John McDermott with Eddie Kramer and Billy Cox, *Ultimate Hendrix: An Illustrated Encyclopedia of Live Concerts and Sessions* (New York: Backbeat Books, 2009), 33.
54 *Jimi Hendrix Exhibition*, 12.
55 "An Infinity of Jimi's," *Life*, October 3, 1969; retrieved from http://www .me.umn.edu/~kgeisler/life.html.
56 Lawrence, *Jimi Hendrix: The Man, the Magic, the Truth*, 61–62.
57 John McDermott with Eddie Kramer, *Hendrix: Setting the Record Straight* (New York: Warner Books, 1992), 42–43.
58 Etchingham and Crofts, *Through Gypsy Eyes*.
59 Kathy Etchingham interview, *Jimi Hendrix: The Uncut Story*, directed by Steven Vosburgh (Passport International, 2004).
60 Redding and Appleby, *Are You Experienced*, 33.
61 Richard Green, "Ex-Animal Adventures," *Record Mirror*, October 29, 1966; retrieved from http://crosstowntorrents.org/showthread.php ?25761-1966-10-26-Scotch-Of-St-James-London.

CHAPTER 4

1 Charles Shaar Murray interview, *Jimi Hendrix: The Uncut Story*, directed by Steven Vosburgh (Passport International, 2004).
2 Kathy Etchingham and Andrew Crofts, *Through Gypsy Eyes: My Life, the 60s, and Jimi Hendrix* (London: Orion, 1999).
3 Chris Stamp interview, *Jimi Hendrix: Hear My Train A Comin'*, PBS *American Masters* television series, aired November 5, 2013.
4 Klas Burling, "Interview with Jimi Hendrix," broadcast on the Swedish radio show *Pop Special '67*, May 28, 1967; transcribed from *Jimi Hendrix: The Uncut Story*.

5   Steven C. Pesant and John McDermott, "30 Years of Experiences: The Making of *Are You Experienced*," *Experience Hendrix* 3 (July/August 1997): 40.

6   Leon Hendrix interview, *Jimi Hendrix: Hear My Train A Comin'*.

7   James Williams interview, *Jimi Hendrix: Hear My Train A Comin'*.

8   James A. Hendrix with Jas Obrecht, *My Son Jimi* (Seattle: AlJas Enterprises, 1999), 82.

9   Chandler interview, *The South Bank Show*.

10 Hendrix, *My Son Jimi*, 120.

11 Leon Hendrix interview, *Jimi Hendrix: Hear My Train A Comin'*.

12 Billy Cox interview with Jas Obrecht, June 22, 1987.

13 Steven C. Pesant, "Shooting the Stars," *Experience Hendrix* 2, no. 1 (March/April 1998): 62.

14 Etchingham and Crofts, *Through Gypsy Eyes*.

15 Etchingham and Crofts, *Through Gypsy Eyes*.

16 John McDermott with Eddie Kramer, *Hendrix: Setting the Record Straight* (New York: Warner Books, 1992), 27.

17 Etchingham and Crofts, *Through Gypsy Eyes*.

18 Kathy Etchingham, "Jimi Hendrix at the Ice Rink"; retrieved from http://www.kathyetchingham.com/jimi-hendrix-at-the-ice-rink/.

19 Mitch Mitchell with John Platt, *Jimi Hendrix: Inside the Experience* (New York: Harmony Books, 1990), 38.

20 Noel Redding and Carol Appleby, *Are You Experienced: The Inside Story of the Jimi Hendrix Experience* (London: Fourth Estate, 1990; repr., Da Capo Press, 1996), 27.

21 Redding and Appleby, *Are You Experienced*, 33.

22 Tony Brown, *Jimi Hendrix: A Visual Documentary* (London: Omnibus Press, 1992), 22.

23 "Interview: Engineer Eddie Kramer on Recording the Beatles' 'All You Need Is Love,'" *Guitar World*; retrieved from http://www.guitarworld.com/interview-engineer-eddie-kramer-recording-beatles-all-you-need-love.

24 Keith Richards with James Fox, *Life* (New York: Little, Brown, 2010), 187. Tuinal is a prescription sedative that combines secobarbital sodium and amobarbital sodium.

25 Richards with Fox, *Life*, 128.

26 Peter Jones, "Mr. Phenomenon," *Record Mirror*, December 10, 1966, 2.

27 Brown, *Jimi Hendrix: A Visual Documentary*, 44.

28 Matt Resnicoff, "Godhead Revisited: The Second Coming of Pete Townshend," *Guitar Player*, September 1989, 83–83.

29 Jann Wenner, "Eric Clapton," *The Rolling Stone Interviews*, vol. 1,

compiled by the editors of *Rolling Stone* (New York: Warner Paperback Library, 1971), 17–18.

30   Mitchell with Platt, *Jimi Hendrix: Inside the Experience*, 30.

CHAPTER 5

1   Bob Garcia, "Our Experience with Jimi," *Open City*, August 24–30, 1967; reprinted in *Hendrix on Hendrix: Interviews and Encounters with Jimi Hendrix*, ed. Steven Roby (Chicago: Chicago Review Press, 2012), 52.

2   Noel Redding and Carol Appleby, *Are You Experienced: The Inside Story of the Jimi Hendrix Experience* (London: Fourth Estate, 1990; repr., by Da Capo Press, 1996), 34.

3   Lawrence Townsend email correspondence with the author, January 31, 2018.

4   Kathy Etchingham, "34 Montagu Square," posted March 13, 2013; retrieved from http://www.kathyetchingham.com/34-montagu -square/.

5   These images can be viewed at http://art-sheep.com/when-jimi -hendrix-got-kicked-out-of-the-beatles-apartment.

6   "Jimi Hendrix's Personal Record Collection," Jas Obrecht Music Archive; retrieved from http://jasobrecht.com/jimi-hendrixs -personal-record-collection.

7   "Jimi Hendrix's Personal Record Collection."

8   "Jimi Hendrix's Personal Record Collection."

9   Redding and Appleby, *Are You Experienced*, 35.

10 Kathy Etchingham and Andrew Crofts, *Through Gypsy Eyes: My Life, the 60s, and Jimi Hendrix* (London: Orion, 1999).

11 Alan Freeman, "Quite an Experience," *Rave*, June 1967; reprinted in Roby, ed., *Hendrix on Hendrix*, 24.

12 Redding and Appleby, *Are You Experienced*, 25.

13 "Keys to the Mystical Kingdom: The Gear of Jimi Hendrix," *Guitar Player Master Series: Jimi Hendrix*, Fall 2003, 25.

14 Steven C. Pesant and John McDermott, "30 Years of Experiences: The Making of *Are You Experienced*," *Experience Hendrix* 3 (July/August 1997): 43.

15 Noel Redding, written correspondence with Jas Obrecht, February 6, 1989. A scan of this document can be seen at http://jasobrecht.com /noel-redding-his-letter-about-the-jimi-hendrix-experience.

16 Billy Cox interview with Jas Obrecht, June 22, 1987.

17 "Jimi Hendrix Joins Track," *Melody Maker*, December 24, 1966; retrieved from http://crosstowntorrents.org/showthread.php?1403 -Newspaper-amp-Magazine-Articles-(Text-Only)-1960-s-1970-s.

18   Jas Obrecht and Bruce Bergman, "Roger Mayer: Electronics Wizard and Designer of Effects Used by Such Rock Greats as Jeff Beck, Peter Frampton, Jimi Hendrix, Ernie Isley, and Jimmy Page," *Guitar Player*, February 1979, 48.

19   Charles Shaar Murray, *Crosstown Traffic* (New York: St. Martin's Press, 1989), 6–7.

20   Transcribed from "Red House—Takes 2–5," *The Complete Are You Experienced* bootleg CD.

21   Chris Welch, "Caught in the Act," *Melody Maker*, December 31, 1966; quoted in *The Jimi Hendrix Companion: Three Decades of Commentary*, ed. Chris Potash (New York: Schirmer, 1996), 3.

22   "More Singles Reviews," *New Musical Express*, December 23, 1966; retrieved from http://crosstowntorrents.org/archive/index.php/t -26502.html.

23   "My Scene," *Record Mirror*, December 29, 1966; retrieved from http:// crosstowntorrents.org/archive/index.php/t-4481.html.

24   "The Upper Cut Club, Part 1—The Rise"; retrieved from http://www .e7-nowandthen.org/2013/07/the-upper-cut-club-part-1-rise.html.

25   John McDermott with Eddie Kramer and Billy Cox, *Ultimate Hendrix: An Illustrated Encyclopedia of Live Concerts and Sessions* (New York: Backbeat Books, 2009), 32.

26   *The Jimi Hendrix Exhibition* catalog, The Jimi Hendrix Scholarship Foundation, London, 1992, 12.

27   Jimi Hendrix, quoted in Tim Morse, *Classic Rock Stories: The Stories Behind the Greatest Songs of All Time* (New York: St. Martin's Griffin, 1998), 168.

28   Sting, *Broken Music: A Memoir* (Dial, 2003); retrieved from http:// www.writerswrite.com/books/excerpts/brokenmusic.htm.

29   Redding and Appleby, *Are You Experienced*, 36–37.

CHAPTER 6

1   Leon Hendrix interview, *Jimi Hendrix: Hear My Train A Comin'*, PBS *American Masters* television series, aired November 5, 2013.

2   Richard Green, "Sex, Gimmicks, and Jimi," *Record Mirror*, January 14, 1967; retrieved from https://crosstowntorrents.org/showthread.php ?25780-1967-01-12-Olympia-London.

3   Mitch Mitchell with John Platt, *Jimi Hendrix: Inside the Experience* (New York: Harmony Books, 1990), 35–36.

4   Graham Oliver, "Jimi Plays Sheffield," *UniVibes* 38, April 2001; retrieved from http://www.univibes.com/JimiPlaysSheffield.html.

5   Brian Southall, *Jimi Hendrix: Made in London* (London: Ovolo Books, 2012), 72.

6   Mitchell with Platt, *Jimi Hendrix: Inside the Experience*, 33.

7   Noel Redding and Carol Appleby, *Are You Experienced: The Inside Story of the Jimi Hendrix Experience* (London: Fourth Estate, 1990; repr., Da Capo Press, 1996), 37.

8   Keith Altham interview, *Jimi Hendrix: The Uncut Story*, directed by Steven Vosburgh (Passport International, 2004).

9   Harry Shapiro and Caesar Glebeek, *Jimi Hendrix: Electric Gypsy* (New York: St. Martin's Press, 1990), 131.

10 Emperor Rosko interview, *Jimi Hendrix: My Story*, A&E *Biography* series, 2004.

11 Keith Altham, "Wild Jimi Hendrix," *New Musical Express*, January 13, 1967; retrieved from http://crosstowntorrents.org/archive/index.php /t-4592.html.

12 Keith Shadwick, "The Genesis of a Legend," *Guitar Player Master Series: Jimi Hendrix*, Fall 2003, 55.

13 Kathy Etchingham and Andrew Crofts, *Through Gypsy Eyes: My Life, the 60s, and Jimi Hendrix* (London: Orion, 1999).

14 Redding and Appleby, *Are You Experienced*, 39.

15 Mitchell with Platt, *Jimi Hendrix: Inside the Experience*, 26.

16 Jesse Gress, "5 Essential Hendrix Riffs," *How to Play Like Jimi Hendrix*, Guitar Player Classic Lessons Series, 2008, 51.

17 Quoted on p. 12 of Michael Fairchild's liner notes for the *Are You Experienced* CD included in the *Jimi Hendrix: The Experience Collection* box set, MCA, 1993.

18 John McDermott with Billy Cox and Eddie Kramer, *Jimi Hendrix Sessions: The Complete Studio Recording Sessions, 1963–1970* (New York: Little, Brown, 1995), 25–26.

19 Chas Chandler interview, "Jimi Hendrix," *The South Bank Show*, ITV, October 1, 1989; retrieved from "Jimi Hendrix Documentary," https:// www.youtube.com/watch?v=pRg9h-XCHKs.

20 Brian Delaney interview with Jas Obrecht, January 16, 2018.

21 *The Jimi Hendrix Exhibition* catalog, The Jimi Hendrix Scholarship Foundation, London, 1992, 20.

22 Hendrix radio interview, transcribed from *Jimi Hendrix: The Uncut Story*.

23 Etchingham interview, *Jimi Hendrix: The Uncut Story*.

24 Etchingham interview, *Jimi Hendrix: The Uncut Story*.

25 Chandler interview, *South Bank Show*.

26 Mike Ledgerwood, *Disc and Music Echo*, January 19, 1967; retrieved from http://crosstowntorrents.org/archive/index.php/t-4590.html ?s=6f17317fe3cb1728d872e5ac172ec921.

27 Chandler interview, *South Bank Show*.

28 Keith Altham interview, *South Bank Show*.

29 *New Musical Express*, January 28, 1967; retrieved from https://cross towntorrents.org/showthread.php?25780–1967–01–12-Olympia -London.

30 Mick Jagger interview, *A Film about Jimi Hendrix*, directed by Joe Boyd, John Head, and Gary Weis (Warner Bros., 1973).

31 "The Weird, Wild, Hit World of Jimi Hendrix," *Disc and Music Echo*, January 12, 1967; retrieved from https://crosstowntorrents.org/show thread.php?25780–1967–01–12-Olympia-London.

32 James A. Hendrix with Jas Obrecht, *My Son Jimi* (Seattle: AlJas Enterprises, 1999), 144.

33 Thom Carlyle Loubet, "Jazzin' the Blues: The Life and Music of Lonnie Johnson" (thesis, Wesleyan University, 1996), 54.

34 Mitch Mitchell interview, *South Bank Show*.

35 Redding and Appleby, *Are You Experienced*, 38.

36 Mitchell with Platt, *Jimi Hendrix: Inside the Experience*, 37.

37 A scan of this set list is viewable at http://www.jimihendrix-lifelines .net/1967jan-june/styled-14/styled-32/index.html.

38 A scan of the Kirklevington ad is viewable at https://picturestockton archive.wordpress.com/2012/09/19/jimi-hendrix-at-the-kirk-c1967/.

39 Redding and Appleby, *Are You Experienced*, 38.

40 Mitchell with Platt, *Jimi Hendrix: Inside the Experience*, 43.

41 Mitchell with Platt, *Jimi Hendrix: Inside the Experience*, 43.

42 Redding and Appleby, *Are You Experienced*, 39.

43 Mike Ledgerwood, "Jimi Hendrix Talks to Mike Ledgerwood," *Disc and Music Echo*, January 26, 1967, 50; retrieved from http://crosstown torrents.org/archive/index.php/t-4600.html.

44 Hendrix, *My Son Jimi*, 129.

45 Ledgerwood, "Jimi Hendrix Talks to Mike Ledgerwood."

46 John King, "Top Pop News," *New Musical Express*, January 28, 1967, 2; retrieved from http://crosstowntorrents.org/archive/index.php/t-4601 .html.

47 "'Pop Think In': Jimi Hendrix," *Melody Maker*, January 26, 1967, 7; retrieved from http://crosstowntorrents.org/archive/index.php /t-4600.html.

48 Jimi Hendrix interview, *Jimi Hendrix: The Uncut Story*.

49 Etchingham and Crofts, *Through Gypsy Eyes*.

50 Chris Stamp interview, *South Bank Show*.

51 Chandler interview, *South Bank Show*.

52 Redding and Appleby, *Are You Experienced*, 38.

53 Jas Obrecht and Bruce Bergman, "Roger Mayer: Electronics Wizard and Designer of Effects Used by Such Rock Greats as Jeff Beck, Peter

Frampton, Jimi Hendrix, Ernie Isley, and Jimmy Page," *Guitar Player*, February 1979, 48.

54 Tony Gale and Steven C. Pesant, "Shooting the Stars," *Experience Hendrix* 2, no. 5, (November-December 1998): 51.

55 Chris Welch, "Caught in the Act: Jimi Hendrix—Who Battle at Saville," *Melody Maker*, February 4, 1967; retrieved from http://crosstown torrents.org/archive/index.php/t-4603.html.

56 Tony Brown, *Jimi Hendrix: A Visual Documentary* (London: Omnibus Press, 1992), 48.

57 Mike Stafford, "Who & Hendrix an Upbeat Team in Saville Date," *Billboard*, February 11, 1967, 34.

CHAPTER 7

1 Quoted in Kevin Swift, "Hendrix the Gen Article," *Beat Instrumental*, March 1, 1967; reprinted in *Hendrix on Hendrix: Interviews and Encounters with Jimi Hendrix*, ed. Steven Roby (Chicago: Chicago Review Press, 2012), 15.

2 Steve Barker, "Jimi Hendrix: The Complete January 1967 Interview with Steve Barker," Jas Obrecht Music Archive; retrieved from http://jasobrecht.com/jimi-hendrix-london-complete-january-1967-inter view-steve-barker/.

3 Noel Redding, "One Nighter—Report by Noel Redding, Bass Man with the Jimi Hendrix Experience," *Beat Instrumental*, April 1, 1967; retrieved from http://crosstowntorrents.org/archive/index.php/t -4604.html.

4 Noel Redding and Carol Appleby, *Are You Experienced: The Inside Story of the Jimi Hendrix Experience* (London: Fourth Estate, 1990; repr., Da Capo Press, 1996), 41–42.

5 Chris Lloyd, "I Interviewed Jimi Hendrix in His Bedroom," *Northern Echo*, January 27, 2017; retrieved from http://www.thenorthernecho .co.uk/history/15054607._I_interviewed_Jimi_Hendrix_in_his _bedroom.

6 Lloyd, "I Interviewed Jimi Hendrix in His Bedroom."

7 Stuart Arnold, "I Bought Missing Jimi Hendrix Guitar for £20," *Northern Echo*, August 29, 2008; retrieved from http://www.the northernecho.co.uk/news/3630437.___I_bought_missing_Jimi _Hendrix_guitar_for___20___/.

8 Lloyd, "I Interviewed Jimi Hendrix in His Bedroom."

9 Redding and Appleby, *Are You Experienced*, 41.

10 Steven C. Pesant and John McDermott, "30 Years of Experiences: The Making of *Are You Experienced*," *Experience Hendrix* 3 (July/August 1997).

11   John McDermott with Eddie Kramer and Billy Cox, *Ultimate Hendrix: An Illustrated Encyclopedia of Live Concerts and Sessions* (New York: Backbeat Books, 2009), 25–36.

12   Eddie Kramer interview, *Jimi Hendrix: The Uncut Story*, directed by Steven Vosburgh (Passport International, 2004).

13   Jas Obrecht and Bruce Bergman, "Roger Mayer: Electronics Wizard and Designer of Effects Used by Such Rock Greats as Jeff Beck, Peter Frampton, Jimi Hendrix, Ernie Isley, and Jimmy Page," *Guitar Player*, February 1979, 48.

14   Brian Delaney, email correspondence with the author, July 17, 2017.

15   James Gurley, interview with the author, September 30, 1978. The entire interview appears in Jas Obrecht, *Talking Guitar: Conversations with Musicians Who Shaped Twentieth-Century American Music* (Chapel Hill: University of North Carolina Press, 2017), 131–154.

16   Andy Johns interview, *Jimi Hendrix: The Uncut Story*.

17   Eddie Kramer interview, *Jimi Hendrix: Hear My Train A Comin'*, PBS *American Masters* television series, aired November 5, 2013.

18   Redding and Appleby, *Are You Experienced*, 42.

19   Eddie Kramer interview, *A Film about Jimi Hendrix*, directed by Joe Boyd, John Head, and Gary Weis (Warner Bros., 1973).

20   John McDermott with Eddie Kramer, *Hendrix: Setting the Record Straight* (New York: Warner Books, 1992), 32.

21   Nicholas Williams, "An Experience in Sound," *Bristol Evening Post*, February 10, 1967; retrieved from http://crosstowntorrents.org/archive/index.php/t-4615.html.

22   "The Jimi Hendrix Experience," *Plaza Bulletin*, February 11, 1967; retrieved from http://crosstowntorrents.org/archive/index.php/t-4617.html.

23   Swift, "Hendrix the Gen Article," 13–15.

24   A scan of this document can be viewed at http://www.jimihendrix-lifelines.net/1967jan-june/styled-16/styled-131/index.html.

25   Lawrence Townsend, email correspondence with the author, January 30, 2018.

26   Redding and Appleby, *Are You Experienced*, 41.

27   Redding, "One Nighter."

28   Redding, "One Nighter."

29   Delaney email correspondence with the author.

30   Delaney email correspondence with the author.

31   Josephine Bayne, *Bath and Wilts Evening Chronicle*, February 21, 1967; retrieved from http://jimihendrix.forumactif.org/t157-bath-the-pavilion-20-fevrier-1967.

32   "Lifelines of the Jimi Hendrix Experience," *New Musical Express*,

March 11, 1966, 12; reprinted in Mitch Mitchell with John Platt, *Jimi Hendrix: Inside the Experience* (New York: Harmony Books, 1990), 42.

33 Redding and Appleby, *Are You Experienced*, 40.

34 "Jimi Doesn't Think He's a Big Name Yet," *Record Mirror*, February 25, 1967, 4; reprinted in Roby, *Hendrix on Hendrix*, 11–12.

35 Paul McCartney, "Paul McCartney Reviews the New Pop Singles," *Melody Maker*, February 25, 1967, 13; retrieved from http://crosstown torrents.org/archive/index.php/t-4628.html.

36 Bruce Fleming and Steven C. Pesant, "Shooting the Stars," *Experience Hendrix* 2, no. 1 (March/April 1998): 58.

CHAPTER 8

1 Bob Garcia, "Our Experience with Jimi," *Open City*, August 24–30, 1967; reprinted in *Hendrix on Hendrix: Interviews and Encounters with Jimi Hendrix*, ed. Steven Roby (Chicago: Chicago Review Press, 2012), 50.

2 "What Goes On," *Crawdaddy*, March 1, 1967, 21.

3 "Jimi Is Here to Stay," *International Times*, March 1, 1967; retrieved from http://crosstowntorrents.org/showthread.php?1403-Newspaper -amp-Magazine-Articles-(Text-Only)-1960-s-1970-s.

4 John McDermott with Billy Cox and Eddie Kramer, *Jimi Hendrix Sessions: The Complete Studio Recording Sessions, 1963–1970* (New York: Little, Brown, 1995), 32–33.

5 Mitch Mitchell with John Platt, *Jimi Hendrix: Inside the Experience* (New York: Harmony Books, 1990), 45.

6 Mitchell with John Platt, *Jimi Hendrix: Inside the Experience*, 45.

7 Jan Waldrop, "Jimi Hendrix Shows His Teeth," *Humo*, March 1967; reprinted in Roby, *Hendrix on Hendrix*, 17–21.

8 Brian Southall, *Jimi Hendrix: Made in London* (London: Ovolo Books, 2012), 93.

9 Sting, *Broken Music: A Memoir* (Dial, 2003); retrieved from http:// www.writerswrite.com/books/excerpts/brokenmusic.htm.

10 Reprinted in Harry Shapiro and Caesar Glebeek, *Jimi Hendrix: Electric Gypsy* (New York: St. Martin's Press, 1990), 170.

11 "Chaos after Police Break Up Crowded Pop Show," *Yorkshire Evening Post*, March 13, 1967; retrieved from https://crosstowntorrents.org /showthread.php?4640-1967-03-12-Gyro-Club-Troutbeck-Hotel -Ilkley-Yorkshire-England.

12 "Pop Fans Amok in Hotel," *Ilkley Gazette*, March 13, 1967; retrieved from http://crosstowntorrents.org/archive/index.php/t-4640.html.

13 Keith Altham, "Hendrix Is Out of This World," *New Musical Express*, April 15, 1967, 4; reprinted in *The Jimi Hendrix Companion: Three*

Decades of Commentary, ed. Chris Potash (New York: Schirmer, 1996), 5.

14 Mitchell with Platt, *Jimi Hendrix: Inside the Experience*, 45.

15 John McDermott with Eddie Kramer, *Hendrix: Setting the Record Straight* (New York: Warner Books, 1992), 47.

16 Kathy Etchingham and Andrew Crofts, *Through Gypsy Eyes: My Life, the 60s, and Jimi Hendrix* (London: Orion, 1999).

17 Barbro Nordström, "Jimi Hendrix: Blast from America's Backyards," *Bildjournalen*, May 24, 1967; translation retrieved from http://cross towntorrents.org/archive/index.php/t-4694.html/.

18 Keith Altham, "Hendrix Is Out of This World," *New Musical Express*, April 15, 1967, 4; reprinted in Potash, *Jimi Hendrix Companion*, 3–6.

19 Noel Redding and Carol Appleby, *Are You Experienced: The Inside Story of the Jimi Hendrix Experience* (London: Fourth Estate, 1990; repr., Da Capo Press, 1996), 45.

20 Redding and Appleby, *Are You Experienced*, 45.

21 John McDermott with Eddie Kramer and Billy Cox, *Ultimate Hendrix: An Illustrated Encyclopedia of Live Concerts and Sessions* (New York: Backbeat Books, 2009), 41.

22 Southall, *Jimi Hendrix: Made in London*, 100.

23 Keith Altham interview, *Jimi Hendrix: The Uncut Story*, directed by Steven Vosburgh (Passport International, 2004).

24 Keith Altham interview, *Jimi Hendrix: The Uncut Story*.

25 Keith Altham, "Walker Surprises," *New Musical Express*, April 7, 1967, 12; retrieved from http://crosstowntorrents.org/archive/index.php/t-4656.html.

CHAPTER 9

1 Bob Garcia, "Our Experience with Jimi," *Open City*, August 24–30, 1967; reprinted in *Hendrix on Hendrix: Interviews and Encounters with Jimi Hendrix*, ed. Steven Roby (Chicago: Chicago Review Press, 2012), 60.

2 Noel Redding and Carol Appleby, *Are You Experienced: The Inside Story of the Jimi Hendrix Experience* (London: Fourth Estate, 1990; repr., Da Capo Press, 1996), 46.

3 "Frenzied Fans at Pop Show," *Evening News*, April 3, 1967; retrieved from https://crosstowntorrents.org/showthread.php?4653-1967-04 -02-Gaumont-Worcester-Worcestershire-England.

4 Chris Welch, "Hendrix: 'Clean Act,'" *Melody Maker*, April 6, 1967; retrieved from http://crosstowntorrents.org/archive/index.php/t-4655.html.

5 Mitch Mitchell with John Platt, *Jimi Hendrix: Inside the Experience* (New York: Harmony Books, 1990), 47–48.

6   Delaney email correspondence with the author.

7   John McDermott with Eddie Kramer and Billy Cox, *Ultimate Hendrix: An Illustrated Encyclopedia of Live Concerts and Sessions* (New York: Backbeat Books, 2009), 42–43.

8   Roger Mayer interview, *Jimi Hendrix: The Uncut Story*, directed by Steven Vosburgh (Passport International, 2004).

9   John McDermott with Billy Cox and Eddie Kramer, *Jimi Hendrix Sessions: The Complete Studio Recording Sessions, 1963–1970* (New York: Little, Brown, 1995), 33.

10   Klas Burling, "Interview with Jimi Hendrix," broadcast on the Swedish radio show *Pop Special '67*, May 28, 1967; transcribed from *Jimi Hendrix: The Uncut Story*.

11   Mayer interview, *Jimi Hendrix: The Uncut Story*.

12   Steven C. Pesant and John McDermott, "30 Years of Experiences: The Making of *Are You Experienced*," *Experience Hendrix* 3 (July/August 1997): 38.

13   Donald Bruce, "Jimi Hendrix Is Racing to Success," *Daily Record*, April 7, 1967, 4; retrieved from http://crosstowntorrents.org/archive/index.php/t-4656.html.

14   Redding and Appleby, *Are You Experienced*, 46–47.

15   Dave McAleer, *The All Music Book of Hit Singles* (San Francisco: Miller Freeman Books, 1994), 124.

16   Lorraine Walsh's recollections retrieved from http://www.newsand star.co.uk/lifestyle/features/article/The-day-a-rising-star-called -Jimi-Hendrix-hit-Carlisle-1813f41e-0ab7-44b7-9c71-378fd82428 ee-ds.

17   RFS, "Release Me from This Noisy Mob," *Derbyshire Times*, April 14, 1967; retrieved from http://crosstowntorrents.org/archive/index.php /t-4749.html.

18   Redding and Appleby, *Are You Experienced*, 47–48.

19   Chris Welch, "Who Says Jimi Hendrix Can't Sing? (He Does!)," *Melody Maker*, April 15, 1967; reprinted in *The Jimi Hendrix Companion: Three Decades of Commentary*, ed. Chris Potash (New York: Schirmer, 1996), 9–10.

20   Disc Spinner, "Teenage Tonsils at the Ready," *Woburn Reporter*, April 18, 1967; retrieved from http://crosstowntorrents.org/archive/index .php/t-4659.html.

21   "Screaming Teenage Girls Raid Stage," *Bolton Evening News*, April 15, 1967; retrieved from http://crosstowntorrents.org/archive/index.php /t-4663.html.

22   Redding and Appleby, *Are You Experienced*, 47.

23   "Me, Vulgar? You Must Be Joking," *Disc and Music Echo*, April 13,

1967, 8; retrieved from http://crosstowntorrents.org/archive/index
.php/t-4661.html.

24 "Jimi's Out for a Double Hit," *Scottish Daily Press*, April 21, 1967;
retrieved from https://crosstowntorrents.org/showthread.php?4668
–1967–04–21-City-Hall-Newcastle-Upon-Tyne-Northumberland
-England.

25 Redding and Appleby, *Are You Experienced*, 47.

26 Hugh Nolan, "For Jimi Hendrix, Colour Means His Shade of Music,"
Disc and Music Echo, April 22, 1967; retrieved from http://crosstown
torrents.org/archive/index.php/t-4667.html.

27 June Southworth, *Fabulous 208*, June 24, 1967; retrieved from http://
crosstowntorrents.org/archive/index.php/t-4667.html.

28 Redding and Appleby, *Are You Experienced*, 48.

29 Redding and Appleby, *Are You Experienced*, 48.

30 "Pop Tours Played Out—Walker Brothers," *Lincolnshire Echo*, April 21,
1967; https://crosstowntorrents.org/showthread.php?4668–1967–04
–21-City-Hall-Newcastle-Upon-Tyne-Northumberland-England.

31 G-Man, "A Stage Full of Pop Stars," *Lincolnshire Chronicle*, April 28,
1967; retrieved from http://crosstowntorrents.org/archive/index.php
/t-4674.html.

32 Southworth, *Fabulous 208*.

33 McDermott, *Ultimate Hendrix*, 46.

34 James Belsey, "Brotherly Act by a Friendly Walker," *Bristol Evening
Post*, April 26, 1967; retrieved from http://crosstowntorrents.org
/archive/index.php/t-4672.html.

35 "Slough's Screamagers No Hit with the Walker Brothers," *Slough
Observer*, May 5, 1967; retrieved from https://crosstowntorrents.org
/showthread.php?4807–1967–05–05-Olympic-Studios.

36 S.A., "Screaming Slough Fans Depress Walker Brothers," *Slough
Express*, May 5, 1967; retrieved from https://crosstowntorrents.org
/showthread.php?4807–1967–05–05-Olympic-Studios.

37 Mitchell with Platt, *Jimi Hendrix: Inside the Experience*, 49.

38 Penny Valentine, "Jimi Looks Like [He's] Becoming a Living Legend,"
Disc and Music Echo, April 29, 1967; retrieved from http://crosstown
torrents.org/archive/index.php/t-4673.html.

39 Tony Brown, *Jimi Hendrix: A Visual Documentary* (London: Omnibus
Press, 1992), 61.

CHAPTER 10

1 *Jimi Hendrix: The Uncut Story*, directed by Steven Vosburgh (Passport
International, 2004).

2 Ann Nightingale, "Just Wild (Parents and Fans That Is) About Jimi,"

Sunday Mirror, May 9, 1967; quoted in David Henderson, *'Scuse Me While I Kiss the Sky: Jimi Hendrix, Voodoo Child* (1978; repr. New York: Atria, 2009), 153–54.

3   Barbro Nordström, "Jimi Hendrix: Blast from America's Backyards," *Bildjournalen*, May 24, 1967; translation retrieved from http://cross towntorrents.org/archive/index.php/t-4694.html/.

4   Keith Altham, "Question Time with Jimi Hendrix," *New Musical Express*, May 13, 1967, 13; retrieved from http://crosstowntorrents .org/archive/index.php/t-4683.html.

5   Keith Altham, "Question Time with Jimi Hendrix," 13.

6   Mitch Mitchell with John Platt, *Jimi Hendrix: Inside the Experience* (New York: Harmony Books, 1990), 28.

7   Charles L. Sanders, "Paris Scratch Pad," *Jet*, May 4, 1967.

8   Charles L. Sanders, "Paris Scratch Pad," *Jet*, June 8, 1967, 28.

9   Jym Fahey, "*Axis: Bold as Love* Turns 30," *Experience Hendrix* 5 (November-December 1997): 28

10 John McDermott with Eddie Kramer and Billy Cox, *Ultimate Hendrix: An Illustrated Encyclopedia of Live Concerts and Sessions* (New York: Backbeat Books, 2009), 48.

11 Fahey, "*Axis: Bold as Love* Turns 30," 28–29.

12 Derek Johnson, "Top Singles Reviewed," *New Musical Express*, May 6, 1967; reprinted in Harry Shapiro and Caesar Glebeek, *Jimi Hendrix: Electric Gypsy* (New York: St. Martin's Press, 1990), 157.

13 Tony Skinner, "An Imperial Victory for Hendrix," *The Leader*, May 12, 1967; retrieved from http://crosstowntorrents.org/archive/index.php /t-4683.html.

14 Nick Jones, "Caught in the Act," *Melody Maker*, May 7, 1967; retrieved from http://crosstowntorrents.org/showthread.php?1403-Newspaper -amp-Magazine-Articles-(Text-Only)-1960-s-1970-s.

15 Penny Valentine, "Hendrix Turns on the Heat," *Disc and Music Echo*, May 11, 1967; retrieved from http://crosstowntorrents.org/archive /index.php/t-4680.html.

16 Samantha Just, "I'm Not Fond of Hairy Men!," *Disc and Music Echo*, May 20, 1967; retrieved from http://crosstowntorrents.org/archive /index.php/t-4688.html.

17 Chris Stamp interview, *Jimi Hendrix: The Uncut Story*.

18 Jimi Hendrix, "Jimi Hendrix Reviews 'Are You Experienced,'" *Rave*, June 1967; retrieved from http://crosstowntorrents.org/archive/index .php/t-25923.html.

19 John McDermott with Billy Cox and Eddie Kramer, *Jimi Hendrix Sessions: The Complete Studio Recording Sessions, 1963–1970* (New York: Little, Brown, 1995), 36.

20 Eric Clapton, *Clapton: The Autobiography* (New York: Broadway Books, 2007), 87.

21 Noel Redding and Carol Appleby, *Are You Experienced: The Inside Story of the Jimi Hendrix Experience* (London: Fourth Estate, 1990; repr., Da Capo Press, 1996), 50.

22 Redding and Appleby, *Are You Experienced*, 50.

23 Gerhard Schizel, "Ich Bin Nicht Mehr der Dumme!," *Bravo*, June 26, 1967; translation retrieved from http://crosstowntorrents.org/archive /index.php/t-4706.html.

24 Hans Carl Schmidt, "Interview with Jimi Hendrix," transcribed from a May 17, 1967, radio broadcast; reprinted in *Hendrix on Hendrix: Interviews and Encounters with Jimi Hendrix*, ed. Steven Roby (Chicago: Chicago Review Press, 2012), 31–35. Portions of the audio can be heard in *Jimi Hendrix: The Uncut Story*.

25 James A. Hendrix with Jas Obrecht, *My Son Jimi* (Seattle: AlJas Enterprises, 1999), 144.

26 Hugh Nolan, "Hip Hamburg Cries 'Heil' to Hendrix! Report by Noel Redding from Germany," *Disc and Music Echo*, May 25, 1967; retrieved from http://crosstowntorrents.org/archive/index.php/t-4694.html.

27 Keith Keller, "Kom til soul-møde med Jimi Hendrix, en troende oprører fra Mars via Cuba," *Expressen*, May 15, 1967; translated and reprinted in Roby, *Hendrix on Hendrix*, 29–30.

28 "The New Madman Is Also Coming," *Helsingin Sanomat*, May 21, 1967; retrieved from https://crosstowntorrents.org/showthread.php?4690 -1967-05-21-Falkoner-Centret-Copenhagen-Zealand-Denmark.

29 Gösta Hanson, "Nervös Cat Stevens och avslappnad Jimi," *Göteborgs Tidningen*, May 20, 1967; translation retrieved from http://crosstown torrents.org/showthread.php?1403-Newspaper-amp-Magazine -Articles-(Text-Only)-1960-s-1970-s.

30 "Rebelsk Pop-Weekend," *Berlingske Tidende*, May 17, 1967, 6; translation retrieved from http://crosstowntorrents.org/archive /index.php/t-4686.html.

31 Hej, "Hendrix er mester," *Aktuelt*, May 22, 1967, 1; translation retrieved from http://crosstowntorrents.org/archive/index.php/t-4691.html.

32 Nils Gudme, "Hendrix—Stærk og bedøvende," *Ekstra Bladet*, May 22, 1967, 11; translation retrieved from http://crosstowntorrents.org /archive/index.php/t-4691.html.

33 Ilpo Saunio, *Rytmi*, May 1967; translation retrieved from http://cross towntorrents.org/archive/index.php/t-4691.html.

34 "Fire Cracker Jimi Hendrix," *Hufvudstadsbladet*, May 25, 1967; translation retrieved from http://crosstowntorrents.org/archive /index.php/t-4694.html.

35 Bosson, *Sydsvenska Dagbladet*, May 24, 1967; translation retrieved from http://crosstowntorrents.org/archive/index.php/t-4694.html.

36 Karre Erichs, "Bristfälligt arrangemang," *Arbetet*, May 24, 1967; translation retrieved from http://crosstowntorrents.org/archive /index.php/t-4694.html.

37 Sven-Oskar Ruhmén, *Aftonbladet*, May 24, 1967; translation retrieved from http://crosstowntorrents.org/archive/index.php/t-4694.html.

38 Transcribed from a bootleg recording of the concert.

39 McDermott, *Ultimate Hendrix*, 51.

40 Lars Weck, *Dagens Nyheter*, May 25, 1967; translation retrieved from http://crosstowntorrents.org/archive/index.php/t-4694.html.

41 "Ekvilibristisk Mäster Gitarrist," *Svenska Dagbladet*, May 25, 1967; translation retrieved from http://crosstowntorrents.org/archive/index .php/t-4694.html.

42 "Hylende Hendrix," *Dagens Nyheter*, May 26, 1967; translation retrieved from http://crosstowntorrents.org/archive/index.php /t-4694.html.

43 "Jimi a Hit in Sweden—Refused Hotel Room," *Melody Maker*, June 3, 1967; reprinted in *The Jimi Hendrix Companion: Three Decades of Commentary*, ed. Chris Potash (New York: Schirmer, 1996), 10.

44 Noel Redding interview, *The South Bank Show*, ITV, October 1, 1989; retrieved from "Jimi Hendrix Documentary," https://www.youtube .com/watch?v=pRg9h-XCHKs.

45 Redding and Appleby, *Are You Experienced*, 51.

46 Germaine Greer, "Jimi Hendrix," *Oz* 30 (October 1970); reprinted in Charles R. Cross, *Room Full of Mirrors: A Biography of Jimi Hendrix* (New York: Hyperion, 2005), 186–87.

47 Redding and Appleby, *Are You Experienced*, 51.

CHAPTER 11

1 Transcribed from the Animals, "Monterey," *The Best of Eric Burdon and the Animals, 1966–1968*, Polygram, 1991.

2 Dawn James, "Wild, Man!," *Rave*, August 1967, 8–9; reprinted in *The Jimi Hendrix Companion: Three Decades of Commentary*, ed. Chris Potash (New York: Schirmer, 1996), 6–8.

3 Kathy Etchingham and Andrew Crofts, *Through Gypsy Eyes: My Life, the 60s, and Jimi Hendrix* (London: Orion, 1999).

4 James, "Wild, Man!," 6–8.

5 Hendrix interview, *Jimi Hendrix: The Uncut Story*, directed by Steven Vosburgh (Passport International, 2004).

6 James, "Wild, Man!," 6–8.

7 Jimi Hendrix, "Message from Jimi on 'Are You Experienced,'" July 8,

1967; retrieved from http://crosstowntorrents.org/showthread.php ?1403-Newspaper-amp-Magazine-Articles-(Text-Only)-1960-s-1970 -s/page3.

8   Mitch Mitchell with John Platt, *Jimi Hendrix: Inside the Experience* (New York: Harmony Books, 1990), 41.

9   Chas Chandler interview, "Jimi Hendrix," *The South Bank Show*, ITV, October 1, 1989; retrieved from "Jimi Hendrix Documentary," https:// www.youtube.com/watch?v=pRg9h-XCHKs.

10 Eliot Tiegel, "Talent's Historical Foundation Fest," *Billboard*, June 3, 1967, 1 and 10.

11 Chandler interview, *South Bank Show*.

12 Noel Redding quote retrieved from http://www.jimihendrix-lifelines .net/1967jan-june/styled-24/styled-370/index.html.

13 A photograph of this inscription appears opposite p. 209 in Sharon Lawrence, *Jimi Hendrix: The Man, the Magic, the Truth* (New York: Harper Entertainment, 2005).

14 Charles R. Cross, *Room Full of Mirrors: A Biography of Jimi Hendrix* (New York: Hyperion, 2005), 187.

15 Paul McCartney, spoken onstage at Toronto Air Canada Center Concert, August 9, 2010; retrieved from https://www.youtube.com /watch?v=8Hr6BbocqdM.

16 Noel Redding and Carol Appleby, *Are You Experienced: The Inside Story of the Jimi Hendrix Experience* (London: Fourth Estate, 1990; repr., Da Capo Press, 1996), 52.

17 Hugh Nolan, "Hendrix: Impact of a 50-Megaton H-Bomb!," *Disc and Music Echo*, June 10, 1967; retrieved from http://crosstowntorrents.org /archive/index.php/t-7500.html.

18 Redding and Appleby, *Are You Experienced*, 52.

19 Norrie Drummond, "Bad Show Brings Jimi Down," *New Musical Express*, June 10, 1967; reprinted in Potash, *Jimi Hendrix Companion*, 11–12.

20 "Hendrix, Wild Man of Pop, Reveals What Makes Him Tick," *Disc and Music Echo*, June 17, 1967, 16; retrieved from http://crosstowntorrents .org/archive/index.php/t-4809.html.

21 Keith Altham interview, *Jimi Hendrix: Hear My Train A Comin'*, PBS *American Masters* television series, aired November 5, 2013.

22 Keith Altham, "Keith Altham Planes West to Cover America's Monterey Pop Festival," *New Musical Express*, June 24, 1967; retrieved from https://crosstowntorrents.org/showthread.php?13716-Jimi -Arrives-In-America-For-Monterey-Pop-Festival-1967.

23 Noel Redding quote retrieved from http://www.jimihendrix-lifelines .net/1967jan-june/styled-24/styled-377/index.html.

24 Mitchell with Platt, *Jimi Hendrix: Inside the Experience*, 53.

25 *Univibes* 16; retrieved from http://www.jimihendrix-lifelines.net/1967 jan-june/styled-24/styled-377/index.html.

26 Altham, "Keith Altham Planes West to Cover America's Monterey Pop Festival."

27 Barry Jenkins, retrieved from http://www.jimihendrix-lifelines.net /1967jan-june/styled-24/styled-378/index.html.

28 Altham, "Keith Altham Planes West to Cover America's Monterey Pop Festival."

29 Joel Selvin, *Monterey Pop* (San Francisco: Chronicle Books, 1992), 5.

30 Mitchell with Platt, *Jimi Hendrix: Inside the Experience*, 54.

31 Redding interview, *South Bank Show*.

32 Redding and Appleby, *Are You Experienced*, 53.

33 Mitchell with Platt, *Jimi Hendrix: Inside the Experience*, 55.

34 Mitchell with Platt, *Jimi Hendrix: Inside the Experience*, 55.

35 Pete Townshend interview, *A Film about Jimi Hendrix*, directed by Joe Boyd, John Head, and Gary Weis (Warner Bros., 1973).

36 Redding and Appleby, *Are You Experienced*, 53.

37 Mitchell with Platt, *Jimi Hendrix: Inside the Experience*, 57.

38 Captions, *The Jimi Hendrix Exhibition* catalog, The Jimi Hendrix Scholarship Foundation, London, 1992, 3.

39 Mitch Mitchell interview, *South Bank Show*.

40 Redding and Appleby, *Are You Experienced*, 53.

41 Mitchell with Platt, *Jimi Hendrix: Inside the Experience*, 57.

42 Selvin, *Monterey Pop*, 3.

43 Jimi Hendrix, *Starting at Zero: His Own Story* (New York: Bloomsbury, 2013), 68–69.

INDEX

Page numbers appearing in *italics* refer to photographs.

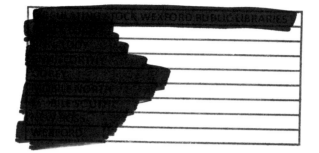